SCREEN LOVE

SCREEN LOVE

Queer Intimacies in the Grindr Era

TOM ROACH

SUNY
PRESS

Cover Image: Juan Pablo Echeverri, *futuroSEXtraños*. 2016. 60 inkjet prints: 400 × 240 cm. Obtained by the artist. Reproduced with the permission of the artist.

Published by State University of New York Press, Albany

© 2021 State University of New York

For information, contact State University of New York Press, Albany, NY
www.sunypress.edu

Library of Congress Cataloging-in-Publication Data

Name: Roach, Tom, author.
Title: Screen love : queer intimacies in the grindr era / Tom Roach.
Description: Albany : State University of New York Press, [2021] | Includes
    bibliographical references and index.
Identifiers: ISBN 9781438482071 (hardcover : alk. paper) | ISBN 9781438482088
    (pbk. : alk. paper) | ISBN 9781438482095 (ebook)
Further information is available at the Library of Congress.

10 9 8 7 6 5 4 3 2 1

In memoriam
Gary C. Thomas
(1946–2019)

Contents

Illustrations

Acknowledgments

I am grateful to Jordan Greenwald, Kelie Montalvo, and the editorial board of *Qui Parle* for soliciting and publishing the conceptual backbone of this book: "Becoming Fungible: Queer Intimacies in Social Media" (*Qui Parle* 23, no. 2, 2015). I am grateful to Leo Bersani, Glyn Davis, Shaka McGlotten, Peter Rehberg, and John Paul Ricco for their feedback on that article. A revised version of it appears as chapter 5, "Becoming Fungible." I am likewise indebted to Thomas Waugh and Brandon Arroyo for soliciting and publishing "Shut Me Up in Grindr: Anticonfessional Discourse and Sensual Nonsense in MSM Media" in *I Confess: An Anthology of Original Essays on Constructing the Self within the Third Sexual Revolution* (McGill-Queens University Press, 2019). A revised version of that essay appears as chapter 6, "Shut Up! in the Digital Closet." I am thankful to Kir Kuiken for inviting me to review Mikko Tuhkanen's *The Essentialist Villain: On Leo Bersani* for *Postmodern Culture* (28, no. 3, 2019). Portions of that review appear in the introduction and chapter 1. Michelle Stewart, my writing partner on "Teaching *Homo Economicus*: Strategies for the Neoliberal Classroom" (*AEQ* 14, no. 2, 2010), deserves credit for formulating the lion's share of that article's key points, some of which I summarize in chapter 1. Finally, a brief section of my chapter "Make Live and Let Die: Michel Foucault, Biopower, and the Art of Dying Well" in Erin Dolgoy, Kimberly Hurd Hale, and Bruce Peabody's edited volume, *Political Philosophies of Aging, Dying, and Death* (Routledge, 2021 [forthcoming]) also appears in chapter 1.

I am profoundly indebted to the peer reviewers of my original manuscript. Your careful reading and constructive criticism undoubtedly made this a better book. I also owe a lot to my editor, Rebecca Colesworthy, who guided me through the publication process with encouraging words and unwavering confidence in the project. Besos to Juan Pablo Echeverri for the amazing cover art; may we never be "future strangers." Sincere thanks to the Bryant University students of LCS 471, "Friendship and Intimacy in the Age of Social Media," for allowing me to experiment with the conceptual premises of this book in the classroom. I am likewise grateful to Bryant University's Department of English and Cultural Studies, College of Arts and Sciences, and Faculty Development Committee for supporting my research and awarding me the most precious of all commodities, time, to complete this project. Special thanks to Sam Simas for revision guidance and to Bryant's librarians and Writing Center staff for hosting biannual writers' retreats. My "field correspondents"—Mark Carpenter, Alan Emtage, Nathan Lee, and Michael Rhodes—deserve a cut of this book's royalties for regaling me with stories of their hookup app experiences. (Your checks are in the mail.) Last but not least, my deep love and gratitude to Jim Greene for putting up with me and keeping me sane through the writing and revision process.

I dedicate this book to Gary Craig Thomas (1946–2019), whose curiosity inspired me, whose knowledge floored me, whose sunniness warmed me, and whose joyful laugh echoes through these pages.

Preface

Since COVID-19 has forced many of us, typically the most privileged among us, to work and socialize from home, screen-mediated intimacies have taken on a new significance. We connect with work colleagues over platforms like Zoom to maintain some semblance of business as usual. We gather with friends in virtual grids to share socially distanced drinks during a quarantine happy hour. We teach and learn from home, through screens, hoping that some iota of knowledge sticks despite various domestic distractions. We teleconference with doctors to avoid infecting others and being infected. In work, play, education, and healthcare, among other places, we are using social media during the pandemic to approximate "normal life" before the pandemic.

I assert that we should do the opposite. Rather than highlight the ways that social media can help us reproduce the pre-pandemic status quo, I explore how screen-mediated connection can help us envision a radically new normal: specifically, antinormative conceptions of selfhood and community. As the race gaps in COVID-19 deaths reveal (Oppel Jr., et al.), and as the activists currently protesting a social order built on the subjugation and murder of Black bodies teach us, systemic racism has been an intrinsic and fundamental feature of "normal life" in America since the birth of the nation. Moreover, even though nearly half of the U.S. population is currently jobless due to pandemic-induced shutdowns (Li), the U.S. stock market proves, once again, that its success depends very little on the health of the American workforce or the unemployment rate (Ratner). We are therefore forced, once again, to reckon with the fact that "business as usual" rewards only the chosen, typically undeserving few, while the vast majority of Americans labor ceaselessly and fight over crumbs. Indeed, the COVID-19 pandemic has made it impossible to ignore that all American institutions—political, financial, educational, and healthcare—have been broken for quite some time, perhaps since their erection. Why anyone even remotely invested in social justice would want to return to that broken world—via social media or any other avenue—is beyond me.

But how can social media help us envision an alternative? Specifically, how can something like Grindr, the self-proclaimed "largest social networking app for gay, bi, trans, and queer people" (grindr.com), prompt us to reconsider who we are and how we relate to others? These questions, in all of their naïve optimism, animate this study. Before I attempt to answer them in earnest, however, it behooves me to state at the outset what this book is *not*. *Screen Love* is not an ethnographic account of Grindr user experience. Nobody was interviewed for this project and no salacious tales of mind-blowing hookups or love at first dick pic are recounted herein. In this regard, the book is not particularly sexy or scandalous—at least not in the conventional sense. In terms of academic discipline or genre, *Screen Love* is less a media studies analysis and more of an interdisciplinary experiment. It is informed primarily by philosophy, cultural studies, and queer theory and interested primarily in ontology, ethics, and politics (with economics and aesthetics bringing up the rear). Ultimately, this study is more *what if* than *what is*: it's a speculative philosophical inquiry grounded in humanities-based textual and visual analysis.

While many prominent thinkers[1] bemoan the bad interpersonal habits social media of all stripes instill, especially in our so-called Millennials and Gen Zers, I do not blame technology for our relationship woes or criticize younger generations for their screen use. I accept that screen-mediated discourse is an integral component of contemporary communication and embrace the fact that we cannot return to some fictional unmediated past. This book, then, is not a nostalgic plea to reinvest in the lost art of face-to-face conversation or a moralizing rant against screen-abetted communicative norms. Rather, it considers what we might do with screen-mediated connection, what it might be doing to us, and how we can harness it to conceptualize alternative models of intimacy and sociality.

The book's title, *Screen Love*, is both a practice and a command. It describes various technologically induced bonds and behaviors: humans loving screens, screens "loving" one another in networked consummation, romantic love or sexual hookups resulting from online and geosocial media, as well as the practice of screening potential partners on dating sites and apps. Screening love on the popular dating app Tinder, for example, entails

---

1. For examples of such critiques, see Turkle, Franzen, and Deresiewicz.

users swiping right on another's profile to express interest and left to communicate disinterest. Often taking the form of crass solicitations and curt rejections, screening love reflects and reproduces a cutthroat relational ethic encouraged in the neoliberal era. Through a neoliberal lens, you're either a winner or a loser, hot or not, someone who shows entrepreneurial potential or someone who fails to produce an attractive self-brand. Dating and hookup app users are socially conditioned to inform fellow users where they sit on this limited spectrum of characterological types. Indeed, *homo economicus*—the key figure of neoliberalism, according to Michel Foucault—ignores or demeans others who do not advance his self-brand.[2] Individualist and hyper-competitive, *homo economicus* perceives himself and others foremost as human capital, as mere vehicles through which cultural and/or financial capital can be accumulated. He stops at nothing to optimize himself and maximize his gains. Although dating and hookup apps may exacerbate *homo economicus's* ruthlessness, they also create a context in which a destructive ego might be humbled. More radically, they create a context in which egos and "selves" are frequently beside the point.

Greg Goldberg notes that users looking for sexual hookups on Grindr tend to objectify one another; they approach, treat, and "use" one another as objects of pleasure ("Meet Markets" 1–2). This instrumental approach to intimacy is widely decried by the political Left and Right because it defies both the ethical norms of liberal-humanist conceptions of civil society and Christian morality. From both sides of the political spectrum, we hear that altruism, self-sacrifice, social responsibility, and interpersonal respect are the moral foundations of a virtuous society. The relational norms of Grindr, Goldberg argues, have more in common with market behavior than with traditional moral principles. Grindr relational norms are transactional, impersonal, and consumerist to the core. Instead of scolding Grindr users for their self-interested and greedy behavior, however, Goldberg explores the political potential of relations grounded *in* instrumentalized intimacy, in what he calls "interobjectivity" (11). He comes to some surprising conclusions. When we objectify one another and consensually use one another as instruments of pleasure, he asserts, we, counterintuitively, respect "per-

---

2. Discussing the shift from a logic of exchange to a logic of entrepreneurship in neoliberalism, Foucault writes: "In practice, the stake in all neoliberal analysis is the replacement every time of *homo economicus* as a partner of exchange with *homo economicus* as entrepreneur of himself, being for himself his own capital, being for himself his own producer, being for himself the source of earnings" (*The Birth of Biopolitics* 226).

sonhood." After all, the Grindr user seeking a quick hookup places very few demands on the users he is objectifying. To him, fellow users are simply skin and skill sets: no real need to get personal, no real need to get to know them. This indifference to knowing the other—especially in a sexual context, given that sexual desire is linked so intensely with "knowing who we are" these days—allows the other to keep himself to himself: indifference to another's difference allows the other to maintain their otherness. Indeed, it is much less violative to mingle impersonally with another than to probe, scrutinize, or force someone to speak their truth. If respecting each other's difference and showing consideration for another's personal integrity is vital to democratic social functioning, then perhaps, Goldberg implies, we can learn these important lessons through virtual cruising and impersonal sex.

Building on Goldberg's insights, I explore how the neoliberal relational norms so prevalent in Grindr, including instrumentalized intimacy and interobjectivity, can help us conceptualize queer forms of sociality. Specifically, I develop two concepts concerning subjectivity and relationality: shared estrangement and fungibility. Both concepts defy liberal-humanist notions of selfhood and intersubjectivity; both likewise repudiate traditional understandings of community, belonging, and membership. Ultimately, it is the task of this book to consider what the connections and collections forged in virtual cruising forums might do for a queer theory of sociality.

Screen Love is therefore not an anti-Grindr polemic. It is instead a measured attempt to glean ethical and political strategies from queer networked experiences. My arguments herein emerge from a personal engagement with geosocial apps for men seeking men (m4m media, herein[3]), as well as from formal classroom and conference discussions

---

3. "m4m" is an abbreviation of "man-for-man" or "men-seeking-men" and is typically used in online chatrooms devoted to men seeking sex with other men. "m4m" is conceptually indebted to "MSM" ("men-seeking-men" or "men-who-have-sex-with-men"), which has been used in HIV-prevention campaigns since the 1990s to destigmatize male same-sex behavior. The logic is as follows: even though a man desires or has sex with other men, he might not identify as gay due to the social stigma attached to that label. Prevention campaigns nonetheless strive to reach a "not-gay" population of men who have sex with men to provide safe-sex information and HIV-prevention services. I use "m4m" instead of "MSM" because "#msm" has come to denote "mainstream media" and is typically used to critique mainstream news coverage. I use "m4m" instead of "gay" because one need not identify as gay to post a profile on m4m platforms. Moreover, like "MSM," "m4m" disentangles erotic desire from social identity, which, for better and for worse, complicates normative understandings of sexuality.

with students and colleagues, informal chats with peers (especially my "field correspondents": friends who report back to me about their m4m media experiences), and, of course, academic research. While scholarship certainly informs my study, I seek to write a quasi-academic book, one that can be understood and appreciated by undergraduates, professors, and curious nonacademics alike.

Throughout *Screen Love*, I emphasize the aesthetic, linguistic, and sensual openings emergent in m4m media: the possibilities they afford for new communicative and relational practices. Nonetheless, I hold fast to a critique of the neoliberal context in which these media emerge and the neoliberal rationality they reinforce. Unlike Shannon Winnubst, however, whose 2015 book, *Way Too Cool: Selling Out Race and Ethics*, is to date the most incisive critique of neoliberal aesthetics and (anti)ethics, I assert that pushing neoliberal logics and relational practices beyond their economic utility might pave the way for other-than-neoliberal futures. Fungibility, for example, is a key component in neoliberal capitalist value extraction. It concerns a law of economic equivalence pertaining to the substitutability of commodities. Human capital in the neoliberal context is fungible: workers are valued as skill sets, brands, and capacities, and are hired and fired accordingly. Instead of seeking a nonfungible point of resistance to thwart a logic of fungibility, as Winnubst does, I explore whether relations and exchanges based *in* fungibility might themselves carry an ethical promise. I am interested in m4m media because I have a hunch they offer a virtual opportunity: a chance to think differently about who we are and how we relate to others, a chance to conceive of subjectivity and ethics in a way that cuts against the grain of normative neoliberal, psychological, and sexological paradigms. Specifically, I wonder if the practice of trafficking in substitutable types on m4m media might push neoliberal relational norms to the point of implosion. Although fascinating work on fungibility is being done in Black and trans* studies,[4] the queer political potential of a relational ethic founded in fungibility has not, to my knowledge, been adequately explored in scholarly literature on social media and neoliberalism. *Screen Love* seeks to fill this lacuna.

July 2020
Providence, RI

---

4. For contemporary work on fungibility in Black and trans* studies, see King and Snorton. For canonical work on fungibility in Black studies, see Hartman and Spillers.

Introduction

Screen Lessons in the Classroom

You have buried one whom you loved; look about for someone to love. It is better to replace your friend than to weep for him.

—Seneca, "On Grief for Lost Friends"

I write this introduction in 2020, which marks my twenty-second anniversary of teaching university-level courses related to women's, gender, and sexuality studies (WGSS). Although my CV reads like the rap sheet of a pedagogical master of none—Introduction to Philosophy, Reading History, Oppositional Cinemas, Gay Men and Homophobia in American Culture, Sexuality and Culture—in every course I teach, I incorporate feminist and queer theory. Come syllabus prep time, I am typically at pains to locate a text possessing that rare combination of accessibility, rigor, and enjoyableness: an essay, chapter, or book that prompts learners to question widely held beliefs about gender and sexuality while simultaneously convincing them to develop a personal stake in the subject matter. The old reliables continue to work their magic: Gayle Rubin's "Thinking Sex," David Halperin's "Is There a History of Sexuality?," Anne Koedt's "The Myth of the Vaginal Orgasm," the Combahee River Collective's "Black Feminist Statement," Adrienne Rich's "Compulsory Heterosexuality and Lesbian Existence," and most anything by bell hooks. More recent gems include J. Jack Halberstam's *GaGa Feminism*, Jane Ward's *Not Gay*, Julia Serano's "Trans Woman Manifesto," David Halperin's introduction to *The War on Sex*, and Dean Spade and Craig Willse's "Marriage Will Never Set Us Free." These texts have helped make WGSS theory, history, and cultural analysis matter to my students; to boot, they have made my time in front of the classroom far more exciting.

Over the years, I've noticed that the pedagogical gems share a few features that students frequently latch on to: personal anecdotes, "current events" case studies, analyses of (actually popular) pop culture texts, and, last but not least, humor. Because my students' cultural worlds are so inundated with heroic against-all-odds success stories, heartbreaking tales of personal trauma, and capitalist rags-to-riches clichés, their ears tend to prick up when scholarly authors reveal a little something about themselves, even simply their personal reasons for writing about the topic at hand. While the political Right has proven itself quite skilled at reaching students by personalizing political issues and individualizing global concerns, the academic Left . . . well, not so much. Of course, this is partly due to the fact that the marketplace of ideas has been coopted by the brutes that shout the loudest, the ones who find no value in reasoned debate and gentle persuasion. These same brutes, moreover, would rather undergraduates spend their precious extracurricular time clockwatching in office cubicles to finance their education. The new normal of students working 40+ hours per week to pay outrageous university tuitions effectively eliminates a fundamental component of higher education: *time* to read, write, and think. In my pedagogical experience, I've noticed that students are more likely to make time to listen to the voices and viewpoints silenced by the shouting demagogues when (leftist) scholars make themselves approachably intellectual, smart but friendly, "relatable," as current business-speak would have it. Astute analyses of news stories, legal cases, and pop cultural texts also tend to leave a lasting impression. When I ask a class general, introductory questions about a course reading—such as, "Overall, what did you think of the author's ideas? What struck you, stayed with you, convinced you, or dissuaded you?"—nine times out of ten, discussion begins with a student recounting an author's personal anecdote, a case study analysis, or an author's take on a pop-culture text familiar to the student. The latter conversation starter can be a bit of a red herring (for example, "I disagree with Halberstam's analysis of *Finding Nemo* for these reasons . . ."), but strong personal reactions make for much more interesting discussions than do indifferent shoulder shrugs or intimidated silences. With any luck, memorable stories and analyses pave the way for an eventual comprehension and appreciation of an author's key arguments.

As for humor, we've learned from this century's satirical news purveyors, not to mention Aristophanes, Jonathan Swift, and Dorothy Parker, that laughing does not preclude thinking. Sometimes the best way to a student's mind is through her funny bone. The political Right paints WGSS scholars and students as cheerless snowflakes triggered by their own shadow, endlessly "virtue signaling" and desperate to create "safe spaces" to silence "free speech" (i.e., alt-right backlash blather) in order to plot the socialist revolution (if only . . .). The WGSS text that can elicit a guffaw while simultaneously stoking feminist passion or queer fury goes some way in undercutting such stereotypical representations. Moreover, that guffaw concurrently ignites and reveals the joy of collective recognition and connection: if I can laugh with you, I might have something in common with you; although we're not the same, perhaps we are alike; perhaps, most importantly, there are others like us. And so the work begins.

I recently designed a course at Bryant University titled Friendship and Intimacy in the Age of Social Media. I conceived the course to work through and experiment with this manuscript's conceptual premise. Teaching the class over the past two years helped me rethink, hone, and clarify my initial ideas; for this, I am thankful to the students of LCS 471. At the risk of turning this intro into a full-scale pedagogical reflection, I describe the nuts and bolts of this course to reveal the key questions that animate this study. All too often the classroom roots of scholarly texts are obscured; here, I want to make it clear that without my students, this book would not exist. It is written for them and for students—whether university registered or not—like them.

The quite verbose course description for Friendship and Intimacy in the Age of Social Media reads as follows:

> Modern Western democracy finds its conceptual roots in ancient understandings of friendship. *Philia*, a Greek concept concerning civic friendships between free men, was the guiding principle of governmental power in the ancient *polis*. Fast-forward 2000-plus years to the founding of Philadelphia, the City of Brotherly Love, and the site at which the Second Continental Congress declared the United States free from British rule. The name and historical importance of this city reveal how deeply *philia* is embedded in the conceptual roots of the modern democratic nation.
>
> Similarly, philosophy itself has roots, both etymological and conceptual, in *philia*, in friendship. Although often translated as "love of wisdom," philosophy might better be understood as a friendship *with* wisdom: a relation founded not in property ("I am yours," "You belong to me"), but, rather,

in mutual respect, humility, and interdependence. Given the foundational role friendship plays in Western thought and society, then, it seems fair to say that a nation's dominant understanding of friendship tells us a lot about how that society functions, what matters most to its people, and what type of life is considered most worth striving for. In other words, the way we understand friendship is intimately connected to the way we understand the "good life."

In these times—the age of social media, the age of neoliberal global capitalism—what model of friendship is considered ideal and why? Has friendship been reduced to business networking and status boosting, or do traditional models of friendship still have relevance? How have global capitalism and social media affected friendship and romance? Should we be hopeful about the democratic potential of social media as they are being implemented in social justice movements such as #blacklivesmatter and #metoo? Or, should we despair that social media are increasingly channels for trolling, racism, misogyny, and political manipulation? What new avenues for creative cooperation and democratic participation become available in the social media context? Which are threatened or foreclosed? These questions will guide us through a philosophical analysis of friendship and intimacy in the age of social media, in which we will pay close attention to non-normative, one might say queer, relationship models through the ages.

The course is divided into three sections: 1) Philosophy of Friendship and Love, in which we read and discuss canonical Western philosophical and literary texts; 2) Neoliberalism and Social Media, in which we analyze globalization and new media theory to assess the relevance of traditional models of friendship and intimacy for the contemporary world; and 3) Beyond *Philia*, in which we explore nontraditional, queer practices of friendship, both historical and emergent, as potential alternatives to current relationship norms that hinder the development of a more just world.

As the ink dries on this manuscript, I've come to realize that this course's goals are far more ambitious than what I set out to achieve here. For example, although I walk my students through an abbreviated and tailored history of the philosophy of friendship and love (*The Epic of*

Gilgamesh, Homer, Sappho, Plato, Aristotle, Seneca, Michel de Montaigne, Ralph Waldo Emerson, and Emma Goldman), I spare the reader of this manuscript such a journey (however much I recommend it!). Although most of my undergraduate students learn about neoliberalism for the first time in this course, I assume here an audience somewhat familiar with its basic principles. For the uninitiated, however, I offer here a very efficient, and hence very neoliberal, bullet-pointed list of what I believe to be the key aspects of neoliberal philosophy:

- Competition governs all aspects of life
- Social inequality is necessary and virtuous
- Society = a collection of self-interested, rational market agents
- Collectivism is suspect; individualism should be cultivated
- Economic efficiency = democratic morality
- Economic freedom = political freedom
- Civic values = economic values
- Social problems exist because individuals make bad choices; social structures, systems, and institutions are not to blame.
- There is a natural hierarchy of winners and losers: winners maximize their entrepreneurial potential and have little need for communal or institutional support networks; losers fail to live up to their entrepreneurial potential and rely on social systems, communities, and other individuals for support.
- All aspects of life are measurable and quantifiable: data driven, cost-benefit analyses should be used to assess everything from work performance to public health to interpersonal relationships.

And neoliberal political-economic goals:

- Unfettered free market ("All boats will rise" if the market functions without regulation)
- Small to nonexistent state (rejection of welfare state and socialism *tout court*)
- Strong private property rights

- Free trade

- Deregulation of industry

- Union busting

- Privatization of public services and spaces[1]

Given that social media technologies flourish in the neoliberal era, I understand them as the "language" of neoliberalism: efficient, utilitarian, and informational. A central question that concerns me is: How does the neoliberal political-economic-technological-cultural nexus affect our ability to relate ethically? Although in my course I cover a broad range of social media and ask "big questions" about their interpersonal and political consequences, I narrow my focus here primarily to m4m media—known popularly as gay hookup apps—to explore an emergent queer relational ethic. Nonetheless, the conceptual premises of the course and this book remain the same: if *philia* is, at least in theory, the building block of Western democracy, does it remain important to modern ethics? To contemporary political life? Should it? If not, are new models of friendship and intimacy taking shape in network culture that can steer us towards alternative models of sociality not grounded in *philia*?

Philia itself is a notoriously slippery concept, and my students and I spend the first third of the course trying to pin it down. In addition to reading chapters of Aristotle's *Nicomachean Ethics* and *Politics*, we look to secondary literature, including an essay by David Konstan that offers a succinct definition of *philia*: "In sum, love and friendship in Aristotle are best understood not as entailing obligations or as based on kinship, but as an altruistic desire which, when reciprocated, results in a state of affairs that Aristotle, and Greeks in general, called *philia*" (212). At first, students typically seem skeptical of reciprocal altruism: Why would anyone want to do something good for another person if they are not necessarily going to be recognized for it? Why would anyone put another's interests before one's own? Isn't all altruism egoism in some form? Eventually, however, they come to find *philia* an inspiring, noble ideal (#relationshipgoals), but are quick to point out that this ideal is all too rare in today's world: social media, in their general estimation, do not lend themselves to the

---

1. This list is culled from the insights of various critics of neoliberalism, especially Brown, Kotsko, May, Monbiot, Read, and Winnubst.

cultivation of shared virtue between friends. Instead, social media cheapen friendship by turning it into a transactional, superficial, popularity contest. Perhaps unwittingly echoing Sherri Turkle's or William Deresiewicz's critiques of social media friendships,[2] students grow nostalgic for traditional relationship models that promote a selfless common good and emphasize the mutual striving toward shared virtue.

Although I am heartened by the fact that ancient philosophy continues to inspire, I do not let *philia* off the hook so easily. Once students seem thoroughly convinced that *philia* is the best of all possible relationship models, I reread a sentence from the course description: "*Philia*, a Greek concept concerning civil friendships between free men, was the guiding principle of governmental power in the ancient *polis*." Several leading questions follow: What does this sentence imply? Why "free men"? Were only men capable of *philia*? What about women? Moreover, doesn't "free men" signal that there were unfree men, that is, slaves? Does this mean that *philia* was the conceptual backbone of a patriarchal, slave society? If so, are sexism and racism—or other forms of social exclusivity and hierarchal categorization—part and parcel of this concept? Has our understanding of governmental power been flawed, then, from the outset? Why would we name one of our nation's most politically significant cities after it? Might *philia*'s emphasis on commonality and shared traits inevitably lead to oppressive social hierarchies? What forms of community and politics might develop from friendships and intimacies that challenge the principles of *philia*?

Admittedly, it's a bit of a straw-man setup. Although Aristotle's discussion of political power in *Nicomachean Ethics* certainly applies exclusively to free male citizens, in the same book, he also expresses his distaste for democracy itself. For him, monarchy is a far superior political system. Of the three types of polity—from best to worst: kingship, aristocracy, and timocracy (in which power is based in private property), democracy is merely a corruption of the worst polity. This usually comes as a bit of a shock to students: according to Aristotle, democracy is a perversion of the least attractive political form. In an interesting twist, however, Aristotle claims that democracy is also the least offensive of the three deviations of the three primary polities: tyranny is the most corrupt deviation (of monarchy); oligarchy is the second worst deviation (of aristocracy); and democracy is the least corrupt deviation (of timocracy). Although friendship's import

---

2. These authors' critiques of screen-mediated relationality rest in quite traditional, more or less Aristotlean understandings of friendship.

varies for each polity, it remains the primary relationship between ruler and ruled and between citizens. In order for governmental power to function smoothly in a monarchy, for example, a king must maintain a friendship with his subjects as a virtuous father would with a son (a tyrant is essentially a bad dad). An aristocrat, moreover, should relate to his inferiors as a husband treats a wife (because the husband's "bloodline," according to Aristotle, is superior to the wife's). Finally, both timocracies and democracies function well when relations between citizens mimic friendships between brothers. *Philia* therefore plays the most crucial role in democracy because democratic citizens are theoretically on equal footing: without daddy or husband to tell them what to do, democratic "brothers" must take care of themselves. "Thus in tyrannies [. . .] friendships and justice hardly exist, but in democracies they exist to a greater extent, because the citizens are equal and so have much in common" (158). A socially harmonious "City of Brotherly Love" therefore rests on an extrafamilial but fraternalesque kinship between citizens. Aristotle repeatedly emphasizes that the common ground between citizens must be cultivated and nurtured in a polity so reliant on *philia*. A crucial problem for democracy, then, concerns the stranger: the one who is not alike, does not share common ground, and therefore does not deserve the same treatment (or rights) as the brother-citizen. "How a man should live in relation to his wife, and in general how one friend should live in relation to another, appears to be the same question as how they can live justly. For the demands of justice on a friend towards a friend are not the same as those towards a stranger, nor those on a companion the same as those towards a fellow-student" (160).

The operative question of the course thus becomes: How are we to treat the stranger ethically in a democracy? Furthermore, if the stranger in antiquity included women, racialized Others, and noncitizens, who counts as a stranger today? Have social media brought us closer to an ethical treatment of the stranger? How would a polity function if hospitality toward the stranger were its foundational principle? Students are typically eager to consider alternatives to *philia* once the gendered, racial, and nativist implications are revealed. I return to another sentence from the course description, this one a Gilles Deleuze and Félix Guattari-inspired musing about the relationship between thought and thinker, to orient us toward a non*philial* understanding of friendship.[3] "Although often translated as

---

3. Deleuze and Guattari begin *What Is Philosophy?* with a discussion of the relationship between thought and thinker: "The philosopher is the concept's friend;

'love of wisdom,' philosophy might better be understood as a friendship *with* wisdom: a relation founded not in property ('I am yours,' 'You belong to me'), but, rather, in mutual respect, humility, and interdependence." A thinker's relationship to thought, then, becomes our initial model of a non*philial* friendship. In my reading of Deleuze and Guattari, thought is that which cannot be fully owned, captured, or privatized by the thinker; it is instead an elusive something that emerges in common with often unrecognized others. Mercurial, ephemeral, and always ready to escape us, thought exceeds our reach as we work to tie it down with words, sounds, and gestures that nevertheless fail to represent it fully. Thought, therefore, is indeed strange and remains a stranger: it exceeds the thinker, holds her at a remove, solicits him, teases her, but refuses a dialectical resolution. As an unassimilable foreigner, thought is best approached defenses down and with the utmost humility. It is, after all, the potential of what we are and how we view the world, the becoming of what we might comprehend and experience. Like death, perhaps the strangest of strangers, thought deserves our respect, our vulnerability, and our hospitality.

The *homophilic* bonds that ground Aristotle's democracy of brotherly love—bonds built on an exclusive commonness—lie in direct contrast to the *philoxenic* bonds at the heart of philosophy itself.[4] Based in receptivity to foreignness, *philoxenic* bonds nurture that which is most alien among friends or citizens: the very differences that are potentially impossible to subsume or assimilate. Like the relation between thinker and thought, this bond is not grounded in property: it resists the terms of belonging (as in, "I belong to *x* group" or "I am yours, you are mine") that turn on an in/out, either/or axis. *Philoxenic* bonds are built on the very things people do *not* have in common, and, most importantly, they resist the desire to fuse, unify, or make those people one. Contrary to a (Hegelian) dialectical conception of intersubjectivity that rests on the subsumption of difference, *philoxenic* bonds encourage a nonassimilative interdependence that valorizes the ontological strangeness of self and other. This

---

he is the potentiality of the concept. [. . .] Does this mean that the friend is the friend of his own creations? Or is the actuality of the concept due to the potential of the friend, in the unity of the creator and his double?" (5).

4. In *Affective Communities*, Leela Gandhi presents *philia* and *philoxenia* as competing political models of friendship, the former indebted to Aristotle, the latter to Epicurus. My understandings of *philia* and *philoxenia* are profoundly informed by her work. See Gandhi, 28–31.

bond, then, works to preserve strangeness, even to amplify it, instead of making it identical. A community or politics founded in *philoxenic* bonds surely offers an alternative to the *homophilic* power blocs that have plagued Western democracy since the outset. But what would a *philoxenic* community look like?

Inventors and early theorists of the Internet sought to show us. The dream of the Internet—and, later, social media—is arguably to construct a *philoxenic* utopia: to flatten *homophilic*, capitalist, and elitist hierarchies built around knowledge production, access, and communication. In this utopia, users connect with and learn from strangers; they become increasingly receptive to foreignness and ultimately transform into cosmopolitan citizens.[5] However much this dream may have become a nightmare of capitalist exploitation, self-segregation, disinformation, and political manipulation, the *philoxenic* utopian impulse lies at the Internet's heart. Alas, if not the Internet, where might we locate a *philoxenic* community? In what context might we access or affirm *philoxenic* bonds?

In "Cruising as a Way of Life," the final chapter of *Unlimited Intimacy: Reflections on the Subculture of Barebacking*, Tim Dean argues that a certain form of *philoxenia*—what he designates "the psychoanalytic ethic"—guides gay men's public, not digital, cruising. For Dean, the public cruising encounter is an exercise in negotiating foreignness in the world and in our selves. It is grounded in a risky receptivity to strangers and a refusal to personalize or get to know another. "The ethics of cruising is a matter not of how many people one has sex with or what kind of sex one has with them (bareback or otherwise) but of how one treats the other and, more specifically, how one treats his or her own otherness" (177). Cruising becomes Dean's model of *philoxenic* ethics because otherness is neither assimilated through identification nor annihilated through differentiation. "[W]hat seems salutary about cruising is how it can involve intimate contact with strangers without necessarily domesticating the other's otherness. [. . .] [I]t is the intimate contact with the other that does not attempt to eliminate otherness that I wish to advocate as ethically exemplary" (180). Unfortunately, however, public access to cruising and even to nonsexual encounters with strangers is increasingly threatened by privatization and profit. Urban redevelopment efforts, for example, tend

---

5. Here I am glossing the more optimistic arguments of early Internet theorists. See Ebo and Rheingold.

to make cities more amenable to tourists and corporations but frequently decrease the amount of social space for variously classed and raced city dwellers to gather and interact. The Internet and hookup apps have likewise transformed public cruising into a privatized experience: the dance of desire becomes, according to Dean, a pleasureless hunt "indistinguishable from Internet shopping" and a dehumanizing experience that rests on "a controlled instrumentalization of the other as an object of use" (194). What these different forms of privatization have in common is a desire to reduce the risk involved in encountering strangeness. Often in the name of safety and security, perhaps the two most commonly deployed political terms since 9/11, privatization efforts work to prevent the radical encounter with otherness that might set in motion a transformative ethical experience. The cruel irony, of course, is that such risk-reduction measures end up making our cities—and our psyches—more hostile and more dangerous. Without interclass and interracial contact cities grow segregated and potentially become powder kegs. Without peaceful and pleasurable encounters with strangers, city dwellers become suspicious and often aggressive. Public cruising is one practice, then, that teaches us how to respectfully navigate foreignness in an increasingly polarized world. With the help of Jane Jacobs and Samuel Delany—thinkers who assert that social and, in Delany's case, sexual intercourse among strangers is essential to a city's livelihood—Dean makes a strong case for *philoxenia* as the ethical foundation of an authentically democratic society. But, beyond cruising, what would such a society look like? What risks are involved in philoxenia?

Because *Unlimited Intimacy* is in essence an analysis of, and often an apologia for, barebacking subcultures, Dean, like the subjects of his study, takes risks. For example, one of his models of ethically exemplary behavior comes in the form of a handsome man at a sex club who consents to anonymous anal penetration from any attendee whomsoever—no questions asked, no visual or aural identification needed. An archetype of *philoxenic* hospitality, is he not? Well, no, not according to my students. Up to this point in the text, Dean has my students in the palm of his hand: they agree wholeheartedly that a basic respect for and openness to foreignness are essential to democratic harmony; they understand the social pitfalls in privatizing public space (the Disneyfication of Times Square, for example) and digitizing intimacy (Grindr, Tinder, etc.). Although cruising is often an uncomfortable topic for them to discuss—not only because they find themselves talking about it with someone their father's age, but also because most of them come to the course with negative prejudices against the practice—they seem to appreciate Dean's argumentative moxie and persuasiveness. The behavior of this sex club participant, however, is where they draw the line: "Is this guy mentally ill? Is he suicidal? Is he on drugs? No one of sound mind would consent to such risky behavior!" It's not long before the pitchforks and torches come out: "He's giving gay people a bad name! He's a public health menace! He should be locked up! And sex clubs should be closed down!"

The recourse to sex panic rhetoric and respectability politics is familiar and unsurprising. As calmly as possible, I explain a few canonical sexuality studies concepts in an effort to quell the outrage. Up first, Gayle Rubin's "fallacy of the misplaced scale": her critique of the excessive amount of *meaning* we assign to sex. Compared to other pleasurable, consensual physical activity, sex is always considered a "special case" that must be adjudicated with unique, and uniquely stringent, moral criteria and legal punishment. Blamed and scapegoated for countless non-sex-related problems, sex in Western culture is deemed guilty before proven innocent. "Heretical sex," blindly consenting to anal penetration in the age of AIDS, for example, "is an especially heinous sin that deserves the harshest of punishments" (11). But whence comes our bloodlust for nonnormative sexual behavior? Religion, social conservatism, biopolitics, homophobia . . . you name it. So as not to get sidetracked by a search for the origins of the "misplaced scale," I simply ask some questions: Are we judging Sex Club Guy so harshly because we are viewing his behavior through an inherited sex-negative lens? Are we extra critical because we are overvaluing sex, that is, making it perhaps more meaningful than it should be? Are we being unfair to sex? Do we judge other consensual physical activity—say, massage, bodywork, even sports—the same way? What about athletes who consent to self-harm and who harm others (boxers, football players), are they too *non compos mentis*? Why do we cheer athletes who violently hurt one another and scorn those who consent to "unlimited intimacy?"

Next, a historical backdrop: Michel Foucault's "perverse implantation," his cheeky term for the sexological invention of a link between sexual desire and social identity (*History of Sexuality, Vol. 1* 36–50). His argument, in a nutshell, concerns the ways in which sexuality becomes a tool of social control in the modern era. By establishing erotic desire as the tell-all secret of personality, psychology, and social behavior, nineteenth-century sexual sciences, including psychoanalysis, performed a great service to law enforcement, criminal surveillance, and population management. In "implanting" perversions into individuals—that is, goading, forcing, and molding erotic confessions—sexologists created "sexuality": a window into the soul, a hermeneutic revelatory of what makes us tick. While in previous eras, according to Foucault, sexual fantasies and fetishes bore little relation to a person's overall character, in modernity they become indicators of *who* we are and *why* we behave the way we do—especially if that behavior is judged criminal. Sexology therefore establishes normative social criteria by which we, the populace, police ourselves and one another. The upshot of our biopolitical work is that population management is far easier for social administrates. What's more, sexology invents a new class of criminals—zoophiles, pedophiles, homosexuals, etc.—that suddenly lurk around every corner. It becomes the moral and patriotic duty of neighbors and psychiatrists alike to rat out the perverts and bring them to justice. In short, and back to the "misplaced scale," we are especially vigilant around and suspect of nonnormative sexual actors and actions partly because we have been trained to be so, for at least a century, by the highest juridical and scientific authorities.

Rounding out the discussion of Sex Club Guy is Michael Warner's critique of sexual moralism: the all too common practice of asserting one's own virtue by sexually shaming another (1–40). Of course, for Warner, this isn't morality at all; it's what sociologists call "downward comparison" (Fischer 52–53). For example, the put-down, "you're a slut," implies: "I am not a slut; you are dirty, and I am clean; you are polluted, and I am pure; therefore, I am morally superior to you." Even "friendlier" expressions of sexual moralism rely on the purity/pollution logic. The not-so-subtle subtext of "no homo," a phrase typically used by straight-identified American men after expressing even the slightest modicum of affection for other men, seems to be: "Don't worry, I'm totally normal, bro; I'm not gay, which would make my affection weird, uncomfortable, abnormal." Again, a declaration of one's sexual normality assures us of their social normality; so-called "real men" have nothing to worry about once the threat of a morally suspect homosexuality is vanquished. Due to both pervasive sex negativity, an overinvestment in the meaningfulness of sex, and a widespread belief that sexuality speaks volumes about a person's character, then, sex is an easy target in moral one-upmanship.

Zoom out, and we see this one-upmanship on a social level: dominant groups frequently secure their social perch by pointing to the supposed sexual immorality of other groups. In male-dominated societies, for instance, a male rapist's criminal behavior is sometimes justified by calling attention to the female victim's alleged sexual impropriety, often ostensibly written on her body in the form of "slutty" clothing or gestures. Groups invested in white supremacy likewise characterize Black sexuality as animalistic and excessive in order to "prove" that minority group's social and moral inferiority. Of course, it's a truism that those with a fragile sense of self shit on people purportedly beneath them in order to feel better. But sex is uniquely positioned to bear the brunt of individual *and* social insecurity. Because shame, anxiety, and embarrassment are part and parcel of sexual desire and development, because we all feel, at one point or another, vulnerable, uncertain, and insecure in regard to sexual matters, it's our collective Achilles heel. Sexual moralism is thus a scoundrel's last refuge: instead of acknowledging that, at heart, we may have something (sexually) in common with people supposedly different from us, instead of recognizing that sexuality is messy, complicated, and *strange* for everyone, the insecure and/or power hungry among us jump at the chance to strike where it hurts most—where it might, in fact, have once hurt the insecure and power hungry most! A nonmoralizing sexual ethics might begin, then, with the following axiom: "If sex is a kind of indignity, we're all in it together" (*Trouble*, 36). A moral code that doesn't take into account that we are all, to varying degrees, humiliated, humbled, and made vulnerable by sex, may be, in the end, immoral.

Discussion around these concepts tends to defuse the situation; reluctant head-nodding and some resigned eye-rolling usually conclude the class session on Dean's work. However, despite the sex panic and moralism, the students ultimately have a point: if we follow *philoxenia* to its logical conclusion we find that the coherence, security, and stability of a *philoxenic* organism is in fact always at risk. Be it a virus infecting an individual body or a noncitizen challenging the laws and mores of a social body, the risk of dissolution and disintegration is ever-present. Indeed, the very identity of the organism is at stake: How can a self or a state define itself, even know itself, if it is unclear where the self/citizen begins and the nonself/noncitizen ends? How can we maintain the boundaries of a self or a state if the stranger is granted all-access entry? How can an organism maintain structural integrity if its very form morphs incessantly? Leela Gandhi, whose staging of the *philia/philoxenia* standoff in *Affective Communities* (13–33) grounds my course rationale, eloquently articulates the stakes of *philoxenic* hospitality: "Poised in a relation where an irreducible and asymmetrical other always calls her being into question, she is ever willing to risk becoming strange or guestlike in her own domain, whether this be home, nation, community, race, gender, sex, skin, or species. So too, the open house of hospitality or the open heart of [*philoxenic*] friendship can never know guests-friends in advance, as one might a fellow citizen, sister, or comrade" (31). Not knowing who we are or whom we might be obliged to welcome is indeed a troublesome prospect. It is particularly upsetting to college students who are striving to hone their self-identities and solidify their value systems; even more so to students working to develop personal brands so as to be competitive on the job market. Whereas *philoxenia* in theory might seem the key to creating a truly democratic and welcoming *polis*, when personalized it becomes a scary prospect. If the wall between self and Other must remain porous, how are we ever to know who we are, let alone empower ourselves to become the best we can be? Tim Dean's argument against the teachings of Christ in the conclusion of *Unlimited Intimacies* becomes the final nail in *philoxenia*'s coffin for many of my students: "Contrary to the Christian ethics of viewing the other as a neighbor and loving him or her 'as thyself,' the psychoanalytic ethic insists that the other's strangeness be preserved rather than annihilated through identification" (212). *Philoxenia* at last reveals its true colors: from my students' perspective it is not only a threat to personal and national identity, it is, worse, an ethical model espoused by unsafe sex addicts and antichrists alike. It's difficult to talk them back from that one.

So, I propose, what if ethics were grounded neither in a *homophilic* nurturing of an exclusive sameness nor in a *philoxenic* embrace of radical difference? Is it possible to relate to one another on a level beyond socially assigned identity, beyond personality, and ultimately beyond difference? Can we become *indifferent* to the sexiness of our own and others' very sexy, very singular psychological depth? What if, instead, we treated one another as nonidentically similar, or as familiar correspondents? Following Dean, what if "getting to know each other" were irrelevant to ethical intimate relations? What if we resisted the temptation to answer to, interrogate, know, and ultimately assimilate and control the Other? Put simply, what if we responded differently to the seductive (siren) song of Otherness: neither fully open to it, nor exclusively against it? What if ethical intimacy begins when we choose *not* to connect with another on a personal level?

Take for example, once more, sexuality: that feature of modern personhood that purportedly tells us so much about who we are. Even though historians of sexuality have provided ample evidence to disabuse us of the illusion that sexual desire is a reliable, transhistorical indicator of personality, psychic interiority, and behavioral motivation, most everything—from our laws to our politics to our manner of dressing, walking, talking, and consuming—continues to rest on this belief. If I'm a straight American man, I *can't* like *x* cultural activity (figure skating, baking, interior decorating); if I'm a gay American man, I probably *should* like *y* (shopping, dancing, drag); if I desire *x* type of person, there's something wrong with me; if I dream about erotic practice *y*, I should go see a therapist. As the army of armchair psychoanalysts among us would have it, everything we do, say, make, or think is revelatory of whom or what we desire and a clear indicator of the type of person we may not even know we truly are: sexuality is an open secret that always gives us away. Although we might take heart in reports that younger generations are less invested in rigid sexual binaries (Lewis)—despite the fact that most Americans continue to believe in the biological basis of sexual orientation itself (Jones)—we need only look to the increasing severity of legal punishments meted out to nonnormative sexual actors to understand how deeply invested we remain in sexuality as a moral barometer of the self that readily transforms into a tool of social control.

The David M. Halperin and Trevor Hoppe edited volume *The War on Sex* explores the recent increase in policing and punishing nonnormative sexual actors. In the introduction, for example, Halperin provides a brief history of U.S. sex offender registries. Since 1994, the year that Congress began requiring all states to maintain a registry, the number of legally identified sex offenders has ballooned. There are currently more registered sex offenders in this country than there are residents of North Dakota, Wyoming, or Alaska (13). The increase has less to do with drastic changes in people's sexual behavior and more to do with the ever-expanding meaning of the label "sex offender." In some states, a sex offense includes public urination, sexting between minors, and many other acts that are either consensual, involve zero physical contact between individuals, or both (14). Although sex offender registries were created to track and survey violent sexual criminals such as rapists and child predators, a shockingly low percentage of contemporary sex offenders—less than one percent in some states—are classified as violent (14). In many cases, killing another person would merit a lesser sentence than a sex offense that involves no physical harm to another and even no contact with another (24). And while contemporary registries systematically discriminate against minority populations (including people of color, transgender youth, and people with HIV), they also discriminate against stigmatized sex *practices* (commercial sex, pornography, intergenerational sex, nonheterosexual sex in general) that cut across social identity lines (39). The label, "sex offender," displayed in red ink across driver's licenses in some states, severely limits vocational opportunities, residential options, and access to public space; it can result in lifelong restrictions on movement, impossible paroles, prison sentences wildly disproportionate to the crime, and indefinite psychiatric confinement (14, 25–26). Gay-identified men are overrepresented among those who receive lifetime psychiatric detention (perversely called "civil commitment") for sex crimes (30). In a cruel historical twist, the fight led by gay males for the removal of public cruising from the first sex offender registry indirectly contributed to that registry becoming a Cthulhu-like monster whose tentacles wend their way into so many aspects of modern life: school, work, public and online leisure. As a result, in the eyes of the police, public health officials, and psychiatrists today, we are all potential sex criminals: guilty until proven innocent.

Excessively punitive American sex laws and offender registries are clear indicators of our continued investment in perceiving sexual acts and identities as barometers of moral character and social worth. A first step toward reforming such draconian measures might be to *care less* about sexuality—but not in a simplistically open-minded "it's all good" sort of way. What I'm suggesting here is that we valorize consensual forms of intimacy in which depth-psychological understandings of sexuality are de-emphasized, if not inoperative. Instead of locating ourselves and one another in sex, we should work to abandon both the self that has been identified and "invented" *as* sexual as well as the intersubjective intimacies that such sexualized subjects nourish. By betraying normative sexual meanings and arrangements, we orient ourselves toward an understanding of the nonidentical sameness—the equivalence—of people and forms. In short, we learn to become fungible.

Between or beyond *philia* and *philoxenia*, then, *fungibilis* is an anti-individualist, collectivist, or, rather, "collectionist" ethics premised on the formal substitutability of the self. For the moment, imagine it as an extreme form of *philoxenia*: an embrace of foreignness so radical that one and another become mutually interchangeable. This self-substitution is voluntary, pleasurable, and sensual: one welcomes the prospect of losing the self, disappearing into a sea of similitude, and becoming a mere equivalence. Through a process of volitional, aesthetic desubjection—momentarily freeing oneself from social definitions and determinations—the self is afforded an opportunity to expand outward, to extend itself horizontally toward similar, desubjected aesthetic forms. Unlike *philoxenia*, then, *fungibilis*—or, less pretentiously, fungibility—nurtures likeness rather than foreignness: it is an ethics rooted in an immanentist ontology that understands substance as internally differentiated, asubjective sameness.

Bear with me: I realize that the previous sentence is a mouthful of philosophy jargon. When I try to explain immanentist ontology in lay terms to students, the first things that come to mind are the hippie-dippiest of song lyrics: the (third) chorus of Joni Mitchell's "Woodstock," which begins, "We are stardust/Billion-year-old carbon," or the title of a (much worse) song by Moby, "We Are All Made of Stars." As saccharine and as naively "we're cut from the same cloth; we are all the same" as the sentiment behind these lyrics is, it's a start. As post–Big Bang subjects, we *are* all made of stars, and in that sense ontologically connected. But if human history teaches us anything it's that the discovery of a shared origin of species does not magically usher in global social equality. The powerful instead willfully misinterpret and manipulate the data to secure their social perch. The very un-Darwinian concept of Social Darwinism, for example, continues to convince many that capitalism is an inevitable part of our evolution and that white supremacy is by design. Rather than emphasizing the constitutive role of interdependence and symbiosis in species' development, as Darwin did, the "victors of history" lay stress on "survival of the fittest," which translates economically to unbridled capitalism and eugenically to white power.

This doesn't mean, however, that we have to give up on the connective thread of cosmic stardust altogether. The fact that "billion-year-old carbon" interacts with the environment, genetic material, and microbiota of each stellar individual can still teach us something about immanentist ontology. Indeed, the billions of microbes—bacteria, protozoa, fungi, and viruses—that constitute the collective microbiome of our species might help us envision an ontological substance grounded not only in "internally differentiated, asubjective sameness," but also, at least to an extent, in *philoxenia*. "All of human development and all the systems in the body have all evolved, or co-evolved, with our microbes," argues neuropharmacologist, John Cryan. "As humans we are very much human-focused and we feel that human cells and genes have primacy, but the microbes were there first" (Davis). And while all humans swim in a common pool of the planet's microbiota, the way it interacts with each socially situated individual is unique: there is infinite variation emergent within and from this communal pool; there is differentiation within sameness, singularity in the common. Moreover, microbiota, caring little for who we are in terms of social identity, welcome us as strangers—at least when they're not trying to kill us. The friendlier of the bunch work with our guts to digest breast milk, and hence help many of us survive infancy, and with our skin to potentially protect us from cancer. In this way, microbiota model a *philoxenic* openness to foreignness by cooperating with our strange and terrible species. And though microbes can escape the human body and live without us, which would effectively spell the end of *homo sapiens*, they've "chosen" to stay with the trouble (Davis). All this in spite of the insulting fact that we've put the cart (the human subject) before the horse (microbiota) for centuries! Indeed, what's becoming clear in this century is that the designation "human" is so *last* century: "Animals and plants are no longer heralded as autonomous entities," biologists Seth R. Bordenstein and Kevin R. Theis declare, "but rather as biomolecular networks composed of the host plus its associated microbes, i.e., 'holobionts'" (1). Once we holobionts accept on a mass scale our microorganismal interdependency, our species and the planet will surely benefit. If we learn to respect the microbiome, show it a little gratitude, and work harder to figure out how to exist with it symbiotically, we might also learn some important lessons about ontology and ethics.

With all due respect to the science of microbiota, the onto-ethical framework I am sketching here—substance (internally differentiated sameness) expressed in various modes (holobionts, geologic cycles, cosmic forces) that become fungible in the search for corresponding forms—is most indebted to the work of Leo Bersani. For Bersani, substance is originary, but actualized and accessible only in its effects. Bersani highlights the way "homo-ness," his word for substance, manifests and re-manifests in aesthetic and sexual experiences. It is concretized in art, for instance, and sensualized in queer forms of sociability—anonymous cruising, for one. In a Bersanian ontology, being is self-contained fullness, and desire does not originate in lack. Consequently, progress or growth is not dependent on assimilating difference. "One way to describe Bersani's entire oeuvre," Mikko Tuhkanen notes in his remarkable *The Essentialist Villain: On Leo Bersani*, "is to say that it seeks other modes of our moving-in-the-world than that compelled by an originary lack" (5). Although Bersani is per-haps best known in queer studies for his psychoanalytic investigations into the self-annihilating sex drive (the so-called "antisocial thesis"), his late work attempts to think beyond the dialectical *sturm und drang* of an anthropocentric psychoanalytic ethics. In this work, he leaves behind both a sadistic ethics of intersubjectivity and a masochistic ethics of self-shattering. What emerges is an ethical subject that develops according to the rhythms of an impersonal, expansive, and even cosmic narcissism. In its becoming, this subject moves from a centripetal retreat towards nothingness to a centrifugal extension toward corresponding earthly and celestial forms and forces. Through aesthetic and sensual encounters that diminish the power of a voracious ego, the subject becomes aware that she is nothing special—or, rather, that her specialness lies in the capacity to recognize and valorize variations of an essential sameness.[6]

By way of an example, one that I explore further in chapter 5, call to mind (or see figure 5.3) Andy Warhol's *100 Cans,* his famous print of the Campbell's Beef Noodle Soup collection. In this image, the soup cans are essentially the same but superficially unique. What makes each can special is its imperfections, its failure to live up to the Platonic ideal of Soup Can. Whether it's a smeared label or a misshapen cylinder, no can is perfect: all of them "misfit" together in an assemblage of serial similitude (Flatley,

---

6. Bersani's conception of subjectivity, his preferred self-subtractive practices (cruising, e.g.), and his antisocial thesis *tout court* have been critiqued, most pointedly by José Esteban Muñoz and Jack Halberstam, as blind to social difference, especially race, and averse to intersectionality. These critiques are of course necessary and have proven quite productive; they are foundational to queer of color critique. I remain interested in Bersani as an ontologist, as I indicate above, and as a methodologist. Methodologically speaking, my project takes a cue from Bersani's total critique: his radical negation of the *value* of liberal society itself and his transvaluation of the antisocial. Total critique, an immanentist methodology credited to Nietzsche, involves not simply championing the negated abject of a dialectical struggle but attacking full force the system that designates and classifies abjection. An absolute negation in this method is conceptually necessary for autonomous creation: *pars destruens, pars construens.* I argue in my previous book, *Friendship as a Way of Life,* that Foucault employs a total critique in his repudiation of sexology and his affirmation of queer friendship. After divesting the homosexual of its sexological essence, Foucault finds in queer friendship "the development towards which the problem of homosexuality tends," and a creation that must be "invented from A to Z" (*Essential* 136). In this project, I likewise valorize a relational form immanent to capitalism—fungibility—in attempt to think beyond the system that exploits it merely for profit. For more on the critique of the antisocial thesis, see Goldberg, *Antisocial Media* 3–5, 25–30; For more on total critique, see Roach, *Friendship* 66–70.

"Like" 92–93). Moreover, because the cans are formally equivalent, they are interchangeable. As pieces of a themed collection, they can be swapped one for the other without much consequence: their being-in-common is unperturbed and they remain united in their inability to be identical or ideal. The ontological lesson here, which resonates with Bersani's work, is that sameness is the structuring framework through which difference manifests. Ethics, consequently, rests not on the primacy of difference (on, for example, the alluring yet enigmatic call of the Hegelian Other), but, rather, on the appeal of an essential sameness that "tempts the subject with nothing that he does not already, in some form, have" (Tuhkanen 157).

On a purely formal level, I see this onto-ethical schematic at work in m4m media. Not unlike the way Warhol assembles his soup cans, m4m media, beginning with Grindr, gathers singular avatars into a collection of fungible objects. The layout of the standard m4m media grid bears both a visual and structural resemblance to Warhol's soup cans (if you don't know what the standard m4m grid looks like, see figures 5.1 and 5.2). This is not to say that all user profile pics look identical, nor is it to cynically claim that the people manipulating the various avatars in the grid are "all the same." It would be ridiculous to argue that m4m media avatars and the people communicating through them are treated equally in the virtual call and response. As numerous scholars and critics have pointed out, prejudices and powerplays based in social identity—racism, effemephobia, body shaming—course through m4m media.[7] Each user brings to the apps the historical weight of personhood—unique histories and experiences, subjective worldviews, and varying degrees of social privilege—and each user must negotiate all of this in profile setup and communicative exchange. Nevertheless, it is the *protocol* of mediated fungibility and the *figure* of the interchangeable avatar-object that interest me here. Just as Foucault argues that the key figure in neoliberal theory is *homo economicus*, I posit that the fungible avatar-object is the key figure of m4m media.

Figures, according to Todd May, are "created and defined by the environment in which they arise. [. . .] They are constructed, in Foucault's eyes, through a series of practices that give rise to them by impinging upon individuals in particular ways" (18). The theoretical figure of *homo economicus* affects and influences actual neoliberal subjects in myriad

---

7. For examples of this scholarship, see Daroya, McGlotten, Rodriguez, Sen, and Ward.

ways. Depending on where we sit in the social hierarchy, we are more or less expected to become *homo economicus* and more or less punished for not living up to its standards. And yet because *homo economicus* is the normative model of subjectivity in neoliberalism, *all* neoliberal subjects are evaluated in relation to it. Similarly, the protocols of m4m media produce the normative figure of the fungible avatar-object: this figure comes to life both in the design of the m4m grid and the app's rules of engagement. By downloading the app, plugging in personal data, and clicking the "I Agree" button, each user, consciously or not, accepts the terms of fungibility and learns to operate in this register. My overriding point here and throughout the book is that we can view this experience as an ethical opportunity: seeing ourselves as a fungible avatar-object in an aesthetic collection can attune us to a radically antisocial experience of subjectivity and relationality that harbors queer political promise. And though I articulate my vision of queer fungibility by analyzing a site of male-specific intimacy, the ethic is not the property of men. In fact, being fungible is the very antithesis of manhood as it has come to be defined in male-dominated American society: individualistic, competitive, controlling, and impenetrable. An ethics of fungibility emphasizes vulnerability, egolessness, and self-substitution; at this historical juncture, normatively socialized American men are arguably most in need of learning fungibility's lessons.

To neoliberal subjects, that is, anyone reading this book in the early decades of the twenty-first century, fungibility may already be a familiar concept: it is, after all, a key component in contemporary capitalist value extraction. As I mentioned in the preface, fungibility, in economic terms, is a law of equivalence pertaining to the substitutability of commodities. It is different from exchange in that it does not require an external principle (such as money) to measure a commodity's value. It is, in other words, an immanentist conception of value determination. "To be fungible," Shannon Winnubst writes, "is to have all character and content hollowed out. It is a relationship of equity that requires purely formal semblance" ("Queer Thing" 92). Beyond commodities, labor can also be fungible; indeed, fungible labor is arguably the dream of capitalism itself. One need not look too far into our past to see this dream take shape in slavery; one need not look too far into the future to envision its logical conclusion in robotics.[8]

---

8. This speculative claim prompts the question: Might we think of neoliberalism as a transitional moment, or, a lynchpin, between slavery and robotic capitalism? The very notion of human capital—a concept predicated on the depersonalization

Indeed, evidence of the capitalist desire for fungible labor can be found throughout history. We can locate resistance to this desire in, for example, the labor activism of A. Philip Randolph and the Brotherhood of Sleeping Car Porters. Beginning in 1925, Randolph, a union leader from Harlem, represented the porters of the Pullman Car Company, a train car manufacturer that was one of the few corporations to hire former slaves after the Civil War. Before unionization, Pullman porters—exclusively Black until the 1960s—were all identified as "George": the first name of the Pullman corporation's founder. The porters were thus made mononymous against their will, robbed of their individual names and personhood, and deemed formally interchangeable by white passengers and management alike. As union leader, Randolph demanded and won individualized nameplates for each porter—a significant step in de-fungibilizing, or individuating and humanizing, the Pullman porter labor force.[9]

Generally speaking, from the standpoint of management, the ideal personnel are impersonnel: labor is most efficient when the all-too-human is removed from the equation. With all due respect to Karl Marx, imagine the Platonic ideal of a capitalist, let's call him Mr. Moneybags, as a deistic god plugging readily replaceable parts (i.e., laborers) into an automatized clock (a corporation). Personalities, individual histories, and social identities are obstacles to this machine's functional efficiency: an inhuman or at least dehumanized labor force is certainly preferable to one with families, desires, and dreams. Left to its own devices, without a moral compass and without so-called nanny states to hinder it, the machine functions best with desubjectified labor. "If actual humans must

---

of labor—has as much in common with slave labor as it does with nonhuman labor. In this sense, Shannon Winnubst's quite compelling claim in *Way Too Cool* that race is the Lacanian Real of neoliberalism is instructive. Her argument, in brief, goes something like this: try as we, neoliberals, might to erase social difference by employing fungible metrics such as human capital, racial injustice will forever haunt the capitalist system. Unlike human capital, race is nonfungible. Because contemporary movements for racial justice, such as Black Lives Matter, call attention to the ways that racial violence and racialized income inequality empower neoliberal regimes, they go some way in thwarting neoliberal progress. Winnubst thus seeks to locate and valorize nonfungible sites of resistance that counter the logic of neoliberal fungibility. By contrast, I explore whether relations and exchanges based *in* fungibility might harbor an ethical promise.

9. For more on Randolph and the Brotherhood of Sleeping Car Porters, see Tye.

be part of the labor pool," Mr. Moneybags declares, "they are best treated as human capital: valued only as skill sets, brands, and capacities." Human capital is a concept fundamental to neoliberal theory and practice, a term spoken without irony or shame in boardrooms around the globe. (Calling attention to the brazen prioritizing of "capital" over "human" in "human capital," Mark Slouka reminds us to "please note what's modifying what" (34).) When a worker is understood first and foremost as human capital, her, his, or their life, like the one of a slave on an auction block, becomes fungible.

While neoliberalism may teach us all to varying degrees about the fungibility of human capital, Black bodies have been branded, quite literally, as fungible labor for centuries. Conceived in the capitalist/eugenicist/ biopolitical imaginary as living outside the fold of the human, as the not yet human, and as the necessary foil to the life worthy of investment, Black lives matter, in this mindset, only inasmuch as they produce white capital, fuel white moralism, and augment white power. And yet, according to Tiffany Lethabo King, even though Black fungibility manifests in horrific social contexts in which Black bodies are utterly objectified, it can counterintuitively signify openness, possibility, and transformation. "The ever-changing and unpredictable violence that makes Black bodies fungible can also be exploited by Black people seeking freedom" (1036). Developing Hortense Spillers's seminal insight that Black bodies in captivity lose all distinguishing characteristics and become "a territory for cultural and political maneuver" (Spillers 67), King discovers in the abstraction of Black lives an opportunity for fugitivity and creativity in a white supremacist society.[10] "Black fungibility here is conceptualized as the capacity of Blackness for unfettered exchangeability and transformation within and beyond

---

10. C. Riley Snorton likewise develops Spillers's work specifically in relation to the mutability of gender in Black captive bodies. "[C]aptive flesh figures a critical genealogy for moderns transness," Snorton writes, "as chattel persons gave rise to an understanding of gender as mutable and as an amendable form of being" (57). Akin to King, Snorton also explores the fugitive potential of (gender) fungibility for chattel persons: "To suppose that one can identify fugitive moments in the hollow of fungibility's embrace is to focus on modes of escape, of wander, of flight that exist within violent conditions of exchange" (ibid.). For more on the role of fungibility in the collateral genealogies of Blackness and transness, see Snorton, 17–97.

the form of the commodity, thereby making fungibility an open-ended analytic accounting for both Black abjection and Black pursuits of life in the midst of subjection" (1023). Although the "blankness" of the fungible Black body serves as a screen on which colonizers and conquistadores project avaricious fantasies of borderless frontiers and inexhaustible natural resources, King emphasizes that the "empty vessel" of fungible Blackness is "an open sign [. . .] that can be arranged and rearranged for infinite kinds of use" (1025). She turns to cultural texts, William De Brahm's 1757 map of South Carolina and Georgia as well as Julie Dash's 1991 film *Daughters of the Dust*, to conceptualize Black fungibility as a (Foucaultian) hetero-topic space: "Dash beautifully and poetically turns porous and stained flesh as well as the noxious zone of indigo processing into heterotopic spaces where the possibility for other kinds of life exist. Black flesh and black spaces as heterotopic spaces function as counter-sites where new possibilities for (more than) humanness and freedom are articulated. The dense, smoky, putrid, and secluded area of indigo processing may have allowed for the enslaved depicted in De Brahm's imaginary and actual plantation landscapes of the 18th century to maneuver and temporarily escape the violent relations of the plantation" (1036).

Screen Love resonates with King's work in that both projects seek to tease out the posthumanist and emancipatory potential of a concept that upon first glance seems irredeemable. Likewise, King's turn to cul-tural texts to speculate about the radical possibilities of Black fungibility corresponds with my attempt to visualize queer fungibility in an aesthetic object: m4m media. That said, I find King's (and Spillers's) configuration of Blackness as "existing outside of current conceptions of the human" (1038) especially important to keep in mind when thinking through the identity political norms of m4m media discourse. As I implied earlier, these norms are not per se this study's purview: one can find insightful analyses of the racial dynamics of m4m media in the work of Emerich Daroya, Shaka McGlotten, and Jane Ward, among others. What I highlight in the pages to come is that the *protocol* of fungibility in m4m media affects users from all backgrounds. By design, all avatar-objects are assembled in a grid that emphasizes the equivalence of forms. Equivalence is *not* the same thing as equality here: avatar-objects stand in an unequal relation to one another in terms of how they signify, in terms of how popular they are, and especially in terms of the social status and situatedness of the people behind the avatars. Still, it's important to keep in mind that the in-real-life person manipulating an avatar-object is, with exceptions,[11] someone who voluntarily chooses to download, join, and open the app—that is, someone who exercises agency to get on the grid. For better and for worse, that someone is afforded the opportunity to experience what it's like to be fungible—a volitional, thoroughly mediated, and, with any luck, pleasurable form of fungibility—in the labor of virtual cruising.

To conclude, fungibility is a significant operating principle in both neoliberalism and m4m media. The aesthetic experience of online cruising mirrors the economic experience of neoliberal laboring. As it is in neoliberalism, so it goes on Grindr: m4m media translate neoliberal labor norms into digital code and bring the job market (and hunt) into the bedroom. The difference, however, lies in fungibility's function and potential in each context. The practice of trafficking in substitutable types on m4m media, I argue, holds the capacity to push neoliberal relational norms beyond their economic functions. While there is zero chance that m4m cruising will put an end to neoliberalism as we know it, it may well train us to relate in ways that exceed neoliberal aims. Echoing King, there is fugitive potential in fungibility. The ethical potential of virtual fungibility, however, is directly proportionate to the degree with which it diverges from capitalist labor fungibility, which holds as axiomatic exploitation and annihilation. Although the parallel systems—neoliberal labor and m4m media cruising—might turn on the same operating principle, and even express the same *ontological* principle of substitutable similitude, their trajectories grow farther and farther apart as m4m media resurrect and reinvent queer practices of antisocial intimacy.

By privatizing, popularizing, and mainstreaming historically queer sex practices, hookup apps of all stripes train users to evaluate oneself and others not as complex individuals with psychological depth, but as images and services. As disturbing as this might seem, as dehumanizing as it is,

---

11. The specific exception I have in mind here is a Grindrbot. Grindr has been plagued in recent years by spambots, colloquially known as "Grindrbots," which are designed to lure users to websites that infect phones with malware or steal personal information. I discuss Grindrbots in more detail in chapter 5. Regarding other exceptions concerning *involuntary* participation in m4m media, I have not encountered in my research a case where an individual was forced, against their will, to download an m4m media app and participate in communicative exchange. While such cases may exist, specifically in the form of sex trafficking, my study concerns consensual, voluntary participation in m4m media.

the media's protocol requires users to recognize first and foremost their *own* replaceability: users learn to understand themselves as merely one transposable option among many. The aggressive ego of *homo economicus* is humiliated in this process: it is tempered by the law of equivalence in a (meat) market of fungible goods, it dissolves in a collection of like things. Just as our microbial friends "teach" us to abandon an ego- and anthropocentric worldview, virtual self-dissolution might also prompt us to set aside a liberal-humanist conception of the subject as a stable, sealed, impermeable fortress and embrace instead the porosity of being. Unlike the increasingly common economic experience of job hopping through the neoliberal marketplace, the aesthetic and sensual experience of bouncing from user profile to user profile might attune us to the rhythms of a queer sociability and "naturalize" us as citizens of an antisocial collection. It is by no means guaranteed that m4m media users recognize or take advantage of this ethical opportunity. It is thus the task of this book to call attention to its presence and its potential: to determine how we might locate and nurture a queer ethics of fungibility in the ether and elsewhere.

As much as I would like people to read *Screen Love* from cover to cover, in the interest of user-friendliness I close with a chapter-by-chapter breakdown of the book's content. My peer reviewers noted, however, that no one chapter stands on its own as a self-contained essay: each chapter develops the arguments and ideas of its predecessor. That said, if you've read this intro, you can likely turn to any chapter of interest and not feel too lost.

Chapter 1, "Screen Lessons in the ICU," begins with an analysis of medical crowdfunding to explore some of the basic tenets of neoliberal theory and society: the absence of a social safety net, self-entrepreneurship as the catch-all solution to social ills, debt as a way of life, and the bald racism that imbues the entire system. The bulk of the chapter unpacks the book's two key concepts: shared estrangement and fungibility. If you're interested in harrowing accounts of life and death in the ICU, AIDS care-giving and activism, anal liberation, modular synthesis, or lesbian-separatist nomads, you might find something worth reading here. Also, if you read this chapter, you'll be well equipped to bounce to any other.

Chapter 2, "Fail Better at Romance!" is a short chapter on the utopian impulse behind sexting and the disappointing relationships where utopian fantasies often go to die. I remind readers that dating app corporations profit from both romantic failure and the demise of traditional, marital monogamy: these businesses need single, adulterous, or openly partnered customers. I then examine how enhanced features on hookup apps might purposely prevent users from hooking up. Instead of bemoaning the death of romance and the horrors of alienated misconnection, I point to ways we might understand screen-mediated communication failure and screen-abetted relationship turmoil as queer blessings in disguise. (For what it's worth, this is my favorite chapter.)

Chapter 3, "Dare to Be Indifferent (or, How to Become a Cat Person)," is in the main an analysis of Katherine Roupenian's short story "Cat Person," which was published to much fanfare amid a #metoo mediastorm in December 2017. I critique the hardly feminist tropes Roupenian employs in the story, while applauding her refreshingly nuanced take on female sexual desire and consent. I also highlight the ways that the story's implied critique of screen-mediated intimacies mirrors longstanding psychological and political critiques of queer intimacies. Finally, I offer an alternative reading of the story's conclusion, queering the two female characters and exploring how they might be models of fungible love.

Chapter 4, "Embodied Echoes and Virtual Affordances," offers some queer historical context for the protocols and norms of contemporary social media. I point to some of the ways that queer erotic practices pave the way for social media engagement and highlight how the virtual realm has proven an invaluable space for gay male communion and identification. Countering critics that insist on the dissimilarities between physical queer spaces and queer digital culture, I emphasize the historical continuities between gay male sexual infrastructures and m4m media. After reviewing relevant scholarship on pre-geosocial m4m media and the generally promiscuous browsing and sharing habits of networked users, I conclude by asserting that online interpassive promiscuity is a virtual affordance that can be mined as a queer ethical resource.

Chapter 5, "Becoming Fungible," is, conceptually speaking, the densest chapter of the book—the chapter, I suppose, for the "theory heads." Following Paulo Virno, I speculate whether connection-as-such, feelings of untethered yet intense connection experienced online, might be put to work in the creation of nontraditional "collectionist" formations that defy traditional understandings of community. Specifically, I wonder if connection-as-such could be the affective foundation of collections of whatever belonging. Inspired by Giorgio Agamben's notion of whatever being, whatever belonging is a form of nonexclusive membership that valorizes a common ontological substance seeking to assemble singularities in nonidentitarian communal forms. I turn to m4m media, despite its

well-earned reputation for aggravating egoism, bigotry, and self-segregation, to locate the rudiments of whatever belonging. Because a collection
of whatever belonging is difficult to envision, I enlist Proust, Warhol,
Magritte, and Foucault to help me sketch its contours.

Chapter 6, "Shut Up! in the Digital Closet," also somewhat dense
theory-wise, conceives of m4m media as a welcome return of sorts to
the (digital) closet. I explore the ethical and political potential of m4m
media's sensual nonsense, focusing on three points: (1) the confession as
the discursive crux of identitarian sexuality, itself the nexus of disciplinary and biopolitical power in modernity; (2) human capital trumping
depth-psychological models of sexuality in neoliberalism and its influence
in m4m media; and 3) the sublime digital closet of m4m media as a site
in which users are afforded the opportunity to practice an impersonal
ethics of fungibility that opens onto nondialectical, post-representational
political imaginaries. If you're a fan of Emily Dickinson (or the Grindr
user who texts only in Dickinsonian verse), this chapter is for you.

The absence of a conclusion is intentional.

Chapter One

Screen Lessons in the ICU

At 3:30 a.m. on Friday, April 25, 2014, my sister, Erin, drove herself to the emergency room of our local hospital in Providence, Rhode Island. Erin had called me the previous day to tell me she was sick with the flu. She had seen her primary care doctor and was taking a prescription flu medication, but she said she felt too miserable to leave the house to pick up some necessary provisions. I put together a little care package of teas and soups and sports drinks, and although she wouldn't allow me into her apartment when I arrived ("You do not want this, believe me"), we chatted at the door for a bit. In a gravelly voice, between coughing fits, she described feeling shivery and terribly achy, but a little better because she had just woken up from an hour's nap—the only hour of sleep she had had in the previous twenty-four. "Ugh, I'm so sorry, that sounds awful," I said, concerned and empathetic, but not terribly worried. At forty-four years old and generally quite healthy, she was medicated under doctor's supervision and reaching out to others to help her through the suffering. What more could she do? What more could I do? It was simply a matter of time before the virus would run its course. Reminding her to call me if necessary, and assuring her I would check in later, I left to spend time with my partner, Jim, in Boston. I was relieved not to hear from her that night: "No news is good news," I thought; "I hope she's finally getting a decent night's sleep." The ER doctor in the early hours of Friday morning also hoped she would get some sleep that night. He did not admit her when she arrived at 3:30 a.m. because she was not yet presenting with pneumonia. "You have a bad flu," I imagine him saying, "go home and get some rest."

The following day, Erin was put in a medically induced coma that lasted two weeks. Intubation, life support, dialysis, eleven lines pumping various medications through her system for fourteen days. A morbidly ironic twist on the "get some rest" directive. In the thirty-six hours since I had seen her, the virus transformed her lungs into a pneumonic morass, infiltrated her heart, shut down her kidneys, and ultimately triggered septic shock. The doctors were not optimistic she would make it through that first night in the Intensive Care Unit. Flash forward one week, and the situation was almost identical. At a less prestigious hospital, at any hospital a decade prior, she would not have survived. With excellent care and a whole lot of luck, she did.

I begin with this story neither to sound the alarm about twenty-first-century superviruses nor to praise or critique the U.S.'s supposedly reformed healthcare system. Rather, I begin here because the experience of waiting helplessly and hoping impossibly during that harrowing two-week period prompted me to reflect on the forms of intimacy emergent in screen-based social media. Although a hospital may seem a strange place to ponder this topic, my work begins here in part because the modern ICU is a palace of screens: waiting room TVs and visitors' smartphones, for sure, but also screens that relay crucial information about a patient's vitals to doctors, nurses, and bedside guests. The particular monitor situated above my sister's hospital bed was a cleanly composed, if somewhat cluttered, multicolored display of graphs and numbers relaying information on heart rate, blood pressure, the amount of oxygen in the bloodstream, and body temperature. (See figure 1.1.)

After a crash course in medical semiotics, generously taught by various nurses and doctors, my family and I became self-proclaimed experts in interpreting the screen's signs. The blips, beeps, and incessantly fluctuating figures gave us something to latch onto, an abstract yet comprehensible representation of what was happening to the unconscious body lying before us. If we could understand the images and numbers, we thought, we might gain some control of a situation resolutely beyond our control, some leverage in a process so utterly indifferent to our presence and efforts. Presumably like many before us, we used the screen as a coping mechanism to distance ourselves from the palpable fear and worry in the room. We analyzed and debated the significance of the monitor's information precisely to avoid discussing the unspeakable outcomes it might reveal. This oracle alternately toyed with us, maddened us, and relieved us; it offered solace on the good days, and frustration and panic on the

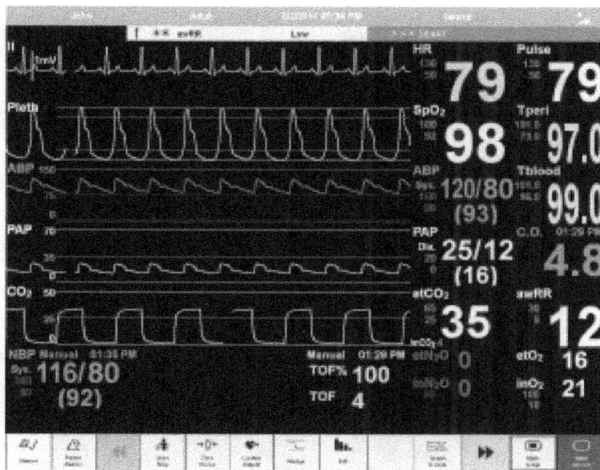

Figure 1.1. Patient monitor similar to the one above my sister's bed in the ICU.

bad. Visibly more vibrant and animated than the systems and processes it represented, the monitor became the simulacrum of my sister, a signifier seemingly more real than its signified, a mercurial creature behaving like a friend one minute and an enemy the next. Although the screen did little to span the impossible distance between our loved one and us, it offered the illusion of intimacy and control. The changing colors and numbers assured us that a living body was animating the display, but the person we knew may as well have been in a different room or a different country. Put simply, the screen paradoxically gave life to a comatose body and dead-ened the connection we felt with the individual. It objectified my sister's personhood in a way that was dehumanizing and disturbing . . . and yet, comforting. As long as the screen remained animated, there was hope. The affective power the monitor lorded over us prompted me to think about the illusions, the limits, and the ethical possibilities of screen-mediated intimacies in the world beyond the hospital walls. The experience of gaz-ing raptly at that monitor while holding my sister's hand was an expe-rience simultaneously alienating and bonding, profoundly intimate and absolutely isolating. The affective ambience in the hospital room was one of helplessness and hope; the relational dynamic—the uncomfortable yet reassuring connection between the screen, my unresponsive sister, and myself—brought to mind a concept I had developed in my previous schol-arship: shared estrangement.

Before diving headlong into an explication of shared estrangement as it relates to screen-mediated intimacies—that topic is the conceptual springboard of the chapter—I wish to relay one more "screen lesson" I learned in the ICU. This one concerns healthcare in the neoliberal era: specifically, the oversized and quite unsettling role social media play in it. During my sister's coma, Erin's doctors and my family were not the only ones glued to screens, hoping for good news. Erin's friends and relatives outside the hospital were also checking Facebook for status updates from me and my siblings. My family spent hours responding to inquiries and "get well soon" messages. As moving and heartening as it was to witness the outpouring of love and concern for my sister, it was also exhausting to manage it, to do justice to it. To help us out, a close friend, Brett, offered to act as a liaison between the outside world and my family. He created a campaign on a medical crowdfunding website called, at the time, GiveForward.com. (GiveForward.com is now part of the larger crowdfunding outfit, GoFundMe.com.) Brett posted medical updates from the family on Erin's GiveForward page, but its primary purpose was to raise money to help Erin pay what were bound to be outrageous hospital bills. Needless to say, when Erin returned home after two months, barely able to walk and still battling a wracking cough, a mountain of bills awaited her: tens of thousands of dollars of healthcare debt. Fortunately, the GiveForward campaign, linked through Facebook and an email list, generated over seventeen thousand dollars in two months. This money helped Erin enormously: it didn't cover everything, but it saved her from having to declare bankruptcy. We are all—my sister, my family, myself—deeply grateful for the crowdfunding site, for the media that spread the word about the campaign, and, especially, for the generous people who supported Erin through her illness.

But this "happy ending" hardly tells the whole story. What if my sister, who fortunately has decent health insurance, had been uninsured? What if she hadn't been "connected," i.e., didn't have a lot of Facebook friends or even a Facebook profile? What if her generally middle-class supporters didn't have the disposable income to part with? When a health crisis hits, are we all poised for bankruptcy but for the kindness of strangers? Is falling ill a personal failure, a character flaw? From a neoliberal perspective, it seems, yes, our illnesses are *our problem*: the individual is wholly accountable for its fate, and that fate is calculated in zero-sum terms of success and failure. Although the body's vulnerability and inevitable degeneration are shared and common facts, in the neoliberal context they are construed as individualized weaknesses to be remedied by strict regimens of exercise, proper diet, and wholesome habits. Because our primary duty as neoliberal citizens is to enhance our human capital and maximize our profitability, if our health stands in the way, well, that's our fault. Like building a resume, personal health becomes a lifelong task of self-optimization. When the body falls out of line, when illness erupts, the lucky ones can count on an individualized support network (a job with benefits, family, friends) to pick up the pieces and compensate for financial shortcomings. The rest, well, that's their problem, indeed, their *fault* for not having taken care of themselves, for not having secured enough capital—human or otherwise.

The contemporary popularity and increasing necessity of medical crowdfunding sites bring into sharp relief some of the basic tenets of neoliberal society. In a social field dominated by the free market and free trade, freedom itself is comprehensible only in terms of consumer choice, entrepreneurial innovation, and competition between calculating market agents. In terms of healthcare, one is free to purchase the appropriate products to stay fit, active, and competitive in order to keep pace with other market agents. Our capacity for human capital maximization, after all, rests on our physical and mental fitness. Self-care becomes a pass/fail test of character: refusing to follow normative health guidelines and practices is a cause for suspicion, a potential sign of moral defectiveness. If one flunks this test and had not the foresight to prepare a disaster plan, crowdfunding sites like GoFundMe offer assistance. Hardly a panacea for, indeed, more a reinforcement of, the systemic failures of corporate, governmental, and public welfare, such websites do of course help—my sister's "success" is but one example. Depressingly, however, success on these sites seems to correlate with how well one has built a personal brand, the financial strength of one's investors (i.e., followers and funders), and the viability of the marketing strategy. To put it bluntly, on GiveForward, as in so many other areas of neoliberal life, it's business as usual: the individual campaigns compete for attention as if in the boardroom of an advertising firm. They lure clients with images, personal narratives, and memorable, investment-worthy hooks. Also akin to political campaigns, crowdfunding success hinges on private donations: the bigger the war chest, the better the chances of winning. But the stakes here are more *Hunger Games* than *West Wing*: winning, more often than not, means securing enough capital to stay alive.

In "Producing a Worthy Illness: Personal Crowdfunding amidst Financial Crisis," Lauren S. Berliner and Nora J. Kenworthy discover that creating a successful crowdfunding campaign requires the ability to market a narrative of "deservingness": a story that appeals to a donor base but has the potential to spread beyond it. Such marketing acumen requires a mastery of neoliberal entrepreneurial skills, among them social media literacy and self-branding. The success of crowdfunding campaigns likewise hinges on social networking fluency, a knowledge of graphic design, advanced reading and writing skills, and an ability to express oneself in a normative, emotionally expressive manner. The ability to access and acquire such skill building is of course dependent on, among other social determinants, economic and racial status. After conducting a "mixed-methods study of a randomized sample of 200 GFM [GoFundMe] campaigns between March and September of 2016" (235), Berliner and Kenworthy conclude that medical crowdfunding campaigns reflect and exacerbate existing population disparities and inequities. They write:

> The high proportion of [medical crowdfunding] campaigns located in states that refused the ACA [Affordable Care Act] Medicaid expansion underscores an emerging divide between Americans experiencing more or less severe contexts of austerity in public health insurance coverage. Geographic inequities are compounded by the social, technological, cultural, and media literacies required to develop successful GFM campaigns. U.S. healthcare and social safety-net systems are strongly premised on ideas of deservingness structured by class, race, gender and immigration status; GFM further legitimizes this logic. Our findings reveal a crucial paradox in the use of crowdfunding for health care. Although it may be most financially critical as a tool for those most vulnerable in the U.S. healthcare system, crowdfunding platforms are constructed in ways that can further marginalize these populations. The importance of certain literacies and forms of social capital on GFM reproduces inequities and reinforces a hyper-individualized system of choosing who is and who is not deserving. (240–41)

So, who *is* deserving of our money? Whose campaigns are funded? Judging by past GiveForward and current GoFundMe splash pages, the fortunate ones are family-oriented, affectionate, and pale-skinned people, "attractive" according to conventional white American, middle-class sartorial and beauty standards. (See figures 1.2 and 1.3.)

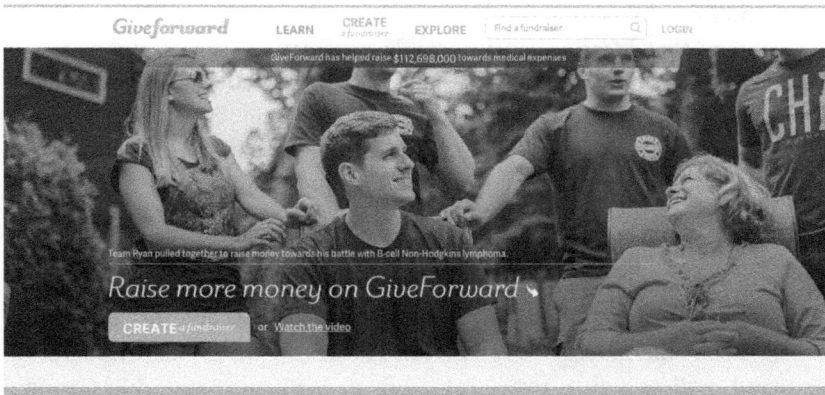

Figure 1.2. Former GiveForward.com splash page (2014).

Figure 1.3. Current GiveForward.com splash page (redirecting users to GoFundMe) (2020).

Although the photographs change with each refresh of the page, the racial and class politics of the imagery is consistent, and its meaning not subtle: the face of health, success, and well-being, the face of innocence, heroism, endurance, and charity is white. Some cry, some laugh, some hug one another in celebration, others relax among family: regardless, the white models are stand-ins for the "average American," a figure so carefully constructed through centuries of racist advertising and popular culture. But the everyman and woman here are also extraordinary: they may be "just like you and me," but they are also winners, survivors, and successful leaders in the brave new world of self-entrepreneurship. Of course, the actual patients used as models here are not to be blamed; they are merely being exploited for their skin color, playing a stock role. The design team at GiveForward, however, should know better. But perhaps it

does? In effect, its willingness to conform to an all-too-common marketing strategy that idealizes and normalizes whiteness speaks to an uglier
truth not only about crowdfunding websites, but about American neoliberal society at large: whiteness, both conceptually and physiologically,
signals success. GiveForward's homepage thus visualizes in distillate the
racialized connotations and economic realities of what is normatively
understood as a successful life in America.

In *The Birth of Biopolitics*, Michel Foucault notes that the neoliberal
social field is one in which "minority individuals and practices are tolerated"
(259), one in which self-development and social mobility are encouraged
for all. Such tolerance is only possible, however, when histories—racial,
gendered, and sexual histories saturated in inequality and violence—are
erased.[1] All indeed are nominally equal in the marketplace—labor is fungible, workers are substitutable—but to get a foot in the door one must
arrive to the job interview *tabula rasa*: devoid of a personal and political
past, merely human capital and skill sets. The celebration of diversity and
difference in neoliberalism is thus purely formal: it works, paradoxically, to
exacerbate racialized disparities in wealth and income.[2] For axiomatic to
neoliberal theory is the notion that competition is not necessarily innate
to human populations: it must be fabricated and continuously secured.
Inequality, if anything, is a catalyst for competition. While neoliberals
assert that poverty and massive income disparity will vanish once the
free market is permitted to do its magical work, historically entrenched
social inequalities (evidential residue, we are told, of liberalism's failure) are
convenient, useful, indeed, integral to neoliberalism's functioning insofar

---

1. Regarding the de-emphasizing or eclipsing of personal identity in neoliberalism,
see Winnubst, "The Queer Thing," 85–87 and Dilts, 136–39. Regarding the racial
dynamics of the biopolitical imperative to "make live and let die," see Stone, pp.
40–41. Glossing Foucault, Stone argues that in a biopolitical context: "Races will
be classified in terms of those worth preserving and those not worth preserving.
The races not worth preserving will have powers applied to them such that, in
their dying, the 'living' of the race worth preserving will be not only preserved
but augmented" (41).

2. Winnubst writes: "[D]iversity is the explicit aim of neoliberalism as so many
have argued (Duggan, Giroux). But because it is following out the logic of fungibility that the market demands, these differences are purely formal—they must be
hollow, stripped of any historical residues, especially if those residues bring with
them the ethical and political conflict of xenophobia" ("The Queer Thing" 94).

as they safeguard competition. The role of the neoliberalized government, then, is to secure, not alleviate, historically entrenched social inequalities—anything else would be social*ism* and hence political suicide.[3]

What results from the deliberate perpetuation of racial and income inequality is a conflation of whiteness with success: a successful entrepreneur—regardless of skin color, emptied of personal and collective history—*achieves* whiteness once s/he maximizes human capital. Historically constructed to connote the norm and the ideal, the typical and the exceptional, whiteness, as witnessed on GiveForward's and GoFundMe's home pages, is the arch-brand through which neoliberalism hawks its wares. Contrary to the neoliberal myth of social mobility for all, the odds of succeeding financially remain more favorable for those whose skin pigmentation aligns with the brand fantasy. The authors of the Federal Reserve's 2016 Survey of Consumer Finances confirm this: "Median incomes for white non-Hispanic families are between 20 and 75 percent higher than for families in all nonwhite and Hispanic groups" (Board of Governors 12). Moreover, Loïc Wacquant argues that the contemporary "Centaur-state," a two-faced Leviathan reengineered over the past three decades to clear the way for the neoliberalization of civil society, speaks one message to the tycoons and another to the poor. The Centaur-state is "uplifting and 'liberating' at the top, where it acts to leverage the resources and expand the life options of the holders of economic and cultural capital; but it is castigatory and restrictive at the bottom, when it comes to managing the populations destabilized by the deepening of inequality and the diffusion of work insecurity and ethnic anxiety" (74). Wacquant argues further that the massive expansion of the penal apparatus in the U.S. as well as the transformation of social welfare to workfare have been essential to neoliberalism's progress—essential, that is, to the intensification of racialized poverty. Even a cursory glance at the skyrocketing rates of incarceration for Black Americans and the disproportionate number of people of color enrolled in disciplinary workfare programs gives lie to the treacly celebration of diversity across the neoliberal landscape.[4] If slavery and segregation

---

3. For more on constructing competition and sustaining social inequality in neoliberalism, see Brown, 4–10.

4. More information on the racial dynamics of American income inequality can be found in the Federal Reserve's 2016 Survey of Consumer Finances. For a summary and visualization of the data from the survey, see Hart-Landsberg, who writes: "[T]he bottom fifth of families saw their net worth fall by 24 percent over

were not enough to ensure social inequality and tip the scales in favor of white success for centuries to come, neoliberal practices of incarceration and punitive, panoptical workfare policies should do the trick.

In a low-income, predominantly Black neighborhood near the home of my partner, Jim, there is a headstone manufacturer whose sign reads: "If a life is worth living, it is worth remembering." It is the conditional tense of the slogan, the "iffiness" of it, that strikes me. As a motto for the Hemlock Society, a right-to-die organization for which philosophical questions concerning quality of life are fundamental, the statement might make sense. As ad copy for a headstone business, however, it beckons its viewers to become philosophers: what type of life *is* worth living? What type of life is *not* worth living? As we see in distillate in medical crowdfunding and writ large in the racial demographics of poverty, the life apparently most worthy of investment, has a face, a skin color, and a supportive community. But the lives not worth living or remembering? Playing on consumer anxiety, guilt, and feelings of inadequacy, as most advertisements do, the slogan implies that the unworthy lives belong to those who cannot afford to purchase an expensive headstone. After all, the ad is pitched to mourners, present and future, as well as those preparing for their own death. It might as well read: "Unless your life or your loved one's life is utterly forgettable, you should buy a headstone from us." It is morbidly ironic that the headstone manufacturer's sign daily confronts the demographic most often forgotten, if not left for dead, in the contemporary biopolitical context: i.e., the poor of color.[5] In addition to being a reminder of their forgettability and their disposability, the sign teases with the opportunity to become "somebody" in death—a high price to pay for social respect. Just as an individual's health and a loved one's concern are monetized in crowdfunding campaigns, a life's worth here is commodified in granite, slate, or marble and quantified in the size,

---

the period 1998 to 2016, while the next lowest income tier experienced an even greater decline, 34 percent. Those in the next two higher income tiers basically treaded water. In sharp contrast, the top ten percent enjoyed a net worth increase of 146 percent over the same period." For more information on the racial divide in American employment, see Irwin, Cain Miller, and Sanger-Katz. For information on racial disparities in American incarceration rates, see the NAACP's "Criminal Justice Fact Sheet."

5. Regarding the racial dynamics of biopolitics, see Foucault, *Society Must Be Defended*, 239–64.

shape, and extravagance of the memorial. The commodification of our best intentions, of our desire to relate, to care, and to love, speaks to the cynicism and opportunism produced and rewarded in the neoliberal era. We cannot blame the charitable for donating as much as they can to a crowdfunding campaign; we likewise cannot blame the family who purchases a headstone beyond their means. It even perhaps does little good to blame the business that exploits the vulnerabilities of consumers who seek to make tangible their grief. The equation "doing good = giving money" is so thoroughly normalized in neoliberalism that we rarely question its ethical implications (Winnubst *WTC* 192–93). An entrepreneur exploits a consumer: whether or not either party in the transaction understands how carefully designed and prescribed this encounter is, the practice is the cornerstone of neoliberal life. In the age of global capital, evading completely the roles of entrepreneur and consumer is next to impossible. But if the language, affects, and behaviors of these prized neoliberal figures are pushed to their limit, if their game is played not to "win" (i.e., to become *homo economicus*) but to generate alternative definitions and images of success, then new forms of subjectivity, different ways of relating, and unorthodox understandings of life's worth might emerge.

Shared estrangement and neoliberalism: the former an existential conundrum endemic to interpersonal relations, the latter a historical disaster aiding and abetting the sixth extinction. Both thrive in a contemporary screen-mediated, communication-obsessed social context. Both, for better and for worse, have lessons to impart. *Screen Love* attempts to tease out these lessons and discover in neoliberal media a means through which we might imagine ourselves and the world differently. I begin this task by explicating two concepts that are simultaneously exploited in the neoliberal context and primed for antineoliberal appropriation: shared estrangement and fungibility.

Shared Estrangement

My 2012 book, *Friendship as a Way of Life: Foucault, AIDS, and the Politics of Shared Estrangement*, goes some way in exploring the relational dynamic of shared estrangement. Because my present study is conceptually quite indebted to *Friendship*, it behooves me to summarize some of that book's key arguments. *Friendship* begins with an analysis of Michel Foucault's peculiar understanding of friendship as "a desire, an uneasiness, a desire-in-uneasiness" (*Essential* 126). For Foucault, friendship rests on a productive tension: it is guided by an ethics of discomfort that nurtures the unknown potential—the strangeness—between friends. Cultivating an impersonal, at times even treasonous, intimacy, Foucault's friends hold each other at a remove and resist assimilating their differences into an identity. Even though sex is typically understood as the defining feature of contemporary relationships—i.e., the presence, absence, quality, quantity or type of sex in a relationship supposedly tells us everything we need to know—Foucault's friends are not subjects of King Sexuality: sex does not make or break his friendships. Because Foucault was so critical of sexuality as we have come to know it (as a marker of social identity, as a window into the psyche) and because he understood the crucial role sexuality plays in biopolitical social control, he theorized—and practiced—a friendship beyond sexuality. Part of this practice involves the mutual refusal of a discourse of transcendence: in Foucault's friendship, two do not become one, souls do not meld, and friends or lovers do not reunite beyond the grave. Foucault's friendship is thoroughly materialist: it is grounded in an anti-intersubjective notion of estrangement, and it is forged in the shadow of finitude. *Friendship*'s paramount goal is to tease out the ethical and political implications of friendship when conceived and practiced as relation of shared estrangement. To this end, I explore the heroic caregiving work among friends during the early days of the AIDS crisis as well as the impersonal, often anonymous, sex practices characteristic of modern queer communities. While caregiving work and impersonal sex may seem profoundly dissimilar at first glance, they find common ground in the relational dynamic of shared estrangement. This ethical bedrock, I argue, gives shape to the creative and effective political work of AIDS activist groups, such as ACT UP.

The groundwork for ACT UP's important work was laid in part by the AIDS Buddy System, a volunteer program established in the early 1980s to assist people with AIDS. In the years before protease inhibitors, people with AIDS and the Buddies who assisted them did not have the luxury of ignoring death—unlike, say, the Reagan administration.[6] People with AIDS and AIDS Buddies were forced to confront death head on, to

---

6. As Tim Dean notes: "Ronald Reagan, for example, refused to enunciate the word 'AIDS' until late 1987, by which point over twenty-five thousand U.S. citizens had already died in the epidemic" (*Beyond Sexuality* 111).

learn how to die, to befriend, or at least become hospitable to death—the strangest of all strangers. As such, the Buddy relation foregrounds an existential paradox: death, the end we collectively share, is the one thing we actually cannot share; although everybody can "relate to" finitude, it is, in the end, unrelatable. We are thus "alone together" in regard to death.[7] That said, a friendship that valorizes an unshareable finitude affords the opportunity to become more creative, more experimental, and more *essential* than ever before. In acknowledging death's immanence to life, or, more radically, in overcoming the fear of death, we experience what Spinoza refers to as "absolute freedom": a condition in which we are simultaneously most dangerous and most artistic (290–98). ACT UP's wildly inventive, daring, and joyful political actions speak to the boundless artistic spirit unleashed in a state of absolute freedom. For instance, "playing dead" in the form of a die-in, one of ACT UP's trademark protests, signals an artistic orientation toward death: not a self-destructive death *wish*, but a fearless affirmation of the art of living. The most controversial of ACT UP's die-ins is arguably "Stop the Church," which took place at Saint Patrick's Cathedral in New York City on December 10, 1989 (Roach, *Friendship* 117, 146). Because during the AIDS crisis the Catholic church actively discouraged HIV-prevention measures (while hypocritically proclaiming their allegiance to "life"), ACT UP responded by collectively "playing dead" during a Sunday service: literally lying down *en masse*, during mass, in the cathedral's nave. Beyond speaking truth to power, beyond a courageous refusal to die quietly in an unjust world, and beyond an embodied reminder of the "unfit" populations so murderously neglected in biopower, this protest form is also a ritual of death preparation. Indeed, a collective mimicking of death, or, rather, a collective playing *with* death, signals a hospitable orientation toward an inassimilable foreigner. In the die-in, we familiarize ourselves with the stranger we've been told to fear, the one that prevents the continuance of "life as usual," however rife with injustice. In short, friendships that refuse to transcend death, friendships that begin at the very point where relating is impossible, friendships

---

7. I use this phrase, somewhat sardonically, to allude to Sherri Turkle's best-selling book, *Alone Together: Why We Expect More from Technology and Less from Each Other*. While Turkle argues that being "alone together" is an unfortunate byproduct of the digital age, I understand shared estrangement as an existential condition that, when valorized, can give rise to radical ethical and political forms.

that welcome, rather than fear, absolute foreignness, ground a politics of
shared estrangement: a radical and formidable politics in which living
artistically—i.e., freedom itself—is at stake.

A political sensibility grounded in an ethics of shared estrangement
can likewise be gleaned from sexual encounters. It is here where the
impersonal character of historically queer sex practices—e.g., anonymous
cruising, sex in bathhouses and darkrooms, S/M, 1970s gay male "clone"
cultures, etc.—becomes important. These erotic practices do not turn on
social identity or psychological interiority; such aspects of selfhood in this
context are, more often than not, liabilities. Rather, the operative features
of these queer sex practices are generic archetypes, bodies and pleasures,
and a sensuality of surfaces. Through such experiments in voluntary
depersonalization, one might sense a commonness that hierarchies of
social difference make inaccessible and yet cannot contain. That is, the
rhythms of impersonal erotic sociability—associations and separations
indifferent to possessiveness, ownership, or even subjectivity—undercut
and destabilize the masterful (Cartesian) self and the social categories
to which it lays claim. Such erotic rhythms have more in common with
geological ebbs and flows (tides, lunar cycles, seasons) and thus permit
access to that which seethes beneath social identity and the social itself:
an asubjective and anarchical "commonism" that precludes and exceeds
identitarian forms.[8] Following Leo Bersani, I assert that through impersonal sex practices our bodies might attune to a common substance that
expresses itself in infinitely diverse forms. The sensual/erotic element is
essential to this attunement. In the words of William Haver: "[T]here is
no sense of the common apart from the sensuousness of the common" (3).

A "training" in impersonal sensuality can also lend itself towards
an activist life. Not only does voluntary depersonalization subtract power
from a voracious ego, a sense of the common gleaned from impersonal
sex may provoke a resistance to privatization and colonization in its
myriad forms. The sense of the common emergent in the impersonal
sexual encounter is a sense of a world beyond the self, indifferent to the
self, a world in which one might locate oneself in various resemblances
and reverberations. Because impersonal sex, like the AIDS Buddy system,
requires a hospitable approach to strangers and one's own strangeness,
because it poses a risk to, if not an abdication of, the self's integrity, it

---

8. Here I am essentially summarizing Leo Bersani's argument in "Sociability and
Cruising." See *Is the Rectum a Grave?*, 44–62.

is an exercise in entrustment and cooperative, consensual collaboration. In the memoirs of David Wojnarowicz, an artist who writes extensively about the transformative ethical possibilities of impersonal sex, I locate a "common sense," a sensuous, erotic force and rhythm, that resists containment in deadened sexual identities (homo/hetero) and normative relational forms (marriage, family). I argue that Wojnarowicz's "common sense" becomes the seed of a *sensibility* that fights for the common—an activist orientation (Roach, *Friendship* 137–47). Even in its most nascent form, a common sense emergent in impersonal sex is an intuition that one belongs to a larger sex public. As Michael Warner notes: "Contrary to myth, what one relishes in loving strangers is not mere anonymity, nor meaningless release. It is the pleasure of belonging to a sexual world, in which one's sexuality finds an answering resonance not just in one other, but in a world of others" (179).

Which brings me back to screens. Although it would be facile, not to mention insulting, to render equivalent the ethical and political significance of AIDS caregiving, queer impersonal sex, and screen-mediated intimacy, I find the relational dynamic of shared estrangement at work in these disparate practices. Because I am most interested in exploring the queer ethical potential of this dynamic in the contemporary context, my study focuses primarily on queer hookup media. Grindr stands in as the metonym for these media for the following reasons: it is the first geosocial smartphone app of its kind; it has become the template for most other hookup apps; it remains the LGBTQ-identified platform with the most users. Throughout *Screen Love*, I emphasize the continuities in pre- and post-Internet queer life and explore the new ethical affordances m4m media might offer.

The dominant narratives of pre- and post-Internet gay culture tend to emphasize the radical break, even the fall from grace, that the Internet set in motion. Since the invention of websites such as Gaydar and Manhunt, so the story goes, gay culture has hit the skids. In this morality tale, scholars and critics bemoan the loss of queer sex publics and seek redemption in a reinvestment in physical queer spaces and communal practices. They claim that the digital turn, i.e., the shift from primarily physical sites of queer connection to virtual ones, hurts the LGBTQ community in numerous ways: it reduces cruising to a joyless, consumerist search akin to shopping; it reduces sex to a transactional exchange; it contributes to the commodification and consequent depoliticization of LGBTQ culture at large; it exacerbates racism, misogyny, gender-normativity, and body-shaming; it desensitizes users both to the humanness of others—their story, their feel-ings, their plight—and the broader sociopolitical context in which LGBTQ lives continue to be endangered. Cruising online, we are told, is a solipsistic, narcissistic, egotistical, psychologically and socially damaging time sink. If that weren't bad enough, it also contributes to the destruction of an already crumbling LGBTQ public infrastructure. If neoliberal privatization schemes, misguided AIDS-discriminatory public health measures, homonormative assimilationist LGBTQ campaigns, and politically popular family-values moralism aren't enough to shutter gay bars, sex clubs, and bathhouses, we, virtual cruisers, will finish the job with our typing fingers. And yet who can blame us? In this story, "we" are an AIDS-traumatized generation seeking safety and control in the virtual realm to overcome a devastating past and begin anew. Although virtual cruising might seem to some like a step forward in LGBTQ cultural evolution, it is actually complicit with social and political forces that work to drive antiheteronormative queer intimacies underground. According to this anti-tech line of argument, in terms of queer ethics and politics, nothing good has come from these media and nothing likely ever will. Our moral duty as radical queers is to unplug and hit the streets: to cruise, to patronize a local gay-owned establishment, and to fight the antigay powers that be.[9]

While this story is quite convincing, I still wonder if something else might be going on in the digital turn: might queers be turning to screens to escape the normative pressures of relationship life now that same-sex marriage is legal and homonormativity celebrated? Might the digital turn "inward" also be a turn away from erstwhile identity-political communal forms? Might it be a turn toward a relational ethos that offers an alternative in the neoliberal era of No Alternatives?[10] That is to say, has the relational dynamic of shared estrangement—cultivated historically in queer imper-sonal sex practices as well as AIDS caregiving and activism—resurfaced in online cruising forums? If so, these new forms of shared estrangement, so steeped in neoliberal principles and practices, certainly reflect but also might exceed their historical moment: they hold the potential to resurrect the past so as to push the present beyond itself.

---

9. The sources of the story I tell here are a combination of popular polemics, academic arguments, and conversational, gay male scuttlebutt. For more on this story, see Campbell, McGlotten, and Mowlabocus.

10. Here I am referring to TINA: Margaret Thatcher's oft-spoken belief that "There Is No Alternative" to neoliberalism.

While screens underscore the distance between people—between my comatose sister and me; between eager, potential hookup partners on Grindr—they simultaneously produce intense feelings of connection, "resonances" in Warner's parlance. Just as "loving strangers" might reveal "the pleasure of belonging to a sexual world," screen-mediated intimacy can similarly provoke the affective experience of what I call connection-as-such—a feeling of connection not necessarily tied to a particular person or group, but to a world of connections, to the experience of connection itself. These feelings of untethered yet intense connection are not exclusive to mediated intimacy: they are produced and affirmed in a larger neoliberal context that rewards rootlessness, flexibility, and contingency. Following Paulo Virno, I speculate in chapter 5 whether such powerful feelings of fleeting connection—powerful precisely because they are fleeting—might be put to work in the creation of nontraditional collectivist formations that defect from contemporary social arrangements and functions. I look to m4m media, despite its well-earned reputation for aggravating egoism, bigotry, and self-segregation, to locate the virtual architecture of these social collections. I argue that the unspoken prerequisite for signing on to m4m media is agreeing to become fungible: submitting to platform protocols that render users equivalent. By clicking "Agree" on Grindr, or any other corporate m4m platform, our singular complexity vanishes into an asubjective plurality of monetized data points. By submitting to Grindr's profile creation protocol, we likewise agree to become part of a collection of aestheticized avatars. By design, Grindr users are represented as one component of a plural mass, one transposable option among many. To the extent that all profiles are held to the same visual constraints—in the Grindr grid all profile photos are the same size, e.g.—subjective singularity becomes accessible only through an engagement with a horde of similarly framed others. In this sense, the crowd comes first, individuality second. At once uniquely singular and blandly plural, then, Grindr users negotiate an interesting existential conundrum. The urge to make one's profile "pop," to work overtime to distinguish oneself from the millions of others, is perhaps an unconscious response to the fear that we're all the same, that we might just be *replaceable*. At the same time, the typical cisgender, masculine "just a regular guy" self-presentations that populate the m4m media landscape speak to a conformist fear of straying too far from conventional gender norms that might be deemed unattractive by other norm-compliant users. As an ethical principle, then, fungibility tarries within the push and pull of singularity and plurality, sameness and difference. It is only through an acceptance of our substitutability within a constituted plurality that we might develop a singular ethics of fungibility—and Grindr, believe it or not, could move us in this direction.

The acknowledgment of death's singularly plural presence in the AIDS Buddy friendship is likewise an acknowledgment of one's fungibility. From the standpoint of the HIV virus—or, for that matter, COVID-19—human bodies are fungible. Although social determinants such as race, class, sexuality, and gender most certainly influence levels of viral risk, exposure, and transmission, in the "eyes" of the virus we are equivalences: all of us interchangeable, cookie-cutter homes to occupy. The HIV-prevention slogan, "AIDS does not discriminate," for example, underscores the radical immanence—the asubjective commonness—of HIV while simultaneously mystifying its biopolitical reality. Although we are all indeed susceptible to infection,[11] some of us—precisely because race, class, gender, sexuality, and nationality so profoundly determine our access to education, healthcare, and, now, pre- and post-exposure prophylaxis (PReP and PeP)—are singularly more susceptible than others. The same goes for mortality: death indeed comes for us all, but due to the deliberate inequalities built into racist neoliberal institutions and eugenicist public health initiatives, it visits poor communities of color more frequently than wealthy white ones. Without minimizing or ignoring the very real social determinants and differences that influence HIV- and COVID-19 infection and mortality rates, not to mention social injustices across the board, I wonder whether the *voluntary* virtual experience of being made an equivalence might afford an opportunity to access a "common sense" that undercuts, even spites, social difference. More precisely, I wonder if willfully becoming part of a collection of fungible aesthetic objects on m4m media holds an ethical promise.

Fungibility

If I were to trace the ancestry of my theory of queer fungibility, the conceptual bloodlines would intersect not only with the work of Leo Bersani and Michel Foucault, but also Guy Hocquenghem. In *Homosexual Desire*,

---

11. For the sake of argument here, I am discounting the estimated less than 1 percent of the *homo sapiens* species that have demonstrated an innate resistance to HIV. See Mendus and Ring.

an *Anti-Oedipus*-inspired queer manifesto, Hocquenghem conceives of desire as ontologically undifferentiated, productive, and wanting for nothing. Desire is transformed into lack and bifurcated into heterosexual and homosexual only when forced into service as a reproductive agent for social and economic institutions: the patriarchal family and capitalism. Male homosexual desire—physiologically and symbolically associated with the anus—is sublimated in both of these institutions so that a phallocentric, competitive, and hierarchical form of sociality can flourish. "Only the phallus dispenses identity; any social use of the anus, apart from its sublimated use, creates the risk of a loss of identity. Seen from behind we are all women; the anus does not practice sexual discrimination" (101). Because the phallus-father dictates our name and our role in the reproduction of the family and capitalism, because, moreover, living up to our name and social role requires the privatization and ultimate repudiation of the desiring function of the anus, a reinvestment in and a desublimation of anality would weaken phallocentric hierarchies, prompting forms of relating and grouping antithetical to society as we know it. Hocquenghem imagines a state of "primary sexual communism" (111) wherein the anus is restored to its desiring function, phallic identities melt away, and impersonal group sex, the indiscriminate plugging in of body parts, becomes a model for a nonreproductive and horizontal (i.e., nonhierarchical) form of relating. "Homosexual desire is a group desire. It groups the anus by restoring its functions as a desiring bond, and by collectively reinvesting it against a society which has reduced it to the state of shameful secret. [. . .] Possibly, when the anus recovers its desiring function and the plugging in of organs takes place subject to no rule or law, the group can take its pleasure in an immediate relation where the sacrosanct difference between public and private, between the individual and the social, will be out of place" (ibid.). For Hocquenghem, "homosexual grouping" takes a circular form yet remains malleable and open to amoeba-like permutations. Group members themselves are movable parts, seemingly divested of individuality and interchangeable: "The anus's group mode is an annular one, a circle which is open to an infinity of directions and possibilities for plugging in, with no set places. The group annular mode (one is tempted to spell it 'anular') causes the 'social' of the phallic hierarchy, the whole house of cards of the 'imaginary,' to collapse" (ibid.).

As is evident, Hocquenghem's communist utopia emerges in the wake of sensual and somatic liberation—specifically the de-privatization and re-eroticization of the anus. Although fungibility as I conceive it sidesteps a repression/liberation framework that guides Hocquenghem's analysis (I learned well from Foucault's critique of psychoanalytic liberationist discourses), I find Hocquenghem's fantasy of a depersonalized and nonidentitarian homosexual grouping—horizontal connections with an "infinity of directions and possibilities for plugging in"—simultaneously appealing and terrifying. I imagine his group as a man-machine assemblage that works something like a self-operating modular synthesizer.[12] Each module/individual in this system has a dedicated function and yet contains versatile internal options. When patched together, singular modules generate new sound/relational combinations. Patches/somatic connections are merely neutral or impersonal conduits that plug part to part; they can be interchanged between and with others to create various forms of sonic/collective synthesis. The patches, then, create a correspondence between modules/individuals that are singular in personality, yet internally variable; patches are indifferent connectors of discreet modules that can be tweaked to create variations on their unique themes. Modules/individuals can likewise be routed through other components/non-human entities to shape, filter, oscillate, and amplify the sound/relational combination. Between the diversity of internal tweaks to proprietary modules and the multiple possibilities for connection between modules and components, sound/relational combinations are nearly infinite. Simultaneously predating and actualized in the infinite sonic/relational combinations of the modular synthesizer/homosexual grouping is the vibrational hum of a brilliantly discordant ontological polyphony.

But what would it feel like to be a fungible module in musical synthesis? What would it feel like if one's personhood were necessary only insofar as it contributed to a composition? Even more radically, in the words of artist Collier Schorr, "Could everything be different if one's image of oneself was that of another?"[13] Though a polyvalent query, I interpret Schorr's words to mean: What ethical model might emerge if subjects conceived of themselves as interchangeable with one another? My explorations into fungibility seek to answer these questions—with trepidation. What worries me most about Hocquenghem's vision of homosexual

---

12. Thanks to B&H Photo's YouTube video "What Is a Modular Synthesizer?" for helping me articulate how a modular synth operates.

13. J. Halberstam discusses Schorr's photographic work in *The Queer Art of Failure*, 162–72. Schorr's question is quoted on 171.

grouping is that it bears resemblance to a fascist military unit: another group in which fungible modules are patched together to form a cohesive whole that serves a higher purpose. While Hocquenghem's goal is the destruction of capitalism and the family, and certainly not the global domination of a master race, both projects are motivated by a desire for a *transcendent* synthesis to a dialectical struggle. Moreover, sex or no sex, fascist fantasies are typically premised on the exclusion of femininity and the glorification of homosocial, phallic bonding. Even if an individual module is versatile as plugger or plugged, as it is in Hocquenghem's vision, the phallic patch remains the crux of the connection. However desirous and liberated Hocquenghem's anus may be, the plug remains the essential relational—and hence ethical—element. As a result, I'm highly skeptical that the "phallic hierarchy . . . collapses" in a gay male group sex fantasy in which the plug/phallus is the fulcrum around which all activity turns.

In *The Queer Art of Failure*, J. Halberstam highlights the "politically problematic connections" (162) between masculinist erotic utopias and fascist realities. He reviews relevant scholarship on the symbolic links between fascism and male homosexuality—including Theodor Adorno's stunner of an observation that "totalitarianism and homosexuality belong together" (157)—and histories of Nazi-condoned homophilia. In the latter context, homosexuality is conceived as a surplus of virility and hence compatible with fascist misogyny and anti-Semitism. Based on the evidence, Halberstam concludes: "[W]e cannot afford to settle on linear connections between radical desires and radical politics" (162). Furthermore, histories of fascist homosexuality must be exposed to prevent "a universalizing and racially specific history of homosexuality" (158) that ultimately benefits what he refers to in a different work as "the white gay male patriarchy" ("The Anti-Social Turn" 152). Taking seriously Halberstam's claims and Adorno's troubling observation, I devote the remainder of this chapter to distinguishing my concept of queer fungibility from fascist erotic fantasies, naïve utopian visions, and totalitarian, phallocentric masculinism.

I begin with a tidbit from the twentieth-century queer archives that stands as an extraordinary model of queer fungibility: the 1970s lesbian-separatist collective known as the Van Dykes. Described by Ariel Levy as "a roving band of van-driving vegans who shaved their heads, avoided speaking to men unless they were waiters or mechanics, and lived on the highways of North America, stopping only on Women's Land," the Van Dykes was founded by Lamar Van Dyke (then, Heather Van Dyke) and Ange Spaulding (then, Brook Van Dyke) in 1977. To become a group member, women were required to disown their family/marital name, invent a new first name, and, you guessed it, adopt "Van Dyke" as their last. The surname itself, an obvious yet hilarious pun, speaks to the Van Dykes's quite serious commitment to lighthearted egolessness and collective identification. The name-change ritual satirizes the then-popular, Anita Bryant-stoked, heterosexual fear of homosexual recruitment. The Van Dykes surely had a laugh literalizing homosexual conversion by defiantly changing what they referred to as their "slave name" to an anti-gay slur. The pack's mononymity was conceived, moreover, as a disruption of heteronormative business-as-usual: "They had a fantasy that a maître d' would one day call out, "Van Dyke, party of four?" and dozens of lesbians would stand up, to the horror of the assembled heterosexuals." Though clearly laced with humor, this fantasy nonetheless bespeaks the subversive power of collectivities grounded in sameness: the image of mononymous, quasi-cloned ranks popping up in unexpected places amplifies the queer mantra, "We Are Everywhere," to the status of a threat. I imagine an army of Van Dykes traversing the nation and multiplying in the most unnatural of ways (recruitment), while working the land, rethinking individualism, and experimenting with small-scale communist self-sufficiency—all of it grounded in voluntary fungibility. For adopting the Van Dyke surname in some respects signals an acceptance of one's substitutability: recruits empty themselves of their personal histories by choosing to become an interchangeable member of a nomadic pack. In this regard, the Van Dykes resemble the most fearsome enemy in the *Star Trek* franchise, the Borg: an alien race of indistinguishable cybernetic beings that combats Enlightenment-inspired, Western colonial progress. Comprised of nameless and depersonalized drones that share a group consciousness and speak in one voice, the Borg defy liberal-humanistic principles of individualism and seek to destroy democracy as we know it. Unsurprisingly, the Borg were introduced into the *Star Trek* franchise in 1989, on the heels of Perestroika (*Borg*). The show's writers used the Borg to make a forceful and quite reactionary political statement: the telos of communist social organization is inevitably totalitarianism; a social investment in sameness is necessarily fascistic. A decade prior, however, the Van Dykes seemed to scoff at such foregone conclusions.

The sexual norms of the Van Dyke collective—promiscuity and non-monogamy—further emphasize the fungible nature of group membership. "When the Van Dykes were running around," Lamar Van Dyke recalls, "everybody was sleeping with everybody. It was chaos" (5–6). Although

Lamar Van Dyke refuses to be considered the group's leader, "hierarchy was considered patriarchal," she claims to hold a special status because she slept with all but one Van Dyke in the collective's three-year existence. If the Van Dykes were at all cult-like—another sensationalized heterosexual concern of the late 1970s—then Lamar was the personality around which that cult revolved. Levy's narration of the decline and fall of the Van Dyke collective, however true or false, is somewhat cliché: it reiterates the well-worn trope that even our best communist intentions will be undermined by individual egoism. According to the author, the interpersonal chaos resulting from the sexual promiscuity—coupled with Lamar Van Dyke's controversial embrace of lesbian sadomasochism in 1979—led to the collective's demise. "What that trip taught me," Chris Fox (Thorn Van Dyke) recalls, referring to the Van Dykes's international adventure, "was that, in the end, people will act more on their personalities than on their politics." Before the road to ruin, however, Fox herself initially deemed interpersonal messiness and romantic heartbreak a reasonable price to pay for the freedom afforded by membership in a lesbian-separatist collective. About her and Spaulding's break-ups with Lamar Van Dyke, Levy writes: "Chris and Ange did not think of themselves as jilted lovers following their ex-girlfriend on a road trip. They were convinced that their struggle to dispense with the straight world outweighed their bruised egos and broken hearts." Jocular self-transformation, chaotic promiscuity, egoless fungibility, and horizontal connectivity: initially, the Van Dykes arguably actualized an anti-patriarchal and nonphallic form of Hocquenghem's homosexual grouping, even a quite fun and voluntary version of Borg-like connectivity. But maybe they weren't Borg-like enough? For when "personalities," in Fox's words, begin to rear their ugly head and conflict with other personalities, when formerly de-emphasized personalities take on self-important authority, the phallic re-emerges in the form of power grabs and competition. One anecdote about the collective's demise speaks volumes about the irrepressible ego: "One night, Heather (Lamar) became jealous when she heard that Brook and Judith planned to go out dancing without her, so she hid Judith's dancing shoes. When, later, Judith found her dancing shoes among Heather's possessions, she retaliated by setting Heather's van on fire."

As I will argue in the pages to come, training ourselves not to be seduced by personality—especially in the throes of sexual/sensual seduction—is essential to a queer ethics of fungibility. Seeking aesthetic experiences that might encourage an indifference to our own and others' personalities is likewise necessary to actualizing this ethos. And though, like Hocquenghem, I analyze queer fungibility in a site of male-specific intimacy, the ethic per se is not solely the province of men seeking men. In fact, as I mentioned in the introduction, being fungible is the very antithesis of manhood as we've come to know it: individualistic, competitive, controlling, and impenetrable. An ethics of fungibility emphasizes vulnerability, egolessness, and self-substitution; at this historical juncture, normatively socialized American men are arguably most in need of learning fungibility's lessons. And how might something as solipsistic and seemingly inconsequential as virtual cruising aid in this education? Because a significant feature of the modern Western personality concerns sexual identity, perhaps it is through sexual practices—not necessarily sex itself—that we might learn to de-emphasize our personalities, to lessen ourselves. The Van Dykes achieved this, initially at least, with self-effacing humor and promiscuous partner swapping. If through the virtual cruising experience men can learn to see and embrace themselves similarly (as less of a self, as a fungible option); if through virtual cruising men can learn to, like the Van Dykes, *laugh at and disavow* socially determined self-identity as opposed to becoming ever more invested in it, then the media merit attention. In this case, with all due respect to Audre Lorde, it could take the master's tools, neoliberal media, to dismantle the master's house: the ego of *homo economicus*. A sexually and socially utopian pipe dream, perhaps, but at this stage in the game—as the Earth warms, seas rise, extinction looms . . . and the megalomaniacs calling the shots continue to make the inane, nihilistic, and homicidal case that global capitalism will save us—we should seek out and exploit any and all possible avenues for social transformation.

That said, it is necessary to qualify my thoughts on how I understand fungibility to operate in the m4m media context. First, in no way am I arguing that race, class, gender or any other significant social identity marker magically disappear in m4m forums. In no way do I believe that users become social and sexual equals in some imaginary online hookup utopia.[14] As many media scholars have noted, quite the opposite is true:

---

14. Leo Bersani laid to rest such magical thinking in the context of gay male bathhouses as well. Despite the fact that men are rendered "the same" by submitting to the uniform protocol of the white towel, bathhouses are hardly communist utopias. In his words: "Anyone who has ever spent one night in a gay bathhouse knows that it is (or was) one of the most ruthlessly ranked, hierarchized, and competitive environments imaginable" (*Rectum* 12).

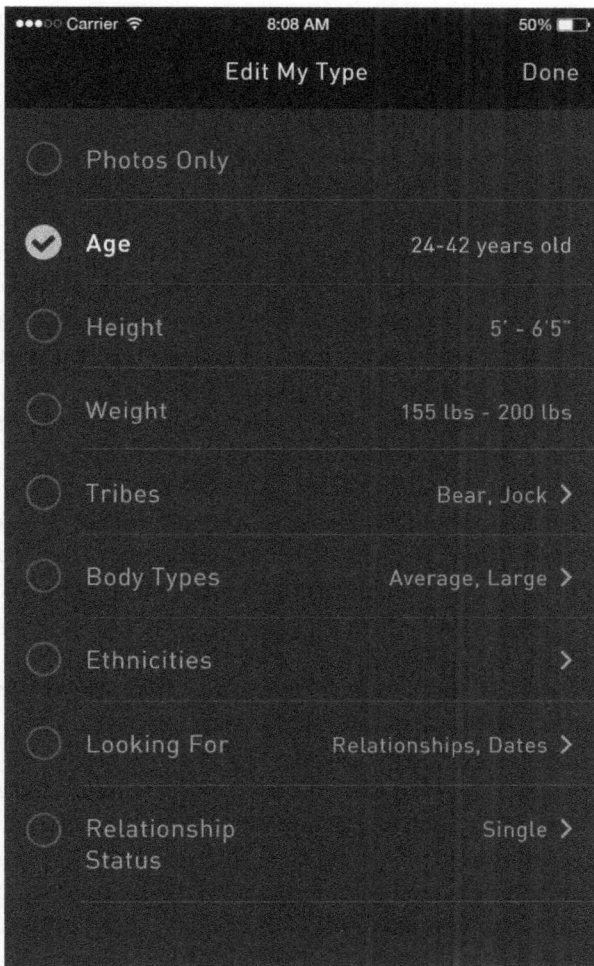

Figure 1.4. Grindr's "My Type" filters.

social prejudices and biases steeped in the sludge of history are more often than not *exacerbated* online.[15] Aiding in this exacerbation, apps such as Grindr reify discursively constructed and historically contingent racial categories (euphoniously designated "ethnicities" on the app) and allow

---

15. For more on the exacerbation of social inequality online see boyd, 153–75.

users to literally racially profile one another while cruising.[16] Grindr's "My Type" feature, moreover, permits users to curate their "collage" (Grindr's name for the grid of user profile pictures) to render invisible any undesirable social types. (See figure 1.4.)

There are no two ways about it: Racism, classism, effemephobia, gender- and body-normativity are palpable in m4m media, and social identity filters help them flourish. Filters work, moreover, to foreclose unexpected connections, reinforce bigotry, and prevent encounters with socially different or atypical (as in, "not my type") others. But what is the best way to rid m4m platforms of all these "isms"? The best way to make these forums sites of more authentically democratic and open-minded participation? Should we demand that media corporations police user behavior more forcefully or remove filters altogether? Is more oversight and less options the answer here? Before jumping to panicky conclusions, it is important to keep in mind an uncomfortable yet axiomatic fact: try as we might, we cannot simply wish away what Bersani calls "the ruthlessly exclusionary nature of sexual desire" (*Homos* 107). As we learned from gay conversion "therapy," personal and institutional attempts to force sexual desire to conform to a spiritual, social, or political ideal are not only barbaric, they rarely work. Andrea Long Chu observes where such attempts most often lead: "Desire is, by nature, childlike and chary of government. The day we begin to qualify it by the righteousness of its political content is the day we begin to prescribe some desires and prohibit others. That way lies moralism only." The history of the social regulation of sexuality is rife with moralizing, panicking, and prohibiting. m4m media's social identity filters make searching for a sex partner convenient in ways that do not align with liberal-humanist and multiculturalist democratic principles. Rather than instituting punitive measures to rid the grid of exclusionary practices, however, we'd be better off sitting with the discomfort to mine it for its ethical potential.

Greg Goldberg does just this. He finds in the self-interested virtual hunt for sex an opportunity to imagine a queer model of antisociality: one grounded in equivalence rather than identification, differentiation, reciprocity, or altruism. Goldberg welcomes the exclusionary, consumerist, choose-your-ideal-product relational norms of the Grindr hunt. Because these norms mirror those of the marketplace, Grindr forces us to reckon

---

16. For more on racial profiling and racism in m4m media see McGlotten (esp. 62–77), Daroya, Sen, and Raj.

with an ethical quandary: "how to engender the formation of social bonds in a milieu that indulges antisocial tendencies" ("Meet Markets" 13). Goldberg continues:

> This quandary is intensified when the relations in question are sexual, insofar as sex already poses a dilemma for ethics: what, if anything, does one owe to another person who provides, enhances, or is in some other way necessary for one's own pleasure? Sex seems to touch an ethical nerve, in part, because it threatens that in a state of pleasure we might abandon (if only temporarily) our obligation to our partners; the more intense the pleasure, the more poignant the challenge to ethics. Sex thus becomes symbolically charged as a practice of sacrifice and discipline, of transcending or taming one's appetite for pleasure, an appetite that requires other people's participation but threatens indifference to their experience. [. . .] In short, if "meaningless" sex is dangerous, it is precisely because of what it means for the social. (13)

Instead of chastising Grindr users, Goldberg appreciates Grindr as a site in which a sexual ethics unbeholden to traditional, Christian values might be carved out.[17] In a similar spirit, I assert that fungibility, based in a formal, protocological equivalence and *not* social equality, is one of those ethical models.

It is not lost on me, however, that when equivalence—or, worse, sameness—is emphasized between social groups with varying degrees of social privilege, the knives come out. Be it the biological, intellectual, and emotional similarities between men and women or the shared experiences

---

17. Goldberg insists, however, that his analysis of Grindr does not concern ethics; it seems ethics, for him, is inherently moralistic because it concerns "how we should treat others" (2). Goldberg seeks instead to explore "the political desirability of objectification" and ultimately claims that "openness to otherness can be established and maintained through objectification" (2). The way I see it, his notion of interobjectivity is an ethical concept: it is an ethics that *begets* an antisocial politics. In other words, I do not find it necessary to draw such a rigid line between ethics and politics. Both, in my estimation, emerge from and through an ontological framework, one that Goldberg and I share: namely, Bersanian sameness.

of oppression between gay men and lesbians, claims to sameness are unpopular across the political spectrum. Dominant groups (in the previous example, men: gay- or straight-identified) often aggressively emphasize their difference from those they deem inferior in order to secure their perch at the peak of the social hierarchy. Progressive, activist groups with members of varying social privilege all too often splinter or dissolve because individuals from socially dominant groups fail to acknowledge the ways their social privilege informs their group input. Moreover, in contemporary "call-out culture" sanctimonious takedowns of morally suspect individuals are sometimes welcomed more than collective strategies for structural social change. So often commencing in and going viral through various social media platforms (I'm looking at you, Twitter), call-out culture can be a hindrance to collective, leftist social progress because it individualizes structural issues. Although calling someone out might rid a spoiled bunch of a "bad apple," it ultimately fortifies the barrel that contains, constricts, and hinders the bunch: it prevents us from realizing better forms of social activism and organization. Commenting on the conflation of structural analysis and individualized moralizing in call-out culture, Asam Ahmad, a self-described "poor, working class poet, writer, and community organizer," notes: "[W]hen people are reduced to their identities of privilege (as white, cisgender, male, etc.) and mocked as such, it means we're treating each other as if our individual social locations stand in for the total systems those parts of our identities represent. Individuals become synonymous with systems of oppression, and this can turn systemic analysis into moral judgment. Too often, when it comes to being called out, narrow definitions of a person's identity count for everything."

The academy itself is certainly not immune to call-out culture, and an emphasis on ontological sameness and immanentism typically draws the ire of the academic left.[18] This is due partly to the fact that a philosophy of difference, steeped in the Hegelian dialectical method, has dominated leftist critical thought since World War II. Arguably in response to fascism, understood as an attempt to eradicate difference *tout court*, the academic left doubled down on an investment in dialectics. A philosophy grounded in the push and pull of opposing forces offered a logical antidote to fascist investments in sameness. From the dialectician's perspective, immanentist

---

18. For an example of this phenomenon, see Timothy Brennan's *Wars of Position*, which essentially calls out immanentist Marxists for their political-theoretical ineptitude.

explorations into ontological sameness are dangerous, naïve, fantastical, or, indeed, fascistic. Adorno's aforementioned claim that "totalitarianism and homosexuality belong together" is, at least on the surface, exemplary of this perspective.[19] Because both practices fail to dialectically engage the Other (e.g., the non-Aryan or the opposite sex) in any ethical way and because, from this perspective, both practices are investments in cultivating sameness, they are similarly dangerous. Their relatedness lies in an exclusion of difference that prevents a necessary *frisson*, one that saves the self from a sociopathic narcissism and the populace from a nativist authoritarianism. Adorno's claim rests on a Freudian connection between narcissism and homosexuality. In one of Freud's many narratives of sexual development, male homosexual desire is at root a narcissistic wish for an idealized version of the self. The adult homosexual, let's call him Leonardo, seeks to locate in another man, Michelangelo, the boy Leonardo imagines himself to have been when he was cared for and coddled by Mom ("Leonardo"). Hence, the call of the proper Other—in this case, the lure of the opposite sex—goes unheeded, resulting in arrested development, neurosis, or worse.

Leo Bersani takes up the gauntlet thrown down by philosophers of difference in embracing the very nondialectical sameness they pathologize. Proposing that a "salutary devalorizing of difference" (*Homos* 7) might be a way to work through the quagmire of a divisive identity politics and an insipid multiculturalism, Bersani creates the concept of "homo-ness:" an ontology that rests on a monist conception of substance, sameness, that is internally heterogeneous, or, inherently different from itself. In Hegelian ontologies, difference (or the Other) is something encountered, reckoned with, sublated, or assimilated by a self; in a Bersanian ontology, by contrast, difference is primordial and internal to Being itself. Self-growth,

---

19. According to Thomas Pepper, "totalitarianism" is mistranslated in Adorno's infamous statement: Adorno actually wrote "Totalität" meaning "totality." Nonetheless, the homophobia embedded within the sentence is not lost in translation. As Pepper argues in *Singularities*: "Here it would seem that the translator, expecting, perhaps, to see the typical attitude of a Jewish grandfather (or father), has read the text through a rather hallucinatory ideological filter. Adorno is making a post-Hegelian commentary on Plato's *Symposium*, a fact which takes the homophobia of the text much further—and much more interestingly so—than the published translation does" (21). Whether totality or totalitarian, any investment in nondialectical sameness remains deeply problematic for Adorno and many other dialecticians.

then, is not the result of the dialectical struggle between self and other, between being and nothingness, but rather an emanation of difference that is primary and constitutive. Because homosexuality has been socially constructed as a love of sameness, Bersani finds it a "privileged vehicle for homo-ness" (10). Even narcissism, when conceived as the cultivation of an internally variegated homo-ness, becomes a desirable condition. When the world in its various extensions is conceived as the self undone, narcissistic egoism becomes an attunement to the world's rhythms and repetitions. Counterintuitively, the very psychological states and sociable forms negatively associated with homosexuality become for Bersani avenues through which to reconceive subjectivity and community: "We might welcome the identification of homosexuality with sameness by insisting on the radical potential in that identification: the potential for our having a privileged role in demonstrating how a sort of impersonal narcissism can break down the defensive organization of the self-congratulatory ego, a breaking down that must take place if the fundamental restructuring of the social is ever to take place" (*Rectum* 33–34).

Bersani, of course, is an outlier in his embrace of nondialectical sameness. In the grand scheme of post-WWII leftist cultural critique, theorists that do not feed the difference-valorizing machine that is the dialectic are often sidelined or skewered. For the right wing, these thinkers are a threat to traditional social hierarchies because they emphasize a commonness that cuts through identitarian lines. For the Left, such thinkers are irresponsible in their naïve attempts to wish away actually existing social inequalities. By following Bersani and calling attention to the radical potential of ontological sameness, my argument seeks to offer strategies for toppling traditional social hierarchies while paying close attention to the inequalities that sustain them. Given the present national context of heightened social division—a divisiveness that is not simply the product of a Trump presidency, but more the consequence of neoliberal policy and biopolitical population control, both of which invest in identitarian difference to reinforce barriers between social groups—this experiment seems a risk worth taking, especially now.

I highlight Bersani's work here because my notion of fungibility is most conceptually indebted to his ontology of homo-ness. Like the modules in the synthesizer assemblage described earlier, the fungible self is at once plurally singular and singularly plural: each contains variegated multitudes—adjustable, mutable, trainable—that express themselves in impersonal connections with other modules. Homo-ness, in this analogy, is the primordial, discordant hum that harbors within it a potentially euphonious polyphony. Such polyphony is (re)actualized when modules connect with corresponding forms, bringing them into attunement. The impersonal patching that links these modules allows for a nearly infinite amount of combinative forms to emerge: compositions that unite components that have little in common save their capacity to connect. Connection does not deplete the singularity of each component. Indeed, the singular only becomes discernible in the plural. The fundamental, anarchical heterogeneity of homo-ness is realized, then, in compositions that highlight a module's singularity-commonality over its identity/difference.[20] In this composition, hierarchies of identitarian difference are disrespected. Singular voices instead become fungible equivalents that can be voluntarily plugged in or unplugged. Though clearly essential to the composition, each voice is interchangeable, substitutable, and only recognizable when in common connection with singularly different yet formally equivalent others. If these voices are self-serving in their longing for connective consummation, they are simultaneously self-effacing in recognizing their substitutability. But fungibility is not a martyrdom to a higher cause: importantly, the harmonious synthesis of modules is by no means guaranteed. There is no transcendence beyond the immediate attunement—discordant, euphonious, or otherwise—of sonic rhythms and flows.

Ultimately, fungibility is an aesthetics that betrays an ethics: to riff on Schorr's question from earlier, fungibility is a willful imaging of a self that is formally substitutable for another. I assert that an aesthetics of fungibility lies nascent in the self-aestheticization and virtual cruising experience in m4m media. I locate in these media a "homo-esthetic," for which, in Bersani's words, "homosexual desire is essential, but which, precisely and paradoxically because of this, can dispense with the concept of homosexual identity" (*Rectum* 31). As I argue in *Friendship*, it is from within the immanence of homosexuality—specifically, in the historical forms of impersonal queer sensual sociability—that we struggle to deplete the power of "homosexuality" as a psychology, an identity, and the crux of self and social management. In training ourselves to become less seduced by sexual interiority, in delinking desire from social identity in sensual practice, we work to disidentify with the homosexuals we've been obliged to be. The voluntary self-subtraction occurring in the sensual (haptic)

---

20. For more on the singularity-commonality dyad, see Hardt and Negri, *Multitude* 217–18.

and aesthetic (visual) experience of virtual cruising might be a chance to pursue this becoming.

I'll conclude this chapter with a handful of the odder questions that guide my analysis: What if we were to approach online cruising primarily *as* an aesthetic experience, one akin to perusing artworks in a museum? What if we treated profile creation as a transformation of our life into a work of art, as an opportunity to become artistic? Following that, might we treat the "art" populating online cruising forums with the respect and reverence typically reserved for museum pieces? Not unrelated, what if we were to think about virtual cruising not as a search to satiate a lack but as something to supplement or enrich a fullness? What if, like the Van Dykes of the digital age, we went online to shed the seriousness of our socially determined selves and laugh our way into new identities and adventures? What if we reoriented the temporality of the search from the futural (I want sex or love in the minutes/hours/days to come) to the present? Is the masturbatory, haptic practice of manipulating our phones in the search for connection itself a sexual practice? Do I become a modern-day Diogenes, masturbating in public, when practicing screen love outside domestic spaces? Might our desire to cruise virtually stem from a love of manipulating screens as much as it does from a longing to interact with another human? The visual stimulation, the sensuous scrolling and tapping, the distracted browsing, the liberating feeling of becoming less of yourself or somebody else altogether: might these aesthetic pleasures themselves hold some ethical promise?

If it hasn't yet been made clear, I am more interested in the durational experience of virtual cruising than in the hookups or dates that might result from it. By reorienting the temporality of virtual cruising to the present tense, I seek to divert attention from the excessively meaningful, normative telos of sex and love. Following Foucault, who in more than one interview declares that "sex is boring" (*Essential* 253; Raskin), I am not terribly interested in the psychological factors that motivate people to seek sex online nor in the particular activities in which they hope to participate. For Foucault, the immoderate significance we assign to sexual desire and behavior, the limited imagination we demonstrate in conceiving of and practicing sex, and the selves we seek to discover, validate, or humiliate through sex are much less interesting than the ways in which our relation *to* sex might open onto an aesthetics of existence: the ways we can use our sexuality, like the Van Dykes did, as a creative act. Foucault writes: "Sexuality is part of our behavior. It's a part of our world freedom. Sexuality is something that we create—it is our own creation, and much more than the discovery of a secret side of our desire. We have to understand that with our desires, through our desires, go new forms of relationships, new forms of love, new forms of creation. Sex is not a fatality: it's a possibility for creative life" (*Essential* 163). Geosocial dating apps for phones—an invention originally developed for men seeking sex or connection with men—is one such creative use of sexuality. Like other pre-Internet features of the gay male infrastructure—clone culture or the so-called "gay ghetto," for example—m4m media are an opportunity to experiment with new understandings of the self, new possibilities of pleasure, and a new platform to inaugurate an aesthetics of existence. These media also afford the opportunity to rethink sexuality as a hardwired essence that needs to be authenticated. Through them, we can come to understand sexual expression as a site for self-care, self-modulation, and self-sculpting.

This is to say that in the timeliest of media we might access the untimeliest of self-practices: ancient forms of ascesis not beholden to religious doctrine, civil law, or normative social identity. Foucault found in ancient Greek ascetics the seedlings of a modern, anti-identitarian sexual politics (Roach, *Friendship* 48–50). The work of the ascetic begins with emptying the self of its contemporary meanings—personality, individuality, "sexuality" as we have come to know it—in order to fashion a new self from an inherent, impersonal alterity. Put another way, the ascetic must recognize his fungibility before he can make anything meaningful, original, or unexpected of himself. He must "get over" himself in order to recognize how his internally differentiated self corresponds with external, equivalent forms. Like a sculptor who chips away at a block of marble to reveal an immanent design—one that was always already there but required training to discern—the ascetic molds a new self into a brilliant work of art only after recognizing the original's blankness, only after realizing that that blank block could take countless forms. Analyzing the durational experience of the virtual cruise, I seek to locate the aestheticized forms that are taking shape in modern gay male culture. Tarrying in the means, I speculate about ends that direct us beyond the paradigms of biopolitical identity and neoliberal relationality. It is in the digital cruise itself that I discern nascent aesthetic forms of queer subjectivity and ethics.

Chapter Two

Fail Better at Romance!

The affective pull of screen-mediated sexual and romantic exchanges seems to hold a unique power. Flirty chats prompt us to withdraw from whatever social situation we might be in; sexting pulls us out of mundane activity and into a virtual realm of fantasy and projection. Positive responses to our unmistakably clever chat contributions make us feel wanted and special. Our phones ding or buzz with a text from a potential lover or hookup, and we are interpellated as a participant in a virtual *pas de deux*. The steps to this dance vary between media platforms: exchanges on Grindr, for instance, tend toward the perfunctory and transactional, whereas more relationship-oriented apps and sites follow more traditional, heteronormative courtship scripts. Irrespective of platform, when caught up in a titillating virtual exchange, we feel elated, giddy, euphoric . . . and profoundly *normal*. Given the importance American culture ascribes to a healthy sex/romantic life, few things are more self-validating and more normalizing than shooting and being struck by Cupid's arrows.

And yet, for the more self-reflective among us, the dialogue of the hunt or courtship can nag at us night and day. "Did I say the right thing?" "What does he mean by that?" "Was I too forward?" "Why haven't I heard back from her?" Just as my family and I became self-proclaimed medical semioticians in the ICU, we all become psychoanalysts, linguists, judge and jury when we parse the mysterious, affectless polyvalence of another's texts. To make matters worse, since the average response time in U.S. screen-mediated communication is now under two minutes (Cohen-

Sheffer),[1] we grow anxious, neurotic, and defensive when our solicitations are not returned immediately. In short, when traversing the virtual romantic or sexual landscape, we feel at times most alone, at others never more in sync. Whether the feelings are good or bad, the emotional extremities and the hope for something better keep us coming back for more.

In *Against Love*, Laura Kipnis, riffing on Ernst Bloch, notes that utopianism "is buried deep in those small, lived epiphanies of pleasure, in sensations of desire, in fun, and play, in love, in transgression, in the rejection of drudgery and work [. . .]" (45). Although Kipnis here is referencing the utopian impulse behind adultery—a practice that, if anything, expresses a desire for a different relational order—one can see how even the crassest of online sex solicitations reveals something similar: a conviction that the world would be better if you and I were physically connected. At once binding and separating users, screens paradoxically call attention to our hypermediated, and hence alienated, social attachments. At the same time, screens goad us to bridge the unbridgeable gap between ourselves and others. An excess of affect tends to brim over screen-mediated exchanges arguably because the screen itself is an impasse: a material manifestation of our irreparable and singular solitude, a reminder of our shared estrangement. As *memento mori*, then, screens nourish a utopian impulse: that dead thing between us—the barrier reminding me, consciously or not, that I am alone—makes me want to reach out all the more. Even the most noncommittal online come-ons, clearly born of boredom, betray an all-too-human desire for connection: a change to the current situation, a chance, à la Beckett, to "fail better" at intersubjective fusion (87).

Hookup apps in particular can nurture a utopian desire to be free from heteronormative relational models, standards, and rituals. At first glance, these media seem to enrich the social-relational mosaic by opening a window onto a world of bodies, pleasures, and fantasies. They make evident that there are alternatives to traditional courtship mores and options for unconventional intimacies. They offer proof that compulsory couple-dom, marital monogamy, and rigid sexual identities are not predestined for all. However dystopian the actual solicitations and rejections may be in these forums—however crude, offensive, bigoted, and deplorable—the call and response itself signals a desire for something different: maybe, in

---

1. Citing data from GSMA Intelligence, Text Request, and the Pew Research Center, Cohen-Sheffer claims: "The fact is that 95% of texts will be read within 3 minutes of being sent, with the average response time for a text being a mere 90 seconds."

the end, not a better world, but at least something other than the current arrangement. And though the temporal orientation of dating app discourse is typically futural ("let's meet, I wanna be with u") users sign up to seek a change to their present—everything from killing time during a boring meeting to experimenting with a new sexual self. "Little did I know," one Tinder user remarks in the app's branded lifestyle magazine *Swipe Life*, "when I used the app last summer, I wasn't swiping for love or anything crazy like that—I was swiping for change" (Cai). At the risk of sounding like a Tinder spokesperson myself, suffice to say that "change" resulting from hookup app use can come in many forms: not just changing one's relationship status, not just getting lucky, but also, perhaps, changing one's #relationshipgoals or sexual identity.

In short, hookup apps can serve the social function of making relationship options visible and accessible. They offer access to diverse sexual cultures and practices that do not necessarily equate "happily ever after" with landing the One. They likewise afford individuals the chance to experiment with sex and identity: the social media nurtured sexual self-definition, "heteroflexibile," being one example. Moreover, hookup apps provide a valuable forum for sexual knowledge circulation, an essential ingredient for a democratic sexual morality. To ensure even the most basic sexual freedoms—from the right to exist as a certain sexual being to freedom of sexual choice—information about diverse sexual practices and communities must be readily available. Because schools, families, and other social institutions ultimately fail us on this front, the Internet and social networking media, for better and for worse, pick up the slack. As Michael Warner notes: "Individuals do not go shopping for sexual identity, but they do have a stake in a culture that enables sexual variance and circulates knowledge about it, because they have no other way of knowing what they might or might not want, or what they might become, or with whom they might find a common lot" (7).

And yet, the utopian impulses nourished in screen-mediated connection set users up for inevitable disappointment. Screens entice us with fantasies of ideal intimacy that ultimately fail, betray, or bore us. Cynically, dating app corporations take advantage of this: they harness the power of screen-generated affect and profit from the inevitable failure of traditional intimacy models. The CEO of Tinder, the most popular dating app in the U.S., puts a smiley-face spin on his target market's dating failures: "We actually embrace the fact that our members are in that dating-as-leisure-activity phase of life" (qtd. in Bromwich). And while Tinder users trend young—per the company, more than 50 percent of its users are ages eighteen to twenty-five—meeting online has become the most popular way for singles of all ages to initiate a first date.[2] To keep users coming back for more, dating apps must emphasize the upside of keeping things casual, not committing too quickly, and playing the field. Jonah Engel Bromwich of *The New York Times* observes: "Tinder and Bumble are desperate to convince you that you're not desperate. Dating, they promise, is fun, *so fun*, that when one date ends badly, it's a barely disguised blessing: You get to stay on the apps and keep on dating!" While online matchmaking entrepreneurs bend over backwards to highlight the love connections their products abet, their companies' bottom line rests on users failing to land Mr., Ms., or Mx. Right. Because being single is socially constructed as a *temporary* state of incompleteness, because the very notion of singledom merely serves to reinforce its normative telos—being un-single, or, coupled—dating apps must play the contradictory roles of singles-maintainer and couples-creator. All the while, they put faith in the promise that younger generations will make do with disposable intimacies as they jobscotch around the neoliberal marketplace. These companies also bank on the moneymaker of a fact that at least 50 percent of married couples will split up. Ironically, then, the very promise that draws most people to dating apps—landing the One[3]—is undercut by a corporate mission to ensure that singles stay single. The expectation of romantic failure is built into a dating app developer's business plan.

But dating apps do not merely bank on romantic failure; they also provoke it. The mountains of marketing material claiming how effective apps are at uniting soulmates cannot erase one inconvenient truth: these apps *break couples up*. After all, breakups are good for business! According to a 2019 YouGov survey about dating app/website usage, 17 percent of people who sign up for dating apps do so with the express purpose "to cheat on my significant other" (Ballard). And while this may shock us, it certainly shouldn't. Who among us has not heard a story about, or has not been personally involved in, a breakup instigated by electronic media? That email from your mistress reminiscing about your most recent sexcapade, that text

---

2. Match Group, the parent company of Tinder and OkCupid, conducts an annual survey of five thousand Americans concerning their use of dating apps. These statistics are culled from its 2018 survey. See Match Group, "Singles in America."

3. According to a 2019 YouGov survey, 49 percent of users on dating apps say their main purpose for signing on is "to find an exclusive romantic partner" (Ballard).

from your fuck buddy arriving just as you and your spouse head out for your once-a-month date night, that mole next to your left nipple betraying your identity on your faceless Grindr profile pic . . . all of it tangible evidence that you are a horrible human being, unworthy of your one-and-only's love. The real problem, however, isn't the media; it's the message: "Make Love Happen" (match.com); "Find Your Perfect Match" (eHarmony.com); "Some things are just meant to bee" (bumble.com). Considering that no single technological advance has yet made marital monogamy foolproof, it is highly unlikely that any new technology will destroy it.

But there's a bigger question to ask here: Is anyone actually worthy of their one-and-only's true love? Even if we're not cruising the apps, our eyes may wander to porn or other bodies, and our minds' extramarital, masturbatory fantasy reels may roll. We can generously understand such "straying" tactics as marital aids (or life support) for long term relationships, or we can view them as acts of quiet desperation painfully performed to maintain the illusion that "love wins." Laura Kipnis prefers the latter interpretation: "[O]ur age dedicates itself to allying the turbulence of romance and the rationality of the long-term couple, hoping to be convinced despite all evidence to the contrary that love and sex are obtainable from one person over the course of decades, and that desire will manage to sustain itself over thirty or forty or fifty years of cohabitation" (55–56). But how did this irrational and sadistic dream become a social mandate? What convinced us to conceive of this inherently failed model as both the norm and the ideal? Forget religion, the modern "domestic Gulag," as Kipnis calls it, is the historical upshot of a cunning business merger between capitalism and psychiatry. As much as we might not want to admit it, the age-old search for economic stability psychologically suffuses the modern hunt for exclusive romantic partnership: a "good match," in the contemporary context and in Jane Austen novels alike, is a solid investment in both emotional and economic security. Although crassly materialist marital motives should not be discussed in polite company, they imbue the consumerist psyches of capitalist subjects who "freely" shop for life partners on apps and sites. Summarizing the insights of sociologist Eva Illouz, Kipnis notes: "The real transformation of modern love [. . .] comes with the fact that ranking mates for material and social assets is now incorporated into the psychology of love and unconscious structures of desire, with individuals having now internalized the economic rationality once exerted by parents, thus 'freely' falling in love with mates who are also—coincidentally—good investments" (63). As any stockbroker can tell you, however, it takes a lot of work to get consistently profitable returns from even the most solid investment. Love and labor, then, tend to become indistinguishable as partners slog their way through the long haul. But take heart, fellow traveler, because we are well trained for this work. Kipnis argues that various social institutions condition us from the get-go to squeeze into the straitjacket of monogamous, romantic coupledom. Beyond cultural indoctrination (Hollywood rom-coms, "classic" Disney, "The Bachelor," e.g.), social institutions with seemingly disparate missions—the family, the school, the office, religious institutions, marriage—work together to convince us that repression is key to life-success. Indeed, a "good" child/ student/employee/parishioner/husband/wife is a master repressor of desires and denier of dreams. Put another way, with a Foucaultian spin on it, social institutions *produce* subjects that idealize a navel-gazing self-discipline they are destined to fail at maintaining. (Cruel optimism, anyone?) A successful graduate of said institutions has a very limited imagination regarding love and happiness: both are impossible without suffering and submission. In order to achieve anything worthwhile in this world—or the next, as numerous religions would have it—we must mortify the flesh and tame the spirit. Historically, one endured such suffering to be in good standing with one or another deity—if I can resist temptation and/or transcend desire, the light of the divine will shine upon me, and my spot in heaven (or whatever afterlife) will be secured. These days, by contrast, love wins. More than just a sentimental slogan deployed in same-sex marriage advocacy, "love wins" gives name to the broad historical shift from the pursuit of divine recognition to the pursuit of a romantic "fulfillment" intimately tied to economic security (Kipnis 90–94). The self-abuse, self-doubt, and anxiety-unto-death previously attending spiritual quests transforms into disciplinary rituals of courtship preparation: dieting, exercising, weightlifting, tanning, hair dyeing, and plastic surgery to ready the body; for the soul, therapy, self-help manuals, and endless, essentialist pop-psychological advice about "what women/men/gays/lesbians *really* want."

Especially since the U.S. Supreme Court legalized gay marriage in 2015, queers are now, more than ever, expected to honor, cherish, and adhere to the rigid relationship rules that straight couples have been failing to follow for centuries. "You asked for it," Mayor Tom Menino of Boston quipped sardonically after the first legal same-sex wedding ceremony in the nation.[4] We asked for it, indeed . . . and what did we get? For one, a

---

4. Menino spoke these words in private after the ceremony. My evidence for the quip is anecdotal, but I have confirmation from a City of Boston employee who was in the room when Menino said it.

massive surge in the number of registered Grindr users: up from 7 million to 27 million between 2013 and 2017 (Dating Sites Reviews). In the age of marriage equality, over 9 million nubile American men seek men on Grindr. Studies show, however, that marriageable boys are not typically cruising the ether looking for a new hubby: the common Grindr profile abbreviations DTF ("down to fuck") or, simply, ↓ speak volumes about the intentions of the majority of Grindr users (Kuhnreich). Even though many of these users are migrating to other m4m apps due to Grindr's indefensible security breaches, unethical data disclosure, and the company president's anti-gay marriage statements (Shadel; Rodriguez), all trends point to an increase in dating and hookup app use for gay-identified men, irrespective of platform (Match Group). In a word, the future of gay sex and courtship is digital. And though correlation does not, of course, equal causation, one can't help but wonder why more and more gay-identified men are signing up for hookup apps at a time when future ex-husbands are legally permitted to walk down the aisle.

Here's a guess: hookup apps afford a momentary breather from the stifling air in which traditional, marital coupledom thrives. The affective power of screen-mediated intimacy merely feeds the promiscuous desires manufactured in the anxious hunt for (or pressure to stay with) the soulmate. Put another way, the byproduct of marriage equality is virtual promiscuity, and the apps in this sense serve two masters: one socially respectable (seeking LTR); the other less savory (DTF). Even though hookup apps can function as a release valve in the pressure cooker of landing or maintaining the happily-ever-after, few things in contemporary America remain more socially validating, morally vindicating, financially rewarding, and culturally celebrated than tying the knot. Despite the purported fun of casual dating and the salacious naughtiness of cheating, monogamous, marital love continues to hold centerstage in our impoverished relationship imaginaries (Geiger and Livingston).[5] It also extracts a toll on our psyches. "As love has increasingly become the center of all emotional expression

---

5. A Pew Research survey published in February 2019 reveals that love—not children, not financial stability, not companionship—is the number one reason people marry. While the percentage of married individuals has remained relatively stable over the last decade at 50 percent, the number of unmarried cohabiting couples has risen 29 percent in that timeframe. In short, almost 60 percent of Americans over the age of eighteen are part of a domestic, romantic couple. See Geiger and Livingston.

in the modern imagination," Kipnis writes, "[. . .] anxiety about obtain-
ing it in sufficient quantities and for sufficient duration has increased to
the point that anxiety suffuses the population, and most other cultural
forms" (Kipnis 65). So, what if we were to champion hookup apps as an
anti-anxiety anodyne? What if we were to *celebrate* the fact that screens
are complicating traditional romantic arrangements? Might our screens
be doing a public service by posing problems for the domestic couple?
Might we welcome the disruption instead of demonizing the technology?

Queer theory itself is arguably founded in the embrace of antinormative models of intimacy. Michel Foucault urges the queer community
to invent "new forms of relationships, new forms of love, new forms of
creation" (*Essential* 163). Leo Bersani works to locate an ethics of intimacy
that "betray the relational modes sanctified by the dominant culture"
(*Rectum* 60) because, for one, "monogamy is cognitively inconceivable
and morally indefensible" (86). J. Halberstam champions the "queer art
of failure" and advocates for disruptive development trajectories and tem-
poralities in personal relationships and activist politics. From the "failed"
friendships of her queer literary forebears, Heather Love gleans "an inher-
itance of historical anxiety and longing" that offers hope for "alternative
forms of relationship and community [. . .] particularly as queers try to
articulate alternatives to marriage as the dominant form of life" (98).
Indeed, Robyn Wiegman and Elizabeth A. Wilson argue that normativity
in all its guises—"heteronormativity, homonormativity, whiteness, family
values, marriage, monogamy, Christmas"—is "queer theory's axiomatic
foe," and question whether queer modes of inquiry are even possible
"without assuming a position of antinormativity from the outset" (1–2).
Given, then, that the celebration of antinormative relationship models is
foundational to queer theory, might our marriage-ruining apps be tools
of queer praxis? Are they carrying forth the tradition of LGBTQ intimacy
innovation so important to the survival of queer communities? Are they
forcing non-LGBTQ folk to rethink the rules of domestic coupledom, to
think more queerly about relationships? In short, is the romantic havoc
our apps wreak a queer blessing in disguise?

One thing seems clear: apps such as Grindr are influencing how
gay men understand sex and romance. Because "DTF" is the intimacy
norm on most m4m platforms, studies show that users tend not to expect
anything more than a hookup when cruising the ether (Mastroyiannis).
The more sophisticated m4m apps, in fact, seem intentionally invested in
training users to accept the failure of romantic intimacy models. Protocols

of communication breakdown and disconnection govern these apps at an almost ontological level. Features such as filters that narrow the search for potential hookups, statistics that reveal the frequency of a user's response, and metrics that divulge the types of men (age, race, body type, etc.) that users normally solicit or respond to all seem designed to prevent people from meeting in real life.[6]

Imagine this scenario: you're cruising the Scruff grid, clicking on profiles here and there, and you come across one profile pic that really catches your eye.[7] Seeing that the user is only 1.5 miles away, you click on the profile, read the minimal self-description (acceptable), note the practices he's into ("Oral, Versatile, Condoms" [acceptable]), and note the types he's into ("Daddies" [potentially me?], "Bears" [nope], "Leather" [well, not really my scene, but I *do* ride a motorcycle . . .]). He seems a bit out of your league, and he's probably not into you as a physical type, but no harm reaching out. Instead of a "Woof," a feature you find somewhat annoying, you decide to be more direct and type a brief, "Hey, handsome, how are you?" message. You notice a few minutes after sending the message that he views your profile: he's thus active online and at least nominally interested in the person contacting him. Still, no response = not a good sign. "Humph," you think, "it's certainly not worth worrying about or feeling bad about, but I'm liking this guy less and less with each passing, unresponsive minute." You return to the grid to see who else might be available but soon pop off to answer a text, read an email, and check your other social media feeds. After about thirty minutes of distracted engagement, you remember that you're not necessarily waiting (but secretly hoping?) for a reply from that cute guy you messaged earlier. Your phone hasn't dinged, so clearly nothing yet. As a last-ditch effort, you go back to his profile and click on the "Insights" feature to dig a little deeper. Although his response rate is high, he mostly answers to hairy, middle-aged muscle guys—oof, *definitely* not you. You want to give the guy the benefit of the doubt (he

---

6. Some of these features are for users who pay for premium versions of the app. Users who do not pay for the premium services have less access to other users' metrics and are also subjected to banner and interstitial advertisements. For information on Grindr's and Scruff's premium services, see "What Is Grindr Xtra?" and "Scruff Pro Features."

7. Scruff markets itself as a "community of 15+ million guys in your neighborhood and around the world" (scruff.com). An image of the Scruff grid appears in figure 5.2.

hasn't responded because he's at work or whatever), but he's logged on, he viewed your profile, and he's most likely read your message. Nothing about this seems to be going your way; if he were genuinely interested, he would have replied by now. You're certainly not going to waste your time holding out hope for someone who is most likely not into you. And, really, his user stats essentially tell you everything you need to know: you're barking up the wrong tree. You go back to the grid, a little bruised because this guy clearly doesn't find you attractive, a little frustrated that, in general, guys you find attractive don't reciprocate, and a little annoyed that you didn't at least get a response, especially because you're convinced he's read your friendly salutation. "Men suck," you think, as you toss your phone on the couch and go out for a walk with the dog. By the time the cute jerk does respond with "ok u?" about four hours later, you're pretty much over it: you're post-horny, you're still convinced that he's not really interested (that he's just being "nice"), and, knowing his stats and preferences, you're next to certain that the whole thing is ultimately a waste of time. Instead of going through the motions to reach the inevitably disappointing conclusion, you don't reply to his apathetic text. Instead, you get back to the grid to see who else might disappoint you.

The very metrics that purportedly enhance user experience may in fact be barriers to user connectivity.[8] While the metrics may keep users logged on for longer periods—a genius bit of software engineering on Grindr's part: the longer users look, the more appealing the app is to advertisers—much of that time might be spent parsing other users' engagement histories rather than chatting, sharing pictures, or making plans to meet up. By overloading apps with features that provide minute details about users' online behavior, Grindr et al. surely receive more advertising revenue and premium membership dollars, but they also frustrate user connectivity. At least in my experience, which may or may not be reflected in the story above, user stats and metrics tend to exacerbate personal insecurities, provoke distrust of other users, and prevent contact. Although user frustration can be profitable, in the sense that it keeps us logged in and seeking fulfillment, it imbues the search with increased levels of cynicism

---

8. Moreover, the masturbatory, haptic pleasures of scrolling and swiping as well as the very common practice of sharing pornographic selfies are sensual/sexual practices in and of themselves, often pleasurable enough to satisfy users. In other words, the immanent pleasures of the virtual cruise are themselves preventative barriers to burdensome, effortful offline meetings.

and even desperation. Self-doubt and second-guessing—what I see as the byproduct of filters, stats, and metrics—give the hunt an added, ultimately pessimistic, affective intensity. What this techno wizardry might prompt, however, is a heightened *indifference* to romantic connection. Snap judgments about others and harsh criticisms of oneself might convince users to lower romantic expectations or give up on dating altogether. The cynicism can also result in users playing it safer, taking fewer risks, and putting up a detached and disaffected front. As a consequence, the interpersonal crevasse between users grows wider and deeper. They remain caught in a communicative limbo rife with trepidation and distrust.

We might bemoan this predicament as yet another instance of being "alone together" in a networked world, an experience that makes us fall out of love with love, distrust our fellow man, and feel ever more alienated, isolated, and hopeless. We might also view it as an opportunity to rethink the terms of intersubjective engagement altogether. In the last chapter, I explained how a model of friendship as shared estrangement could prove useful for a radical queer politics. Here my aim is similar. Keeping in mind that conceptualizing alternatives to normative intimacy is axiomatic to queer theory, I speculate that the havoc hookup apps wreak on marital monogamy and the cynicism they inspire towards romance are a queer blessing in disguise. The romantic cynicism and intersubjective indifference produced in m4m media could move us to envision alternative models of subjectivity, intimacy, and sociality. Moreover, experiences of online disconnect can help us imagine relational models that sidestep intersubjective merging altogether.

As I've been arguing, dating apps in general bank on the failure of romantic intimacy: although a utopian impulse might lure users into the dating game, the projected fantasy of unlimited intimacy is dispelled by limited relationship options and the constrictive terms of romantic coupledom. m4m apps likewise entice users with the promise of "anything goes," but the DTF norms as well as user cynicism and indifference work to banish hopes of romantic salvation. Although the telos of the digital cruise is generally understood as the sexual hookup or public date, the experience of digital cruising itself is one of shared estrangement: a moment in which a desired, transcendent connection is ceaselessly *coming*. In the cruise, we are left to tarry within the means; in the cruise we are *failing* to achieve the normative goal, but perhaps failing better by experimenting with alternative #relationshipgoals. The connective limbo of the digital cruise situates users in suspension, balanced by the (un)shared virtual space between, a space in which new iterations of intimacy might be formulated.

In *Receptive Bodies,* Leo Bersani discovers in D. H. Lawrence's *Women in Love* a cosmic version of screen-mediated shared estrangement. Birkin, Lawrence's angst-ridden, existentialist protagonist, views ideal love neither as intersubjective fusion nor as an annihilating mastery of the other, but instead as an "intimacy grounded in spiritual isolation and separateness" (*Receptive* 61). Bersani writes: "He [Birkin] admits to wanting 'a strange conjunction' with Ursula [Birkin's love interest]: 'not meeting and mingling . . . but as an equilibrium, a pure balance of two single beings—as the stars balance each other' (*WL* 201)" (ibid.). This "star-equilibrium" finds lovers alone together in a sexless stillness, synced by the forces of the universe and with each other. The untraversable field that separates the lovers maximizes their collective potential while respecting the singularity of each. Celestial forces, an outward force of thermal pressure and an inward force of gravity (Redd), generate and sustain the star-lovers' balancing act.[9] These forces care little about the psychological interiority—the desires, sexual or otherwise—of the star-lovers they suspend: the lovers pay fealty to the forces between them, which determine and stabilize the lovers' proximity to one another. In star-equilibrium, then, the egos of the balanced lovers are irrelevant, but the force field betwixt is brimming with collective possibility. In Bersani's words: "The nearly unimaginable oneness of a new duality would preserve, in each of them, an ego-free individuality. [. . .] The subordination of individual character to a utopian project of a new social collectivity could, it seems to me, be reformulated as the blurring of psychologically distinguishable personality in favor of collective lines of force" (26, 56).

In virtual cruising, these "collective lines of force" are also *connective* lines of force: the cellular ether that balances m4m media users in a virtual equilibrium is itself a space rife with social-utopian potential. Before the physical encounter, for the duration of the digital cruise itself, users are formally fungible: interchangeable data points generated and sustained by the space between. Prior to any transcendent physical consummation, the virtual cruise offers a digitized vision of a star-equilibrium wherein users are physically separated but united in cyberspace. The grid, more-

---

9. Stars do not truly balance each other; thermal pressure and gravity stabilize a star. Nonetheless, as a metaphor, star-equilibrium is quite useful in visualizing the form of shared estrangement I discuss here.

over, unburdens users of their psychological interiority: in flattening their "selves" into two-dimensional avatars, users become serialized in a network of similitude. Held to the same visual constraints and typically mimicking the media's hegemonic looks, poses, and gestural norms, users become indistinct, their collective sameness more apparent than their individual differences. In the machine-like serialization and effacement of individuality, users become mere surfaces, modules, parts to plug or unplug. In this context, I wonder if the collective forcefield that suspends m4m media users might harbor potential, might urge us, that is, to envision as yet unforeseen forms of queer sociality. I wonder, more precisely, if in a medium that purportedly caters to the fulfillment of individualized sexual desires we might discover the inconsequentiality of both sexuality and the navel-gazing individualism that bolsters it.

Bersani notes that he finds "nothing [. . .] more moving" than the fact that Lawrence's mouthpiece for his theory of silent, stellar equilibrium is the novel's most garrulous and angsty character (26). Birkin prattles on and on about his love ideal throughout the novel, but the impoverished romantic vocabulary he has inherited—that *we* have inherited—fails to conceptualize the fuzzy form he seeks to clarify. What Bersani finds moving about Birkin's failure, I think, is Birkin's strident, all-too-human *effort* to decenter sex and romance as the nucleus of human connectedness. His trial-and-error experiment to define ideal love fails continually because his words are steeped in unimaginative, centuries-old lovespeak. Bersani is quick to connect Birkin to Beckett's characters, many of whom also chatter endlessly, futilely, seemingly meaninglessly (63). Like Birkin, they too seek to define and reach a state of connected disconnect, a cosmic equilibrium, where language, sex, and individual desire are superfluous. If our dominant relational models fail us and our vocabularies are ill-suited to conceptualize alternatives, then perhaps all of our hookup app jabber is a search for different forms of connectedness. Perhaps in all of our compulsive swiping and clicking and chattering we too are struggling to articulate and realize forms of intimacy and collectivity that exceed our cognitive and linguistic grasp. Perhaps our repeated failures to connect are thwarted conceptualizations of new forms of connection. Indeed, there is nothing more moving than witnessing our pathetic attempts to fail better at intimacy.

Chapter Three

Dare to Be Indifferent
(or, How to Become a Cat Person)

"Cat Person," a short story first published in *The New Yorker* in December 2017, speaks to both the utopian impulse provoked in the screen-mediated exchange as well as the paucity of socially acceptable alternatives to traditional, romantic relationship models—especially for heterosexual-identified women. Written by Kristen Roupenian, the story chronicles the courtship, one-off sexual encounter, and breakup of Margot, a twenty-year-old college student, and Robert, a thirty-four-year-old "cat person." Thematically, the story tackles the ups and downs of texting-enabled interpersonal communication, the gendered dynamics of heteronormative courtship scripts, and what has been dubbed "gray zone" sex: sex ambivalently or begrudgingly consented to (Bennett). Although hardly breaking new ground in terms of form or content—it resonates with countless other female-centered narratives about finding Mr. Right, from *Pride and Prejudice* to *Sex and the City*—this tale of romantic communication breakdown nonetheless hit home with an enormous number of people. "Cat Person" was the most-read *New Yorker* short story in 2017, and the magazine's second-most-read piece of writing for the year—second only to, appropriately enough, Ronan Farrow's exposé on Hollywood mogul Harvey Weinstein's sexually predatory behavior (Luo). As is well known, Farrow's article on Weinstein, published in October 2017, helped set in motion a new iteration of the "Me Too" movement, a feminist social justice movement seeking to: a) illuminate, so as to eradicate, sexual harassment against women in the workplace and elsewhere, and b) to offer solace and solidarity to victims of sexual assault by giving them a chance to tell their stories, to "see" one another, and to recognize their strength in numbers. Although "Me Too" was founded by Bronx activist Tarana Burke a decade earlier (Scott), the 2017 Twitter-based, Alyssa Milano-inaugurated iteration, "#metoo," became such an essential part of the American conversation that *Time* magazine declared #metoo "2017 Person of the Year" (Zacharek et al.).

The popularity and vast readership of "Cat Person" are partly due to the story's publication date, smack dab in a #metoo media storm, but also the result of the story's social relevance. Although the first text message was sent to a mobile phone (from a computer) in 1992 (Arthur), the norms and ethics of text-driven, screen-based intimacies are still a sizzling hot topic of public debate. Opinion pieces, editorials, and critical analyses of "Cat Person" appear in most every notable American periodical—*The Atlantic, The New York Times, The Washington Post,* and countless others—and responses in the Twitterverse are especially passionate. On the whole, female-identified columnists and Twitter users tend to identify with the story's protagonist, Margot. They find her a flawed, albeit sympathetic character whose experience in navigating the contemporary American dating scene accurately represents the plight of the modern American single woman looking for love. The following selection from Rebecca Fishbein's *Bustle* article, which explores the strong reaction "Cat Person" provoked, highlights some of the key themes that resonate with female-identified readers:

> The discussion elicited by "Cat Person"—about how we deal with sex and dating in the texting and Tinder era, about how women are taught or not taught to take agency over their own bodies and pleasure, about when and how it's OK to say no, and about how compelled women feel to trade in their own comfort and needs to ensure they're not upsetting anyone or making waves—is an important one, and everyone, regardless of their gender identity, is encouraged to take part in it. The more we talk about the unsaid burdens women carry, the more we can parse out why these burdens exist, and maybe spare future generations from suffering muddled, awkward sexual experiences that leave both parties burned and confused.

The dominant critical response from male-identified Twitter users, by contrast, reflects the current—more accurately, centuries-old—backlash against increased female social power and sexual agency. As seen in the "Men React to Cat Person" Twitter account, a compilation of the most dismissive responses to the story written by men, the quite fierce, angry, and misogynistic tone of numerous tweets reveals that the story likewise struck a reactionary nerve (Twitter). From diagnosing Margot's behavior as sociopathic, to declaring Margot's sex partner, Robert, a victim of women's narcissism and "mixed message" communicative style, to dismissing altogether literature about and by women, tweets featured in this account confirm that the very gender inequities the story addresses are quite noxious and quite real.

"Cat Person" incorporates generic conventions of both romantic comedy, especially the "bad first date" trope, and realism: for example, the characters speak, think, and text in contemporary American slang. The narrative concerns, among other things, the communicative norms of screen-mediated heterosexual courtship and the gendered social assumptions and expectations endemic to it. While the popular response to the story tends to traffic in essentialist gender discourse—as in, "men are like this; women are like that," or the universalizing feminine "we" in Fishbein's statement, quoted earlier—cat person is actually about the romantic trials and travails of one white, cisgendered, likely upper-middle-class, female American college student named Margot. Roupenian's omniscient narration allows readers access to Margot's thoughts and feelings as she flirts, texts, dates, has sex with, and ghosts on Robert—a character whose interior life is the mystery that propels much of the narrative. Because Robert reveals next to nothing about himself while courting Margot, the fact that he does tell her that he has two cats—that he's a "cat person"—becomes quite significant. Although it's never spelled out exactly what the "cat person" label signifies, Margot seems to interpret it to mean that Robert is a decent person, that he cares for other living things, and that, ultimately, he's a "good guy." This tidbit of personal information notwithstanding, Robert avoids discussing feelings, thoughts, and details of his life history throughout the couple's screen-mediated courtship. Instead, Robert deflects self-expression, as a psychologist might say, by using humor, sarcasm, and passive aggression. It becomes Margot's singular duty, then, to decipher Robert: to draw him out and to decrypt his thoughts and feelings. In this sense, despite heaps of mainstream feminist praise, "Cat Person's" narrative framing device—young woman seeks romance and must wrack her brain to interpret man's inscrutable desires, emotions, and intentions—is hardly a radical feminist premise. It is more attuned, in fact, to a coercive patriarchal ideology that, as Adrienne Rich observed some forty years ago, idealizes heterosexual romance as "the great female adventure, duty, and fulfillment" (242). Rich continues: "The lie [of compulsory female heterosexuality] is many-layered. In Western tradition, one layer—the romantic—asserts that women are inevitably, even if rashly and tragically, drawn to men; that even when that attraction is suicidal (e.g., *Tristan und Isolde*, Kate Chopin's *The Awakening*) it is still an organic imperative." (244). This "lie," moreover, is "beamed to her from childhood out of fairy tales, television, films, advertising, popular songs, wedding pageantry" (237). Or, in the case of "Cat Person," the lie is beamed through *The New Yorker*. "Cat Person" is in many ways *Sex and the City* for the digital age: both stories involve nominally independent white women whose self-esteem rests on their ability to succeed in the rat race of landing Mr. Right. Indeed, "Cat Person" even fails the most simplistic form of feminist textual criticism: the Bechdel test (*Bechdel*). This test, first appearing in Alison Bechdel's comic *Dykes to Watch Out For* and migrating to feminist cultural blogs and magazines, asks three basic questions about (typically filmic) narrative content: Does the story have two female characters? (In the case of "Cat Person," yes.) Do these characters have names? (Again, yes: Margot and Tamara.) And do these named, female characters have conversations about anything other than men, romance, or the art of finding a soulmate? (Not so much.) In essence, "Cat Person" is premised on decidedly antifeminist tropes: women's work and women's passion involve deciphering the mysterious male psyche; "female intuition" must be honed to avoid the negative consequences that might result from reading men incorrectly. Although the story casts a critical glance at some of the unjust social expectations that burden women in the pursuit of heterosexual love—among them that women are trained to put men's happiness before their own and that female submission to a man's mostly unwanted sexual advances is preferable to making a scene—"Cat Person" perpetuates the myth that women's lives are only interesting, or, more to the point, only marketable, if their stories revolve around the pursuit of male attention.

That said, Roupenian deserves a fairer shake. Despite my crassly second-wave feminist criticism of "Cat Person," I find the story remarkable for its unapologetic spin on the complexities of sexual desire and arousal in the age of #metoo—an age in which sexual consent is so often construed as a thoroughly rational, consumer choice. The story begins with Margot and Robert meeting at Margot's place of employment, an arthouse cinema. From behind the concession stand, Margot flirts with Robert out of boredom and in hope of a tip. After Robert commands Margot to hand over her number ("Concession-stand girl, give me your phone number"), the relationship takes off in the ether, via texting. What separates "Cat Person" from the legion of "young love" narratives written for adults is its attention to texting as a form of intimate exchange. Margot and Robert's *pas de deux* is set in motion and scored by the dinging and buzzing of phones. The virtual call and response interpellates these potential lovers into a realm of fantasy and projection. "She still didn't know much about him because they never talked about anything personal," Roupenian writes of the texting courtship, "but when they landed two or three good jokes in a row there was a kind of exhilaration to it, as if they were dancing." The couple's unwillingness to discuss "anything personal" in their thrilling text exchanges, Roupenian implies, lands Margot in some trouble: a "gray zone" sexual experience, wherein Margot lukewarmly consents to Robert's porn-scripted, cringe-inducing advances so as not to make a scene, so as not to bruise his ego. "It wasn't that she was scared he would try to force her to do something against her will but that insisting that they stop now, after everything she'd done to push this forward, would make her seem spoiled and capricious, as if she'd ordered something at a restaurant and then, once the food arrived, had changed her mind and sent it back." Here Margot masochistically submits to a sexual exchange that she somewhat narcissistically believes is solely of her making—that she, not Robert, is the only sexual agent in this scenario. In other words, Roupenian complicates questions of sexual consent. In order to please Robert, Margot indeed performatively reiterates internalized, sexist social scripts that place male satisfaction over female needs, but she also finds pleasure and power in imagining herself as both sexual gatekeeper and an "out-of-his-league" fantasy.

> As they kissed, she found herself carried away by a fantasy of such pure ego that she could hardly admit even to herself that she was having it. Look at this beautiful girl, she imagined him thinking. She's so perfect, her body is perfect, everything about her is perfect, she's only twenty years old, her skin is flawless, I want her so badly, I want her more than I've ever wanted anyone else, I want her so bad I might die. The more she imagined his arousal, the more turned-on she got [. . .].

Conceiving of sexual consent and desire in remarkably psychoanalytic terms, Roupenian explores the complex, gendered dynamics of the classic Lacanian formulation: "Man's [sic] desire is the desire of the Other" (38). As mentioned, Margot's desire for Robert is both masochistic and narcissistic: like any "properly" socialized young woman, she seeks his attention and approval and longs to fulfill what she perceives as *his* fantasy—a "beautiful girl" that drives him wild, and ultimately secures him in his manhood. Indeed, outside the controlled environment of the clever text exchange, Robert only seems comfortable when he is allowed to play traditional masculine roles of provider and protector: when, for example, he buys Margot late-night studying snacks at 7-Eleven, or when the underage Margot is turned away from a bar and weeps out of embarrassment. About Robert's response to Margot's teary-eyed bar rejection, Roupenian writes:

> But when Robert saw her face crumpling, a kind of magic happened. All the tension drained out of his posture; he stood up straight and wrapped his bearlike arms around her. "Oh, sweetheart," he said, "Oh, honey, it's O.K., it's all right. Please don't feel bad." She let herself be folded against him, and she was flooded with the same feeling she'd had outside the 7-Eleven—that she was a delicate, precious thing he was afraid he might break. . . . [I]n his eyes, she could see how pretty she looked, smiling through her tears in the chalky glow of the streetlight, with a few flakes of snow coming down.

Although one of Margot's first impressions of Robert is that "his shoulders slumped forward slightly, as though he were protecting something," she learns only by enduring an awkward first date and bad sex that that "something" is a very fragile sense of self—a man trembling in his masculinity. And yet, Roupenian repeatedly highlights the narcissistic thrill Margot gleans from performing her dual, two-sides-of-the-same-coin roles as damsel in distress and seductress, virgin and whore. In the passage quoted earlier, Margot notices how attractive she looks while playing the role of the emotionally distraught sufferer. She understands that her submission pleases and relaxes Robert, and she proceeds to use this so-called feminine wile to orchestrate, at least initially, the sexual encounter. Roupenian's point here is astute: when it comes to heteronormative romance, women continue to have very limited options. Either coddle fragile, masculine egos and eventually submit to male domination or, at best, transform that coddling and submission into *tools* of domination: therein lie your options, ladies. As feminist theorists have been telling us for decades, however, sexual power—the power to lure and dominate men by coddling, faux-submission, playing hard to get, etc.—is not only a very individualized and limited form of power, it affirms the game of master and servant that men have initiated and played (to disastrous, bloody, destructive ends) for centuries. Flip-flopping the master/servant roles in the end does not change the game: it does not bring about structural social change or gender equality. Rethinking the game altogether, however, just might.

Roupenian complicates the master/servant game by blurring traditional active/passive conceptualizations of sexual desire and arousal. Since antiquity, active desire has been understood to be the provenance of men, phallus bearers, and "tops": the ones who express their vigorous sexual lifeforce through acts of penetrative domination. In this reductive telling of the sexual story, women, bottoms, and nonphallic types of all genders merely submit to the will of the active desirer by performing the role of empty vessel, their desires "active" in as much as they yield to the sexual agent (power bottoms notwithstanding, of course). Roupenian refuses to accept this antifeminist and antiqueer understanding of desire: active does not always translate as "male/powerful" and passive as "female/weak." By wedding Margot's egoistic feelings of sexual power and control with uglier feelings of self-abjection and repulsion, Roupenian implies that sexual desire, arousal, and consent are conflictive, somewhat irrational, and quite messy affairs. In Margot's case, sexual arousal involves feelings of humiliation as much as it does egoism:

> When Robert was naked, rolling a condom onto a dick that was only half visible beneath the hairy shelf of his belly, she felt a wave of revulsion that she thought might actually break through her sense of pinned stasis, but then he shoved his finger in her again, not at all gentle this time, and she imagined herself from above, naked and spread-eagled with this fat old man's finger inside her, and her revulsion turned to self-disgust and a humiliation that was a kind of perverse cousin to arousal.

At once aroused and disgusted, at once sexual agent and victim (the traumatic sexual experience of bodily dissociation is clearly referenced here), Margot becomes a testament to the complexities of the sexual psyche and the consent it is now expected to affirmatively give. In bestowing upon Margot sexual agency replete with contradictory yearnings to be active and passive, femme fatale and delicate flower, Roupenian refutes a reductive sexual ethics that overrationalizes desire and intention. Instead, the author raises complex ethical questions that cannot be adequately addressed by affirmative consent campaigns: What do we do with sexual ambivalence? Is all sexual desire, to varying degrees, ambivalent? Considering that sexual desire is haunted by social and cultural forces such as gendered social expectations and the shame, disgust, and anxiety that attends them, is consent the best metric for sexual ethics?

Joseph Fischel asks precisely the latter question and answers a resounding "No!" in his book, *Screw Consent: A Better Politics of Sexual Justice.* One of his claims, quite salient for an analysis of "Cat Person," is that the social and cultural norms that make consenting to bad sex easier than not going through with it—e.g., gendered expectations that women put men's needs before their own and social assumptions that the male sex drive is innately active, barely controllable, and must be sated or domesticated—encourage people to consent for all the wrong reasons. All too often decisions to consent have much less to do with "I genuinely want this" than with "I think I should do this because it's what I'm supposed to do; it's what's expected of me as a woman, a man, a gay person, etc." In a brief summarization of some of his book's arguments, Fischel writes:

> Finally, maybe consent is more often the problem than the solution to bad sex. Why do people, too often girls and women, consent to sex that is immiserating, painful, unwanted and unpleasant? What social, cultural and economic forces make consenting to awful sex less costly than saying no? Far from being solved by consent, *that* problem is constituted by it. Consent does not solve all our social problems or intimate injustices. Just like we consent to deadening jobs, we often consent to injurious sex. Right-wing talk show hosts decry that some in the #MeToo movement have confused rape with bad sex, but it's critical that we make bad sex, and not just rape, a primary target of our sexual politics. I don't mean bad sex as in mediocre sex, say, when nobody comes. I mean sex that is persistently unwanted, or painful or begrudgingly acquiesced to, or requires illicit substances to endure. ("What Do We Consent To?")

Cases of blatantly nonconsensual sex should be legally punished—this much should be obvious. But how should we behave toward a partner after an ambivalent sexual experience that leaves us disgusted at ourselves, especially if that self-disgust was part of the turn on in the first place? As Roupenian herself notes:

> I have more genuine sympathy for Margot, but I'm also frustrated by her: she's so quick to over-read Robert, to assume that she understands him, and to interpret his behavior in a way that's flattering to herself. I think it's telling that the moment of purest sexual satisfaction she experiences in the story is the one when she imagines what Robert sees as he looks at her: she's seduced by the vision she's created of herself—of someone perfect and beautiful and young. So much of dating involves this interplay of empathy and narcissism: you weave an entire narrative out of a tiny amount of information, and then, having created a compelling story about someone, you fall in love with what you've created. (Treisman)

Lying in bed alone while Robert retreats to the bathroom after sex, Margot seems unable to process the sensory, emotional, and ethical overload resulting from ambivalent sex. Dazed and confused, she dreams up a future boyfriend, one not dissimilar from the fantasy-Robert she created in the texting courtship, who laughs with her about this "awful yet hilarious" and all-too-real sexual experience. Meanwhile, the actual-Robert completely misreads Margot's somewhat traumatized, daydreamy silence and proceeds to spill his guts. He confesses feeling incredible anguish during their texting courtship, that he was even convinced Margot betrayed him by sleeping with a (nonexistent) old flame over her school break. In essence, through his confession Robert reveals that this relationship—replete with projection, fantasy, misrecognition, narcissism, and anxiety—has been a Lacanian trainwreck for both characters. Roupenian implies throughout the story that the ultimate cause of this romantic disaster is the affective excess endemic to screen-mediated intimacies: the utopian impulses as well as the corporately engineered anxiety.

Moreover, if one of the ethical questions raised by "Cat Person" is, "How should we deal with sexual ambivalence?" both Margot and Robert devise terrible answers. Licking her wounds, the day after the bad sex experience, Margot consoles herself with the thought that Robert willfully misrepresented himself, that he lied about being a cat person. "She remembered that he'd talked a lot about his cats and yet she hadn't seen any cats in the house, and she wondered if he'd made them up." So as to fortify her bruised ego and regain a positive view of herself, Margot resists admitting that her perception of Robert was flawed; instead, her loathing for him becomes "vastly disproportionate to anything he had actually done." She does, however, acknowledge that the Robert she invented during their texting courtship was a fantasy projection. Days later, still in a funk, "she'd realize that it was Robert she missed, not the real Robert but the Robert she'd imagined on the other end of all those text messages during break." Nonetheless, Margot cannot bring herself to break it off with the flesh-and-bones Robert; her fantasy of the text-invented Robert continues to linger and entice. In the wake of ambivalent sex, Margot thus becomes a classic Freudian melancholic. Although her skin crawls when she thinks of or hears from real-Robert (via text, of course), she is unwilling to break up with him because fantasy-Robert—who, as Roupenian notes, is actually Margot's narcissistic, idealized projection—is difficult to let go of. It takes Margot's roommate, Tamara, tired of Margot's hemming and hawing, to break the melancholic paralysis: Tamara grabs Margot's phone and texts a cold dismissal to Robert. Upon receiving Robert's surprisingly conciliatory and grammatically correct response ("I am sorry to hear that. I hope I did not do anything to upset you."), Margot is at once relieved and guilt-ridden. The gendered shame of displeasing a man coupled with the pain of squelching an ego-pleasing fantasy prompt Margot to reconsider: "Perhaps she was being unfair to Robert, who really had done nothing wrong, except like her, and be bad in bed, and maybe lie about having cats, although probably they had just been in the other room." Once restored to the status of cat person, fantasy-Robert lives another day, rekindling in Margot a melancholic self-satisfaction . . . until, that is, the insecure and aggressive real-Robert rears his ugly head. "Cat Person" ends with a series of texts Robert sends to Margot after spotting her and a male friend in a bar a month after the Tamara-composed text-message breakup. The conclusion is worth quoting in full as it encapsulates some of the lessons of this morality tale about the potential pitfalls of screen-mediated intimacy:

> Curled up on her bed with Tamara that night, the glow of the phone like a campfire illuminating their faces, Margot read the messages as they arrived:
>
> "Hi Margot, I saw you out at the bar tonight. I know you said not to text you but I just wanted to say you looked really pretty. I hope you're doing well!"

"I know I shouldnt say this but I really miss you"

"Hey maybe I don't have the right to ask but I just wish youd tell me what it is I did wrog"

"*wrong"

"I felt like we had a real connection did you not feel that way or . . ."

"Maybe I was too old for u or maybe you liked someone else"

"Is that guy you were with tonight your boyfriend"

"???"

"Or is he just some guy you are fucking"

"Sorry"

"When u laguehd when I asked if you were a virgin was it because youd fucked so many guys"

"Are you fucking that guy right now"

"Are you"

"Are you"

"Are you"

"Answer me"

"Whore."

In the conclusion to "Cat Person," Robert becomes the personification of our worst tendencies and habits when using screen-based media. He expresses in capsule form all the ugly feelings endemic to screen-mediated intimacies: the anxiety and anger felt when a message isn't instantly

replied to; the worry and catastrophic thinking provoked when a loved
one/love interest is inaccessible or unresponsive; the competition created
when romantic commitment is measured by the quantity and quality of
screen-mediated input. If "Cat Person" is making a social statement, it is
that modern communication technologies produce interpersonal thrills
and misery in equal measure. Indeed, the story suggests that smartphone
companies should include "increased levels of euphoria, giddiness, and
mania as well as insecurity, distrust and paranoia" on their consumer
warning labels. These affective excesses, it seems, are built into the devices
themselves, and tech giants certainly profit from our quasi voluntary
enslavement to screen-mediated self-sabotage.[1]

Robert's self-sabotaging anxiety grows increasingly aggressive with
each passing moment in the solipsistic experience of texting, essentially,
himself. When his defenses-down confessions are met by silence, he lashes
out in an infantile, yet nasty, name-calling tantrum. His unresponsive
interlocutor, moreover, affirms his comforting, self-fulfilling prophecy of
romantic betrayal: "She's the bad actor, not I." As the story would have
it, then, it's the screen *cum* self-protective wall that conditions all of this
contradictory, excessive behavior: the making vulnerable as well as the
making monstrous. Although Roupenian emphasizes the role that toxic

---

1. To test this hypothesis with students, I ask them to go for a solo thirty-minute
walk in the woods on campus, a cross-country running trail, without any electronic devices: no phones, no music, no Fitbit, no watch. (I offer an alternative
assignment for disabled students and the option of taking a companion along for
those who do not feel safe walking alone. However, silence and zero electronics is
the rule for all.) I ask them to write about the experience in a journal entry: what
they saw and heard; how they felt, etc. Nine out of ten students describe some
form of anxiety. A typical response, paraphrased and composite, goes something
like this: "I was worried that something bad might have happened to my mom
and she couldn't get a hold of me; I was worried that if I fell and hurt myself I
wouldn't be able to contact anybody for help." A surprising number of students
display quasi paranoid and catastrophic thinking, expressing certainty that something terrible was happening or was going to happen specifically in that phone-
free thirty minutes. My response: has there ever been a better business plan for
a commodity in the history of consumer society? If we feel so lost without our
phones—if their absence causes such distress and anguish—then we will be damn
well certain to make sure the latest models are in our pockets for as long as we
live. That we are expected to be available 24/7 to text, chat, or work—let alone
expected to build a personal brand on social media—only adds insult to injury.

gender socialization scripts play in Margot and Robert's communication breakdown, she also clearly blames the discursive norms of texting. Prompting us to keep things short, to the point, witty, and entertaining—in a word, superficial—these norms discourage interlocutors from revealing too much and consequently encourage "reading minds" rather than asking questions. By the time Margot and Robert actually meet up for the first date, their mutual misrecognition of each other—a misrecognition mired in projection and fantasy—dooms them to awkward silences, misread cues, and unarticulated hopes. In this regard, the overarching moral of the story is: do not think you know and certainly do not invest in the stranger on the other side of a screen. More specifically, in the case of romance: do not believe in the screen-generated fantasy of the Other as it's ultimately a narcissistic, self-defeating trap. In the age of phishing and catfishing, trolls and bots, these aren't the worst warnings to reiterate. However, they ultimately reveal and reinforce skepticism, if not cynicism, toward virtual intimacies of all stripes. No one wants to end up like Margot or Robert, so your best bet is to take screen-mediated exchanges with a grain of salt, to resist the ego-boosting thrills and ego-crushing silences. You'd best screen love—scrutinize, interrogate, distrust it—and be wary of both the affective excess and the inevitable failure of virtual intimacy.

That said, we cannot ignore the ways that this story's moral, which reiterates many popular warnings about screen-mediated intimacy, mirrors historical critiques of *queer* forms of intimacy. In other words, the socially stigmatizing judgments leveled against those straying from traditional, heteronormative courtship rituals and romantic models resonate in contemporary warnings about the dangers of virtual intimacy. Shaka McGlotten argues that, since their inception, screen-mediated intimacies have been popularly denigrated as fake, failed, even perverse approximations of "true" heterosexual romantic ideals. He notes:

> [V]irtual intimacies are failed intimacies that disrupt the flow of a good life lived right, that is, a life that involves coupling and kids, or at least, coupling and consumption. From this critical point of view, virtual intimacies approach normative ideals about intimacy but can never arrive at them; they might index some forms of connection or belonging, but not the ones that really count; they are fantastic or simulated, imaginative, incorporeal, unreal. Such characterizations resemble dominant beliefs about queer intimacies as pale imitations or

ugly corruptions of the real deal—monogamously partnered, procreative, married, straight intimacy. (6)

For J. Halberstam, however, one (straight) man's failure is another queer's success: resisting and reimagining heteronormative logics and metrics of success are part and parcel of queer identity. Screen-mediated intimacies might be celebrated, then, as one avenue through which queer failure might be cultivated. "What kind of rewards can failure offer us?" Halberstam asks. "Perhaps most obviously, failure allows us to escape the punishing norms that discipline behavior and manage human development with the goal of delivering us from unruly childhoods to orderly and predictable adulthoods" (3). The "wasted time" spent on dating and hookup sites, the fact that so many chats and dates amount to "nothing," can be reframed, then, as queer investments in disrupting normative conceptions of development and productivity—ones that defy capitalist and reproductivist notions of time, telos, profit, and fertility. Even the coarse, often merciless communicative norms of m4m media—especially that most despised of chat behaviors, ghosting—can be understood through the lens of queer failure. In the age of 24/7 accessibility, for instance, we (queerly) fail each other if we refuse to follow, what Illouz designates, the "therapeutic model of communication" (71) that fuels neoliberal capitalism. This class-based psychological ethos emphasizes "emotional competence"—in the form of self-awareness, identifying and talking about feelings, and empathizing with others—and is necessary for career advancement in a precarious labor market in which emotional management and collaborative cooperation convert to capital. "For, in having become a property of the middle-class workplace, the therapeutic ethos makes men and women far more ready and able to cope with the contradictions, tension, and uncertainties that have become intrinsic to and structurally embedded in contemporary biographies and identities" (73). As I will discuss in detail in chapter 5, the discursive norms of m4m media demonstrate a recalcitrant disregard for the therapeutic model, thereby signaling a discontent, however individualized or unconscious, with the communicative norms of neoliberal capitalism.

Ghosting, for instance, a dismissive gesture quite common in m4m media, is typically understood as self-centered and rude. As a failure to fulfill *another's* requirements for insight, explanation, or closure, however, ghosting in the m4m media context might also be understood as a queer form of self-care. Maya Binyam makes the case that ghosting can be a strategy for people of color (POC) to defy attempts to resolve racial conflict. In "Letter of Recommendation: Ghosting," she describes the exhaustion and frustration she experiences as a woman of color when asked by non-POC interlocutors to help them make sense of racism. These interlocutors turn to Binyam for "expert knowledge" and to assuage their white guilt. They position Binyam as a spokesperson for her race and expect her to educate, appease, and comfort. Instead, she ghosts. Ghosting becomes, for Binyam, a way to escape a role forced upon her by solace-seeking others; it's a way of letting her non-POC friends sit with racial discomfort. It is also a silent refusal to entertain the racist assumptions that motivate their will to know. In her words: "Because society demands that people of color both accept offense and facilitate its reconciliation, we are rarely afforded the privacy we need. Ghosting, then, provides a line of flight. Freed from the ties that hurt us, or bore us, or make us feel uneasy, finally we can turn our attention inward."

But isn't such behavior profoundly selfish and irresponsible? Does not an unwillingness to engage in intersubjective dialogue signal a quite serious mental defect? Isn't this gesture, in a word, *narcissistic*? Ah, yes, narcissism: Not only a stigmatizing label historically affixed to homosexuality—as a form of desire, a subjectivity, and a culture—but also, so the experts tell us, a byproduct of social media use. As Greg Goldberg notes, narcissism has historically served as a catch-all diagnosis for various social and cultural ills, including "the emergence of mass society and the concomitant marketization of social relations, the decline of the family, the rise of fascism, the advent of identity politics, and now the breakdown of social relations at the hands of social media" ("Through the Looking Glass" 10). Indeed, medical doctors, psychologists, and the popular press all seem to agree: social media have made us more narcissistic.[2] Evidence Margot creating a fantasy of Robert in her own self-image in their texting courtship; note the studies contending that male Instagram users demonstrate higher rates of narcissistic personality disorder the more selfies they post (Arpacia et al.). And m4m media? In the popular imaginary, it's a cesspool of narcissistic exhibitionists who have found their ideal platform to bask in self-love. Should we be surprised, then, that m4m media users frequently ghost one another? If gay men are the true heirs to the mythical figure so obsessed with his own reflection, then, no. Indeed, Narcissus himself essentially ghosts the world by becoming deaf to the siren song of Otherness. He refuses to engage difference and fails to play by the rules of

---

2. A quick Google search for "social media narcissism" returns 10,100,000 hits: everything from peer-reviewed psychological studies to concerned parents' blogs, many "confirming" the link between excessive social media use and narcissistic personality disorder. See Arpacia et al.

a therapeutic communicative ethos; he becomes, rather, a template for the socially irresponsible subject. Most radically, Narcissus breaks the contract of intersubjectivity that grounds liberal-humanist conceptions of sociality, development, reproductivity, and futurity.[3] Indeed, traditional dialectical (and psychoanalytic) conceptions of subjectivity and civilization posit that self- and social development rests on exploring the enigmatic mystery of Otherness—an Otherness all too often formulated in heteronormative terms. From this vantage point, a narcissistic investment in sameness and self-love is not merely homosexual, but, but potentially sociopathic.

However, the antisociality of queer narcissism—the refusal to heed the other's call and the defiant lack of interest in "personhood" altogether— might be reconstrued as an experiment in impersonal ethics. If, for the narcissist, difference is not a point of fascination, if the narcissist has little interest in probing the other's otherness, then s/he is likewise unphased by the psychosocial motives for intersubjective violence—motives that stem from a desire to assimilate difference, to make it less threatening (Bersani, *Thoughts* 2). For the impersonal narcissist, difference is simply a red herring, something to distract us from a more compelling similitude. As Bersani and Adam Phillips note: "If we were able to relate to others according to this model of impersonal narcissism, what is different about others (their psychological individuality) could be thought of as the mere envelope of the more profound (if less fully realized, or completed) part of themselves which is our sameness" (*Intimacies* 86). If individualism emphasizes personal development, impersonal narcissism works to realize collective potentiality. When identitarian difference becomes less interesting than the force of non-identical similitude the loved "self" becomes simultaneously multiple and nonexistent at once; it is infinitely replicated and endlessly interchangeable.

---

3. Goldberg critiques the popular discourse of narcissism as a "self-evident wrong" ("Through" 1). Employing Bersani's notion of impersonal narcissism in his analysis of selfies, he seeks "to problematize the diagnosis of narcissism as rooted in a normative project that works to produce responsible subjects, and to suggest that this project is compromised by a queer indifference to difference, as critics fear" (2). An "indifference to difference" is the Bersanian building block of antisocial (queer) communal forms; "critics fear" such indifference, then, because it destabilizes the very foundation of sociality as it is conventionally conceived. Goldberg, like Bersani, welcomes such destabilization as it presages a form of relating not founded on intersubjective violence. See also Tuhkanen's explication of Bersanian impersonal narcissism, pp. 162–64.

Impersonal narcissistic development expands the self centrifugally beyond an anthropomorphic psychological interiority. It opens that interiority onto a world of fungible, corresponding forms, human and otherwise. If, as Bersani has it, "individuation is a metaphysical error" (*Arts* 140), then a narcissism that refuses to treat the Other as a mystery that must be solved, a narcissism that refuses to engage the world dialectically in the form of annihilative, intersubjective subsumption, a narcissism, instead, that interchanges the world for the self and attunes that self to the world's forces and rhythms, might go some way in correcting—or, rather, failing better at trying to correct—that irreparable, ontological error. As I have been suggesting, the narcissistic, superficial, and promiscuous sociability of m4m media might point us in this direction.

Screen-based communicative media are also widely accused of abetting two other social ills: attention-deficit and shallowness. The medical establishment seems at pains to prove the link between screen time and attention deficit disorder (Ra). The popular press and the populace alike have a field day mocking the vapidity of social media platforms and the superficiality of screen-based discourse. The Age of Distraction, the Attention Economy, the demise of grammar, punctuation, and eloquence in the Age of Texting: all fodder for the pop-psychological, twenty-four-hour sensationalized news cycle. In terms of interpersonal relationships, distraction and shallowness are commonly considered romantic deal breakers: the inability to focus on a romantic partner (to have a "roaming eye") as well as the inability to make meaningful conversation—to express intellectual and emotional competence—are absolute relationship no-nos. They are also, unsurprisingly, two vices historically associated with gay men. The promiscuous eye of the gay male and his preternatural inclination to gossip are normatively construed as symptomatic of his innate failure to love or communicate in proper, meaningful ways.

These two vices, however, also hold a counterintuitive promise as practices of queer sociability. For Bersani, queer sociability is a fleeting form of connection devoid of possessiveness and psychological investment. It is a flitting about, a "no strings attached" promiscuous engagement with others and the world. Cruising, for Bersani, is exemplary of this type of impersonal intimacy, but he likewise highlights aesthetic practices that might prompt similar ego-lessening, self-dissolutive pleasures and benefits. Distracted viewing, for one, which Bersani and his writing partner Ulysse Dutoit articulate through analyses of Assyrian art and Caravaggio's paintings, is a promiscuous visual practice that overlooks the main event.

The wandering eye refuses to focus on the objects, figures, or features it is supposed to notice and scrutinize. In the case of Caravaggio's late paintings, Bersani looks beyond the erotically appealing boys positioned front and center and into the "nonerotic sensuality" (*Caravaggio* 79) of the forms that mingle and merge with the main subjects. What he gleans from this distracted viewing practice is the centrifugal pleasure that occurs only when one disengages from the commanding presence of enigmatic Otherness—the main subject's psychology, desires, interior life—and reorients the gaze toward surrounding forms that correspond superficially with the figure. Tuhkanen describes Bersani's cruisy aesthetic method as follows: "The spectator gains access to the centrifugal pleasures of Caravaggio's art only after having learned to become unresponsive to the commanding appeal of the models' sexiness. Suggesting that the loosening of sexuality's spell constitutes the self's impoverishment, Bersani follows Foucault, who argues that it is primarily sexuality that has territorialized the modern self with significance" (55). Bersani's aesthetic method, then, informs his sexual ethics: What one might gain from an unresponsiveness to another's most significant and enigmatic feature—their sexuality—is access to a world in which things or people become newly meaningful, in which various forms—including the self—begin to correspond with one another despite their socially significant differences. Distracted viewing affords the spectator the chance to disseminate the gaze and reorient attention to the "allness"—the likenesses, the correspondences—of the scene.

Similarly, superficial and empty chatter can be another exercise in de-emphasizing psychological interiority and enigmatic otherness. Freud, as we know, took empty chatter quite seriously: he required his patients to "free associate," to blather on and on, so that he could access the secrets of their psyches. But what if, unlike Freud, we were not to seek psychosexual meaning in blather? What if we instead took pleasure merely in the discursive rhythms of call and response? In terms of sex, what if we resisted the urge to transform the immanent pleasures of superficial association into something transcendent like a "relationship?" In other words, what if digital cruising is an experiment in queer sociability?

If distraction and superficial connection are both the bane of modern relationships and the unfortunate byproducts of screen-time, then we see the worst of both worlds in m4m media. The wandering eye of the (nominally) gay male finds solace scrolling promiscuously through the Grindr grid; the superficial chatter of gay male culture is translated into clever quips, inarticulate come-ons, and vapid chat. None of it, supposedly, does any good for individual queers or the community at large. But what if it is cueing us in to a different form of subjectivity and sociality? Because we are so trained to look for meaning "beneath" words or "between the lines," because we are so obliged to discern and decode another's "true colors" in her or his sexual behavior, because we are so encouraged to make meaningful the discovery of the singular, star-crossed lover, m4m media could serve as a platform that redirects us from all this profitable meaning making—a practice that has done little to topple identitarian hierarchies of social difference and lots to line the pockets of CEOs. A training in the art of meaninglessness—be it impersonal chatter or desexualized intimacy—is an apprenticeship in self-subtraction and consequent self-dissolutive expansion. The reduction of the self to the status of a serialized visual object that chatters mechanically may be the prerequisite to a self that becomes exogenous: one that learns to "dilate the self beyond the self" (Davidson, 137), one that seeks to correspond with like forms and amenable forces. Put another way, the desensitizing sensuality of online cruising—the glazed expression, the mobile vision, the haptic twitching—can be understood as an ascetic practice of self-emptying, one that could serve as a catalyst for new forms of connecting and collecting. For when the self loses itself in a sprawling mass of sameness, it might seek horizontal correspondences with emptied-out others—despite identitarian difference.

Fake, failed, unproductive, incommunicative, immature, narcissistic, unfocused, fleeting, and superficial: slurs used to disparage mediated intimacies are likewise used to delegitimate queer intimacies. As I've been arguing, such disparagement is all the more reason to explore the connective tissue between these forms of connection: namely, to discover what mediated intimacies might do for a queer ethics. With that in mind, I conclude with a return to the finale of "Cat Person," a story that warns us about the dangers of both traditional hetero-romantic courtship norms and of the impossible fantasies generated in screen love.

Throughout the story, Roupenian makes clear that virtual chat is no substitute for face-to-face communication and "natural" connection. In the story's final sentence (before Robert's rant), the phone screen becomes "like a campfire illuminating their [Margot's and Tamara's] faces." Far from a wilderness setting wherein these characters might have had a heart-to-heart (about boys?) while basking in the glow and warmth of one of the four fundamental natural elements, Margot and Tamara stare silently into a void illuminated by unnatural light, bracing themselves for the textual vitriol native to this caustic environment. Given that Margot is "curled up on the bed with Tamara" in this harshly lit scene, however, one must wonder: is Roupenian making a (homophobic) connection between the unnatural glare of the phone and the "crime against nature" that might be unfolding on the bed (i.e., Tamara and Margot curling up)? Or, given that heterosexual romance distresses Margot so, is the implication here that the best thing for Margot is actually a cuddle with Tamara? Might we read this conclusion queerly, optimistically, as a new beginning? Although Margot certainly didn't find Mr. Right in Robert, her failed attempt at heterosexual normalcy—an attempt that ran its course through the inherently failed medium of texting—lands her in bed with Tamara. Might all this heterosexual and communicative media failure be the necessary precursor to queer intimacy? Might Margot "fail better" with Tamara? Lest we forget, not only does Tamara snap Margot out of her lovelorn, narcissistic melancholy, but she does so by unapologetically grabbing Margot's phone and breaking up with Robert, in Margot's name, via text message. Clearly, Tamara is good for Margot: she is exactly what Margot needs to move on. Interestingly, Margot's uroboric melancholic cycle is broken only when Tamara *stands in for* Margot, when Tamara speaks in Margot's name. Tamara's forceful gesture transforms Margot into a failed gendered subject: once Tamara takes over, Margot ceases being the good girl who puts male needs before her own, the good girl seeking redemption in a man. However, Tamara is not Margot's double. She is not, psychoanalytically speaking, Margot's liberated id behaving the way Margot *really* wants to. Because Margot's melancholy generates intense uroboric pleasure, her unleashed id would retaliate *against* any force or friend seeking to stanch it. Tamara is also not Margot's shame-inducing superego. Given that Margot's romantic behavior is so informed by toxic gendered scripts, that superego would likely instruct her to give Robert another chance. After all, that's what good girls are supposed to do. No, Tamara is neither Margot's double nor super-ego; she is her *substitute*. By becoming Margot, Tamara affords Margot the opportunity to transform her melancholic solipsism into an expansive narcissism whereby her "self" becomes fungible and interchangeable with another. Tamara invites Margot into a different form of subjectivity and sociality by silencing the call of the Other (Robert's annoying texts) and repudiating intersubjective *frisson*. And while the upshot of Tamara's invitation might be new queer sexual pleasures—after all, this scene is the first in which Margot seems comfortable lying with another—it might also have little to do with sexuality at all. Put another way, perhaps Tamara encourages Margot not to apply the normative terms of traditional heterosexual romance to a person of the same sex, but instead to reconceive both her understanding of herself as lacking and her understanding of desire *as a lack* that can only be sated in intersubjective fusion. Perhaps what we witness here in the final scene is what Bersani understands as a desire *without* sexuality, "a desire that is satisfied just by the proximity of the other" (Bersani, *Homos* 121), one that is indifferent to the secrets of the sexual psyche. If this is the case, then Margot, not Robert, becomes the titular cat person after all. Well-known for their blasé, take-it-or-leave-it approach to human intimacy, cats quite often seem "satisfied just by the proximity of the other," hardly demanding access to the psychological interiority of their human companion. If Margot misreads Robert's cat ownership as a sign of his affection for vulnerable others—i.e., as a sign of his moral goodness—she learns through her failed experiment in psychosexual decipherment that maybe there is no "there" beneath the call of enigmatic otherness. In becoming cat-like, Margot can become indifferent to difference: after all, maybe a pet is just a pet, a stroke just a stroke, and, ultimately, it doesn't really matter who's doing the work as long as it's welcomed. Perhaps because Tamara introduces Margot to the pleasures and benefits of becoming fungible, Margot can lie in peace with her interchangeable other and shake off the pathetic backlash that inevitably occurs in relationships grounded in intersubjectivity. Perhaps the unnaturally glowing screen between Margot and Tamara is the forcefield, rife with collective potentiality, that balances these two new lovers in a star-equilibrium.

Chapter Four

Embodied Echoes and Virtual Affordances

"If Facebook didn't exist," my partner, Jim, once remarked, "queers would have had to invent it." What Jim is implying here is that social media platforms mimic—and exploit for financial profit—forms of intimacy and rituals of connection long familiar to queers. Generally speaking, social media coopt, monetize, and often desexualize, queer erotic practices of shared estrangement: on Facebook and Instagram, and even more so on Grindr and Tinder, everybody to varying degrees becomes a cruiser, a voyeur, or a lurker seeking some form of connection. Moreover, the rules of engagement for many queer subcultural erotic practices and social media platforms are similarly determined by protocols, defined by Alexander Galloway as "conventional rules that govern the set of possible behavior patterns within a heterogeneous system" (7). Just as communication and interaction in S&M and leather subcultures is governed by formal rules (sex roles, semiotic codes, ritualized behavior), the interaction of users on social media platforms is likewise constrained by design and engagement protocols that formalize the means of connection.[1] The protocols that govern S&M and leather subcultures, then, serve the same formal function as the protocols of connection (design, interface, input) on social media platforms. Although these protocols do not determine content—there is room for creativity and variability within both S&M scenes and social media engagement—they do regulate the form of the encounter. Dom/sub

---

1. I credit this insight to the anonymous author of a quite brilliant essay I (double blind) peer reviewed titled "Networked Boredom: Grindr, Norm, and Protocol." Thank you, whoever you are.

roles and safe words are as protocological in S&M as the 280-character limit is on Twitter; flagging, a practice in which the color and bodily placement of a hanky/bandana communicates sexual preference, is as protocological for leatherfolk as the "Like" button is for Facebook users. To varying degrees, then, the protocological nature of queer subcultural connection infuses mainstream virtual connection. Even and especially in contemporary heterosexual-oriented digital media, historically queer connective rituals dominate. Swiping right or left on Tinder to express one's like or dislike of a fellow user, for instance, mirrors the bold solicitations and no-nonsense rejections in the gay male bathhouse or back room. Posting a personal ad on backpage.com or Craigslist Personals (both sites now shuttered) likewise resonates with scrawling a "for a good time, call . . ." message on a gender-segregated public bathroom wall.[2] Indeed, as Shaka McGlotten notes:

> [V]irtual intimacies encounter and rework historical antecedents particular to queer, especially gay male, sociality: chiefly cruising and hooking up. [. . .] Transitory and often anonymous, these intimacies were nonetheless vital in the formation of queer social networks well before the advent of specifically digital communications technologies. The queer network has a longer history. There were the networks produced through word of mouth, spaces of contact and encounter (like bars or zones tied to cruising), through medical and educational tracts, through jurisprudence, and through earlier communication media. (4)

The extent to which the rituals of queer subcultural connection have been normalized in social media is not my main concern in this chapter. The fact that LGBTQ-identified folk maintain a special relationship to digital culture, however, is. In his insightful *Gaydar Culture: Gay Men, Technology, and Embodiment in the Digital Age*, Sharif Mowlabocus explores this relationship primarily in pre-mobile m4m media. He notes that because the LBGTQ community has had a fraught relationship with the public sphere throughout its history, because, moreover, Western LGBTQ social identity and culture were forged mainly in capitalist metropoles inaccessible to many, the virtual realm has provided an invaluable space

---

2. For more on the history of queer communicative and connective forms, see Meeker.

for queer communion, identification, and empowerment. For gay men in particular, digital technology has been instrumental to erotic connection: from pre-Internet Computer Bulletin Board Service and Internet Relay Chat to Gaydar and Grindr, digital culture has, since its inception, pervaded and shaped gay male erotic rituals. Thus, for Mowlabocus, when it comes to being "in the life," the typically rigid line drawn between the virtual and the physical, between online and IRL, is exaggerated, perhaps fictitious. In gay male erotic practice, the two realms have overlapped at least since the 1970s liberationist era, mutually reflecting, informing, and inventing one another.

Mowlabocus further argues that the very architecture of m4m digital media is rooted in two key facets of pre-Internet gay male culture: the pornographic gaze and panoptical surveillance. Through its appropriation and exploitation of modern masculine archetypes (the construction worker, the cop, the biker; essentially, the Village People), gay porn became essential to gay male legibility. Porn archetypes not only helped gay men recognize one another but also played an important role in the formation of a publicly visible social demographic (again, think the Village People). This practice continues in the virtual realm. We can witness gay porn's centrality to m4m digital media in the porn types mimicked in profile pictures—the boy next door, the jock, the lumberjack—as well as the fantasy narratives and porn dialogue employed in chats. More profoundly, the pornographic gaze itself is the structuring principle of m4m media: the "active looker/ passive looked at" power dynamic of pornographic visual pleasure is embedded in the media's digital architecture and complicated through user interaction. Moreover, in addition to being the objects and subjects of a pornographic gaze, gay men have been targets of a legal-juridical gaze. Hidden cameras in tearooms, two-way mirrors in psychiatric institutions, and watchful eyes in so-called "civil commitment" detention centers: surveillance has played an integral role in identifying and pathologizing the LGBTQ community. According to Mowlabocus, gay men in particular have internalized a panoptical gaze. He sees this gaze at work in m4m media practices: in so-called "body fascist" corporeal norms and exclusionist "no fats, no femmes" proclamations. While perhaps less motivated today by a fear of being discovered and ruined (although that fear is still quite real for many), gay male self- and other-policing is typically a bid for normalcy: a desire either to demonstrate features of conventional attractiveness, to declare one's membership in a gay tribe (such as bears), or to offer proof that LGBTQ individuals deserve a place at the table.

Being a "normal gay" today means being a responsible neoliberal citizen. Announcing one's commitment to safe sex, monogamy, or marriage; dressing well, eating right, and buffing up at the gym; representing oneself as accountable, affiliated, and worthy of social validation are common ways of demonstrating one's adherence to contemporary, neoliberal, LGBTQ norms. And though m4m media do their part in encouraging normative conformity, they also offer a respite from it. Building off of Mowlabocus's insights, I contend that these media operate in at least two counteractive ways. On the one hand, they reproduce panoptical (and neoliberal) measures designed to induce self-consciousness and motivate normative, masculine self-optimization—fitter bodies, better self-marketing, or a "just a regular (white) bro" attitude, sometimes packaged in a proud effemephobia or an unsubtle racism. On the other hand, m4m media provide a space for the continued development of antinormative, socially disreputable imaginaries: not only said effemephobia and racism, but also deviant fantasies, antisocial desires, and disidentificatory experiments that are anathema to a respectable, "out of the closet" politics.[3] As such, they are the thorn in the side of assimilationist LGBTQ campaigns. m4m media at once, then, reproduce the pornographic gaze that has been indispensable to gay legibility, perpetuate gay-baiting surveillance tactics by turning the panoptical eye inward, and ultimately undermine political efforts to normalize or whitewash the less savory aspects of gay male erotic practice.

Mowlabocus hints at the subversive political potential of m4m media in their current mobile incarnations. He argues that m4m smartphone apps (and, before that, "Bluejacking," or, flirting digitally with strangers using a Bluetooth-enabled phone) bring cruising back to the public sphere: out of ethernet-wired interior space and into the streets. Due to geolocation technology and the untethered mobility of the smartphone, Grindr et al. also further dismantle the digital/physical binary and offer up new iterations of queer space—turning anywhere into a gay bar, so to speak. Ultimately, and refreshingly, Mowlabocus is quite optimistic

---

3. Concerning the latter, my beloved field correspondents made a point of sending to me screenshots of some of the more unusual introductory requests made by fellow Grindr users. The most memorable reads as follows: Grindr user: "You into scat by chance? I want to be shit on." Field correspondent: "Not my scene, sorry! But have a good day." Grindr user: "Your loss. I can eat a lot of shit. Hit me up once you get over your hang-ups." Indeed, a socially disreputable, antinormative sexual imaginary—with attitude.

about the queer future of geosocial connectivity. He argues that mobile digital cruising harbors political potential for a population that through history has been migratory and "placeless": "The political potential of such connections may not be fully realised [sic] by users of Grindr or Purpll or by those who Bluejack one another during the daily commute, but through their engagement with such technologies and practices, these men are identifying and challenging prevailing hegemonies encountered in public space" (210).

Nonetheless, for many m4m media users, mobile apps merely serve the function of the old-fashioned, pre-Internet gay male public infrastructure: tearooms, saunas, and sex clubs. Kane Race argues that "the design features of online hook-up devices can only really be understood with reference to preceding infrastructures and environments that have shaped gay sexual practices and desires historically. [. . .] [P]receding sexual infrastructures have informed many of the design features, templates, and functions that make online hook-up devices intelligible, familiar and appealing to certain gay male dispositions" (499; 503). Like Mowlabocus's work, Race's scholarship is refreshing in that it counters dominant critical and popular currents that typically emphasize the discontinuities and differences between physical queer spaces and m4m media. Race is more interested in the similarities between gay male spaces of yore and m4m media as well as the new affordances these media offer in the ongoing creation of queer intimacies. Grindr's "cascade" or grid, for example, assembles user profiles into a collection that alludes to historic communal gay male spaces such as bathhouses or bars. This design feature is significant in that it visually interpellates users into a *group* of digitized avatars—unlike, say, the predominantly heterosexual-oriented Tinder, which individualizes the cruising experience by presenting, one-by-one, profiles that fit users' "matching preferences."[4] That the interface of the original geosocial hookup app takes the form of an assemblage of users is significant in other ways as well. The Grindr grid is a collection of often faceless seekers: from a visual standpoint, this online collection is not perforce a "gay community" looking to affirm a political identity or earn rights. What binds this group is a desire for bare connection, which takes multiple forms: chat buddies, porn-selfie swapping partners, hookups, and boyfriends, for sure, but also perhaps

---

4. Of Tinder's 57 million users, 88 percent are heterosexual-identified; 12 percent are gay-identified. See Iqbar.

unexpected alliances and affiliation between people who, in terms of social identity, are quite unlike each other. Noting the "undulating mass of naked male bodies, spread wall to wall" upon his initial visit to a gay bathhouse, Samuel Delany concludes: "The first direct sense of political power comes from the apprehension of massed bodies" (qtd. in Race 506). Although the mass of Grindr "bodies" are mere digital traces of users, the effect of viewing and perhaps understanding oneself as part of a collective/collection can be reassuring, even empowering. It would be silly, of course, to claim that Grindr's grid works as a consciousness-raising tool for gay politics—an awakening akin to Delany's bathhouse experience, I imagine, happens rarely, if ever, on Grindr. However, it is significant that m4m media does not necessarily traffic in sexuality as we have come to know it: as an innate desire inextricably enmeshed with who we are and how we signify socially. In the m4m media universe, not all users are gay-identified, and those who disidentify with gay identity are not by default tragic, self-deceiving closet cases. Instead, they might be questioning or resisting the binary conceptions of sexuality that have proven quite useful as a form of social control. For Foucault, delinking erotic desire from social identity—i.e., denouncing the subjective truth of sexuality as we have come to know it—is a significant gesture of refusal: it signals a longing to defect from the biopolitical management of life (Roach, *Friendship* 91–95). Because biopolitics, as a form of population management, relies so heavily on social identity categories—allocating the lion's share of available resources to social groups deemed viable, on the one hand, while willfully neglecting groups classified as a hindrance to social progress, on the other—refusing to honor social identity categories could be a step toward toppling the social hierarchies built upon them.

Furthermore, it's important to remember that Foucault understood the "invention" of sexuality—the sexological creation of a link between sexual desire and social identity—as the crux of biopolitical control (ibid., 97–99). The policing of sexual identity—on the individual level, the conformity to hetero- or homocultural behavioral norms; on the social level, the management of populations through the institution of marriage, reproductive health statistics, and other actuarial public health measures—is instrumental to biopolitical functioning. Divesting in sexual identity, then—not trying to "find ourselves" in our erotic desires—could be a springboard to an anti- or post-biopolitical understanding of self and community. "If sexuality today is a system of social control," Steven

Seidman writes in a summary of Foucault's sexual politics, "then ironically sexual liberation might involve freeing ourselves from the idea of sexuality" (10). In other words, the less tethered we are to our sexual identity, the less constrained we might be by cultural and institutional norms that tell us who we are, what we should desire, and how we ought to relate to one another. The less we allow social identity at large to dictate our life choices, the greater our capacity to extend ourselves outward, to seek connection and common cause with diverse others. Only in leaving behind or becoming indifferent to biopolitically administered social identity might we recognize a common project that works collectively to create new self-definitions, better ways of life, and alternative forms of assembly that respect internal differences and yet unite in struggle. While I have no illusions that cruising the Grindr grid makes anti-identitarian revolutionaries out of any of us, the experience might lend itself toward a realization that sexual identity is not only an impoverished frame of intelligibility to conceive of a self, but also an increasingly irrelevant one in the quote-unquote "real world" where workers are treated as fungible skill sets rather than unique individuals.[5]

But back to Grindr. The app's "collectionist" interface likewise recalls—however unintentionally and however morbidly—another aspect of the historical LGBTQ infrastructure: the NAMES Project AIDS Memorial Quilt.[6] (See figure 4.1.) Founded in 1987 to "create a memorial for those who had died of AIDS, and to thereby help people understand the devastating impact of the disease" (NAMES Project), the AIDS Quilt is a collection of approximately forty-eight-thousand, three-by-six-foot panels, each one typically commemorating an individual life lost to AIDS. Displayed as a grid wherein each panel touches at least two others, the quilt simultaneously calls attention to the connectedness of AIDS deaths and the uniqueness of each lost life. Unlike, say, the generic white crosses that honor fallen, Christian WWII soldiers at the Normandy American Cemetery in France, each panel of the AIDS quilt is its own individualized cultural artifact, often designed and assembled by loved ones of the deceased to represent her or his interests, passions, and personality. The

---

5. I explore this last claim, that sexuality is increasingly irrelevant in the neoliberal context, in chapter 6.

6. I thank Andrew Cook for calling my attention to this connection.

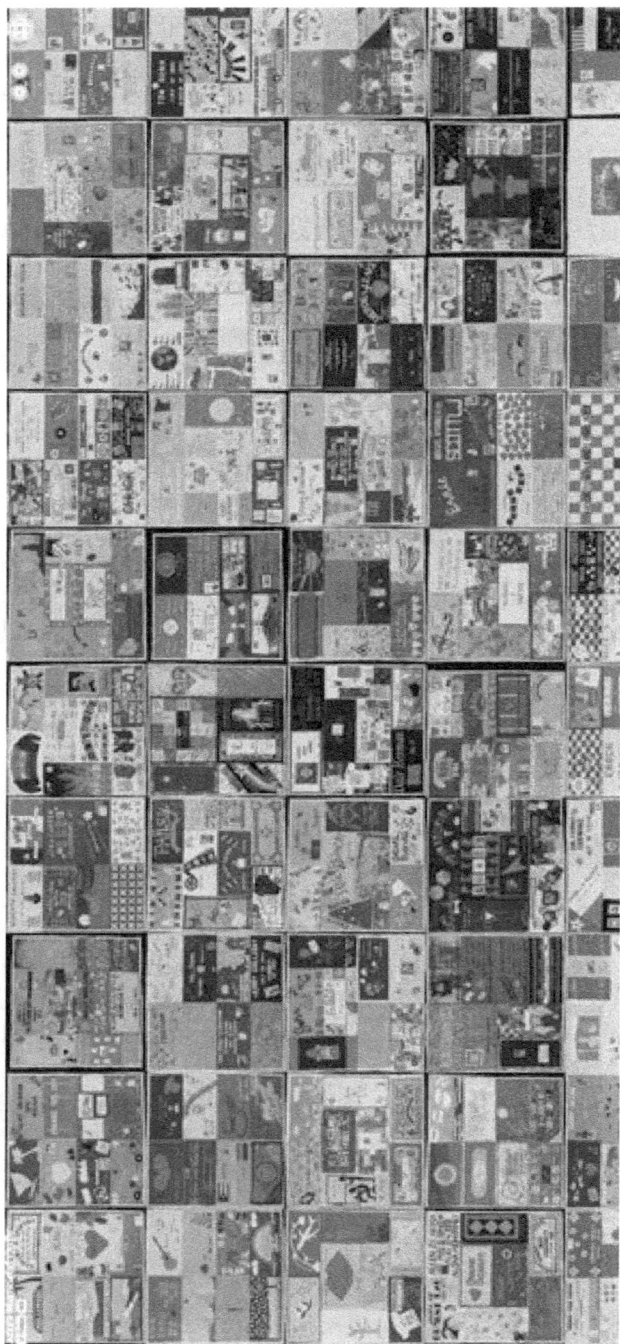

Figure 4.1. A portion of the NAMES Project AIDS Quilt.

quilt's "ontology," if we can call it that, thus rests on a conception of life as singularly plural.[7] While the orderly rows of white crosses in Normandy emphasize the impersonality of a soldier's function—i.e., his or her role as a cog in a military machine—the multitude of personalized AIDS quilt panels reminds us that each death is as singular as it is collective. The quilt's "interface" thus commands us to vacillate between the mathematically sublime and the utterly mundane. From afar, the quilt is a sea of similitude; up close, a one-of-a-kind tribute. Importantly, and again, not unlike the Grindr grid, the singular is only accessible through the plural: even if we seek to view only one, specific panel, we must peruse, parse, and process many similar-looking others. Because all panels are held to identical measurement constraints, no one is exceptional. A panel commemorating a celebrity like Rock Hudson is, in terms of form, no different from one celebrating the unsung achievements of the boy next door. AIDS is the common denominator, and AIDS regards humans as fungible types. This, I would argue, is the most powerful lesson that the quilt can teach us. It encourages us to question an understanding of our life's uniqueness while not abandoning it. It allows us to recognize that while we might be special, we are also interchangeable. As a mass grave for distinct, inimitable lives, the quilt paradoxically de-emphasizes individualism while emphasizing our singular-commonness. If m4m media holds any ethical promise, it lies in its translation of the quilt's ethical lessons into a format available and accessible to so many.

Beyond the interface, the relational norms of m4m hookup apps likewise resonate with those of pre-Internet gay male sex publics. Race observes that the no-strings-attached, unencumbered intimacy conventions of m4m media mimic those of the erstwhile gay male infrastructure (500–2). The impersonal and no-nonsense sexual conventions of tearooms and cruising grounds find their contemporary, virtual home in a less committal, more convenient, and hyper-mediated setting. For gay-identified men seeking no-strings sex, for queer-curious men who have little or no access to physical sex publics, or for men who disidentify with "gay" as a social identity but nonetheless seek sex with other men, m4m apps can be a godsend. They serve these populations, respectively, as a convenient way to hook up with other gay-identified locals at home or away, as an introduction to queer cruising culture, or as a catalyst for depersonalized sexual encounters that complicate issues of social identity.

---

7. For more on an ontology of singular plurality, see Nancy.

For the latter populations, queer-curious and "not-gay" men—Jane Ward's term for men who have sex with men while remaining resolutely invested in heterosexual identity for the social privilege it confers (*Not Gay*)—virtual cruising sites afford at least two opportunities: on the one hand, to experiment with same-sex erotic desires that might otherwise remain unconscious, unacknowledged, or unexplored; on the other hand, to compartmentalize desires and behaviors that a user might deem incompatible with his social self-perception. In a different but related context, this experimentation with and compartmentalization of same-sex desire resonates with the Down Low (DL).

A media sensation in the mid-2000s, the DL refers to a social scene wherein heterosexual-identified, often married, Black American men have sex with men. While journalists and political pundits exploit the phenomenon to reinforce racist stereotypes concerning an irresponsible and irrepressible Black male sexuality, Brad Eliot Stone views the DL as "an act of transgression and as a kind of heterotopia that could serve as a space of resistance against racism and heterosexism" (42). Stone begins his analysis of the DL by highlighting the historical co-constitution of race and sexuality in biopower. Following Foucault, he argues that the sexological conceptions of sexuality that served as a lynchpin between individual and social control in the formation of modern biopolitics are awash in racist, often eugenicist, assumptions. A racialized conception of sexuality thus plays a crucial role in determining a life's worth in the allocation of federal and public resources. In a biopolitical governmentality, socially privileged groups are encouraged or mandated to follow normative health and safety directives to reproduce both their "kind" and the social hierarchies that favor them. Less privileged groups—and race plays a key role in determining this privilege—are deemed a threat to their "superiors'" survival and therefore either neglected, targeted, incarcerated, murdered, left to die, or a combination thereof. Erstwhile eugenicist conceptions of Black sexuality as excessive, uncontrollable, and even threatening to homo sapiens' viability continue to bolster white social power. With Blackness as its foil, whiteness is conflated with healthy, decorous, generative sexuality and deemed worthy of investment. In the DL, Stone observes Black men shouldering the weight of this history and struggling to unburden themselves of it. The DL becomes "a heterotopic space in which real blackness, masculinity, and even heterosexuality can come together [. . .] in a way that contests and reverses the biopolitical strategies placed upon black masculine bodies" (48). Black men on the DL also, according to Stone, challenge a racially charged American ideal of masculinity. The violent, heteronormative fantasy of dominance and invulnerability projected most intensely onto Black male bodies is negotiated and resisted. Moreover, by providing a space for queer-curious Black men who might feel no affiliation with a gay male culture popularly represented as white, the DL affords Black men the opportunity to momentarily escape oppressive models of Black sexuality and to invent communities and identities that confound biopolitical, sexological understanding. In this sense, the Down Low complicates the dominant in/out mentality of the gay liberationist closet narrative: "The Down Low presents itself as a sexual contradiction in a way that being in the closet does not. It is almost as if the Down Low welcomes and savors the contradiction in a way that closeted gay life does not" (48).

As I will explore in chapter 6, m4m media likewise savors contradictions in their social function as a digital closet of sorts for gay-identified and not-gay men alike. For out gay men, m4m media use does not necessarily signal a return to the closet per se. Instead, these media, can act as an "adjacent room" of sorts, into which one might sneak to escape the social pressure of finding a mate or the marital discontents of already having found one. For not-gay men, as Ward concludes, m4m media can serve as a platform to double down on misogyny, racism, and heteronormativity (*Not Gay* 149–52). In quite contradictory, one might say heterotopic, ways, then, m4m media users reinscribe, test the limits of, and confound social identity categories, relational norms, and etiquette conventions. With their messy mishmash of progressive boundary pushing and regressive backlash, m4m media are a contemporary site in which traditional sexual identities and intimacy mores are being negotiated, reworked, and often defied.

However, for men seeking more traditional, interpersonal connections—dates, boyfriends, husbands—the virtual cruise can be an exercise in frustration. Although, in the United States, online platforms are the most popular way for men to meet (Match Group), one need not look far to find testimony about the horrors of looking for love on m4m media. Blog after blog and article after article highlight the bigotry, rudeness, and flakiness of m4m media users, their unwillingness to commit to dates rather than hookups, and the ways the apps themselves exacerbate the psychological damage that gay men experience collectively, though variably, as a social minority.[8] Although this psychological damage is arguably caused by social factors rather than technological ones, many m4m media critics individualize the problem and blame the media for exacerbating it. For example, Jack Turban, a gay-identified psychiatrist and medical writer, has become the go-to critic of Grindr for news outlets far and wide. His sex-panicky and fear-mongering diatribes about the dangers of m4m media use appear in *The New York Times* and *NPR,* among other respected outlets. In a particularly overwrought piece in *Vox,* Turban argues that m4m media have a negative impact on gay men's mental health and the LGBTQ community's public reputation. He warns that Grindr use might not only hamper a gay man's ability to invest in lasting love but also risks compromising the social acceptance of LGBTQ communities.

Turban begins his polemic by comparing the lure of m4m media to the lure of hard drugs: "Neuroscientists have shown that orgasm causes activation of pleasure areas of the brain like the ventral tegmental area while deactivating areas involved with self-control. And these patterns of activation in men are strikingly similar to what researchers see in the brain of individuals using heroin or cocaine. So when a neutral action (clicking on Grindr) is paired with a pleasurable response in the brain (orgasm), humans learn to do that action over and over again." He again sounds the addiction alarm by noting that m4m apps, like slot machines, produce pleasure by offering rewards at variable and unpredictable intervals: "Now imagine a slot machine that rewards you with an orgasm at unpredictable intervals. This is potentially a powerful recipe for addiction [. . .]." The author's deployment of the addiction narrative here is nothing new in the critical discourse on social media use. In *It's Complicated: The Social Lives of Networked Teens,* danah boyd offers a brief cultural history of the concept of addiction: from its early use in nineteenth-century medical journals addressing substance abuse to its contemporary abuse in sensationalized

---

8. Because of all the bad press (for examples, see Sen, Shadel, and Turban), Grindr unveiled the Kindr initiative in September 2018, seeking to "help foster a more inclusive and respectful community on its platform." The initiative involves "a combination of new community guidelines, stricter enforcement policies and awareness-raising videos that highlight user experiences of discrimination in-app." In a public relations statement, Grindr refers to Kindr as "a rallying call for Grindr and our community to take a stand against sexual racism and all forms of othering." See *Grindr,* "Grindr Takes a Stand against Sexual Racism and Discrimination with 'Kindr' Initiative."

criticism of online activity (77–99). She traces the origin of the concept of "Internet addiction" to psychiatrist Ivan Goldberg. In 1995, Goldberg jokingly coined the term to parody the way that even the most mundane activities, such as Internet browsing, are pathologized in American public discourse. Despite its parodic beginnings, the term took on a very somber life of its own: evidence Turban's humorless polemic. boyd argues that Internet addiction rhetoric becomes a potent tool in limiting civil liberties for all, but it affects adolescents most acutely. Since the 1980s, parents and lawmakers have been restricting teen agency—in the name of safety—at increasing levels. Legal curfews, prohibitions on public space, overreaching truancy and loitering laws, and extracurricular over-programming all purportedly work to keep teens out of trouble and in low-risk environments. According to boyd, such measures actually make adolescents ill prepared for life outside the domestic sphere. Due to legal restrictions and helicopter parenting, American teens today are less socially adept, less street smart, and less resilient than they were in the pre-cellphone era. boyd argues that teens use social media to reclaim the individual agency and collective sociality that they have been denied. Parents, lawmakers, and psychiatrists strike back by pathologizing screen use as "addiction" and scapegoating any digital technology that enhances adolescent freedom. "There are teens who do struggle significantly with impulse control," boyd writes, "and we should not ignore the difficulties they face in managing their priorities. But instead of prompting a productive conversation, addiction rhetoric positions new technologies as devilish and teenagers as constitutionally incapable of having agency in response to the temptations that surround them" (83).

In his *Vox* think piece, Turban deploys addiction rhetoric to demonize Grindr use. Just as lawmakers and helicopter parents infantilize adolescents, Turban likewise infantilizes gay men: they too need to be protected, they too know not what is good for them. His paternalism is especially noxious because it weds screen addiction to sex addiction. He adds a plot twist to both addiction narratives by implying that the gay male sex drive, in its very essence, is *prone* to addiction: it is a force inherently excessive and in need of social control or psychiatric surveillance. In this sense, Turban pays homage to his gaybaiting professional forbears. He resurrects a number of quite damaging psychiatric myths about gay male sexuality: it is uncontrollable and immature; indeed, it is stuck in an adolescent stage of arrested development. Like his forebears, he uses his psychiatric bona fides to pathologize gay male desire and concoct new ways to curb its social expression. What might seem like a compassionate plea to improve the mental health of his beleaguered brethren becomes a moralizing, anti-sex, homonormative rant. The narrative logic of the essay bears all the hallmarks of what Gayle Rubin refers to as "the domino theory of sexual peril" (14). This theory rests on an essentialist understanding of sexual desire as a socially destructive force. It assumes that the social constraints that hold sexual desire in check are necessary to civic life. If removed, if, for instance, we give an addictive-prone gay male desire the freedom to cruise the virtual ether, chaos will ensue. For Turban, when these two formidable forces meet—an inherently promiscuous social media and an inherently excessive gay male desire—all hell can break loose.

And while the mental health of gay men may be cause for concern—Turban cites a study claiming that up to 50 percent of American gay-identified men suffer from depression—the author clearly has more in mind than improving it. He argues that while m4m apps can offer temporary relief from loneliness, anxiety, and depression, in the long run, they tend to leave users ashamed, guilty, and self-hating. This psychological static consequently affects gay men's willingness to commit to long-term relationships. With a virtual bathhouse offering easy sex and intermittent ego satisfaction in their pocket, Turban argues, gay men are loath to invest in complicated interpersonal relationships. This, for Turban, is both an individual and a social catastrophe: a gay man's desire and ability to invest in long-term, marital-modeled relationships is directly proportional to his state of mental health and social worth. m4m media therefore prevent gay men from becoming fully realized individuals and optimally productive members of society. Even if app users want to follow the virtuous path toward a long-term relationship, Turban worries that they might have a tough time doing so: once Grindr sinks its hooks in us, it's hard to escape. He offers strategies for users unequipped to break the vicious cycle of app addiction on their own. Unsurprisingly, his recommendations for a full Grindr-free recovery involve psychiatric intervention. Quite surprisingly, however, the interventions include chemical treatments for compulsive behavior and hormonal implants to "make sexual cravings less intense." Recalling pre-Stonewall, de-homosexualizing, psychiatric tactics like aversive conditioning, which sought to weaken homosexual desire by means of electric shock, nausea-inducing drugs, and waterboarding, Turban's recommendations to live a Grindr-free life have more in common with gay conversion "therapy" than with gay pride parades. This is especially perplexing because the author's primary clinical and scholarly research focuses on *ending* conversion therapy for trans children (Brammer). But here his expertise serves reactionary purposes. Turban's takedown of digital m4m sex cultures is ultimately a bid for inclusion in a heteronormative social hierarchy. He shamelessly advocates for the desexualization of gay male culture—literally, depleting gay men's sex drives!—to secure a place at the table for *normal*, nuptial gays. His ultimate concern is not the mental health of gay men. Rather, it is the seamless assimilation of the *good gays* into a profoundly inequitable mainstream. He concludes: "As we continue to fight to bring gay relationships into the mainstream, we need to keep an eye on Grindr and how it both reflects and affects gay culture. The bathhouse is still around. It's now open 24/7, accessible from your living room."

Nonetheless, much to Turban's chagrin, queer intimacies and erotic practices once pitied and pathologized for their failure to live up to heteronormative standards—casual sex, promiscuity, impersonal hookups—are more socially accepted today in part due to the steady normalization of virtual connection, online dating, and LGBTQ culture at large. Of course, such "risqué" intimate arrangements are also perfectly compatible with a neoliberal gig economy rife with one-off jobs, side hustles, noncommittal labor contracts, and precarious long-term job security. To succeed in the new corporate order, employees are advised *not* to get too comfortable in any one place: flexibility, rootlessness, and adaptability are keys to success. What better way to cope with such instability than an app offering disposable intimacy?

In *Labor of Love: The Invention of Dating*, Moira Weigel calls attention to the ways in which intimacy conventions and courtship language reflect economic principles and trends. In the contemporary neoliberal context, the language of finance capital worms its way into the discourse of romance: "People conduct 'cost-benefit analyses' of their relationships and cite the 'low risk and low investment costs' of casual sex. They try to 'position themselves' to 'optimize' their romantic options" (23). Likewise, the heterosexual "hookup," both the term and the practice, saw a spike in popularity during an economic boom, the 1990s tech bubble, and gained traction as a cultural norm once the service industry—fueled by affective labor and transactional intimacy—asserted itself as a dominant economic force (70–72). Put simply, the personal is not only political; it is political-economic. What we are doing in the bedroom is intimately connected to what's going on in the boardroom.

For better and for worse, queer culture has historically been at the forefront of "optimizing" intimacy options. Weigel notes that the first heterosexual singles bar in the U.S.—a New York–based TGI Fridays, of all places—was created with the explicit intent to "make a gay bar, but for straight people" (66). Moreover, as mentioned, Grindr, the original dating/ hookup app for smartphones, was first to incorporate location-based, geosocial technology into the online pursuit of sex and love. As a tech pioneer, Grindr quickly became the phone app industry standard for gay *and* straight dating culture. From a business perspective, then, queers have surely been "ahead of the pack" in terms of intimacy "innovation." And though these innovations are laudable as the creative inventions of a community excluded from heteronormative institutions, they are also products of larger economic forces.

For instance, the "no-strings-attached" sexual norm in pre-Internet and digital gay male cultures alike reflect and reinforce the transactional intimacies that ground the service and entertainment industries. Throughout the short history of the "homosexual" community, a large number of gay-identified men have populated careers requiring expertise in affective labor: nursing, teaching, hairdressing, or serving up cocktails by day while working toward a big break on Broadway by night (Roach, *Friendship* 109–10). Success in these fields requires the skill to turn emotions on and off instantaneously, to instrumentalize affects for financial gain. Such affective labor finds its erotic analog in impersonal hookups—a practice part and parcel of the gay male sex infrastructure. Likewise, sexual promiscuity, another practice historically associated with male homosexuality, also reflects the job precarity LGBTQ-identified individuals face in a heterosexist marketplace.[9] Although the Supreme Court ruled in June 2020 that LGBTQ employees are protected from workplace discrimination under the Civil Rights Act of 1964 (Liptak), prior to that ruling no fed-

---

9. While job precarity is an intrinsic feature of neoliberal capitalism—lest we forget, union busting is one of its fundamental tenets—American LGBTQ-identified workers have historically been more vulnerable to the firing whims of management than straight-identified employees. And while as of June 2020 it is illegal to terminate an employee for identifying as LGBTQ, the Equality Act—a proposed federal bill to prohibit discrimination on the basis of sex, sexual orientation, and gender identity in employment, education, housing, healthcare, public accommodation, and other areas necessary to survival—has yet to pass (*Congress.gov*). Although I argue in chapter 6 that social identity comes to play second fiddle in a neoliberal marketplace that values human capital over personal history, gender, sexual, and racial inequities are exacerbated under the guise of neoliberal "diversity."

eral law prohibited bosses from firing workers for identifying as LGBTQ. Such anxiety-producing insecurity—"If they find out, where am I going to work or live?"—surely encourages individuals to invest only in the short term; without social protections, who's to say that everything—including love—will not be taken away tomorrow? On the one hand, promiscuity has bedeviled the queer community: psychiatrists once preached (and heterosexist moralists still do) that homosexuals are constitutionally incapable of long-term attachments. According to this logic, it's not that LGBTQ folks are socialized into anxious short-term thinking nor, more radically, simply unimpressed with and uninterested in mimicking failed heterosexual romantic models, it's that they *innately lack* the ability to do so. On the other hand, promiscuity arguably saved queer culture. As Douglas Crimp contends in "How to Have Promiscuity in an Epidemic," sexual promiscuity taught gay men and lesbians to care for strangers—a practice that would become essential not only to AIDS caregiving and activism, but to the very notion of a unified LGBTQ community. Whatever the extent to which promiscuity has been a blessing or a curse to queer culture, one thing remains certain: forms of intimacy historically associated with gay men inform online engagement across the board. Network promiscuity in particular has arguably become the new normal for the digital denizens of screen-obsessed societies.

According to media/queer theorist Robert Payne, promiscuity best describes our contemporary engagement with network culture. "As a *modality* of networked media engagement [promiscuity] is a structuring presence for a range of intimate relations among media users, and between users and their media" (2). Unfortunately, according to Payne, the once subversive potential of queer erotic promiscuity is blunted in network culture. Online participatory media foreclose "the opportunities for multiple intimate relations which might force a reinscription of ethics, precisely where the coherent self and its capacity for ethical violence would be threatened" (56). This foreclosure is necessary, however, to propel the Web 2.0 dream of a user-generated Internet: a dream predicated on the myth of a coherent and willful (Cartesian) agent. Anything that threatens the illusion of agentic mastery and stability is a threat to network culture at large. According to Bersani and Dean, whose work Payne engages, the ethical benefit of erotic promiscuity is the potential shattering of the illusion of agentic mastery; network culture, however, cannot accommodate subjective incoherence. For this reason, promiscuous network engagement, which tempts users with the pleasure of "losing themselves," is paradoxically welcomed and feared by corporate media platforms that monetize user interactivity. Network promiscuity is vilified by, for example, digital journalism outlets seeking the lion's share of the information attention market. These companies detest our brand-disloyal, clickbait habits of news gathering because they take our eyes away from their advertisers' products. By contrast, the "frictionless sharing" of user content introduced by Facebook in 2010 was a boon for tech giants and their partner companies.[10] This feature integrates Facebook users' activity with third-party websites that "relieve" users of the burden of sharing—an algorithm does it for them. When from within Facebook a user clicks on a link requiring authorization—a link, for example, that asks for Facebook log-in information—the user's data will be shared *promiscuously* with other corporations. The user thus shares promiscuously, but, more often than not, without her, his, or their consent. By removing the user from the sharing equation, Facebook not only deviously disseminates user data—to disastrous ends, as we found out in the aftermath of the 2016 election[11]—it also tracks the stories and sites the user clicks on and

10. Facebook inaugurated its Open Graph frictionless sharing scheme in 2010. It goes like this: in your news feed, you see a story that a friend recently read. You click on the headline and instead of being linked to the article, a pop-up appears requesting that you install an app or authorize your Facebook log-in credentials in order to read the story. Your friend clearly did this already, and you really want to read what she's reading, so you go ahead and do it. What you've actually done is waive your right to consciously and intentionally share new stories: every story you read automatically gets shared. As tech blogger Molly Wood notes: "When Facebook unveiled Open Graph at the f8 developer conference this year, it was clear that the goal of the initiative is to quantify just about everything you do on Facebook. All your shares are automatic, and both Facebook and publishers can track them, use them to develop personalization tools, and apply some kind of metric to them. [. . .] So, publishers and Facebook in particular really, really want you to click those little Add to Facebook buttons so that everything you read, watch, listen to, or buy will get shared to friends who also authorize the app and share to friends who also authorize the app and so on and so on into eternity and hopefully riches. It's all just part of the plan."

11. In the months following the 2016 presidential election, we learned the extent of Facebook's promiscuous sharing practices. The biggest scandal involved Cambridge Analytica, which purchased American Facebook users' personal data with the intent to sway voter opinion and manipulate election outcomes. For more on the manipulation of the 2016 presidential election, see Madrigal.

shares that information with both other users and corporations. Because users essentially lose control of the whereabouts of their online selves (i.e., their personal data), it has become Facebook's primary duty to ensure the illusion of user agency.

Whether celebrated or denigrated, network promiscuity is constrained within a market rationality of consumer choice. The freely choosing, freely sharing, rational consumer is the fantasy that generates income in the Web 2.0 marketplace. If Facebook fails to produce the experience of autonomy—i.e., if users *feel* they have lost control of their feeds, their posts, and their sharing—the corporation's bottom line is threatened by user disengagement: a trend that has plagued the tech giant since the 2016 presidential election (Rosoff). To keep users logged in and to make more money off of them, Facebook et al. must master a delicate dance: online engagement must be enhanced and made easier, but users still need to feel in control of their activity. Algorithms that predict searches and tastes, curate newsfeeds and contact lists, and outsource sharing to partner corporations are certainly moneymakers, but they risk exposing the fact that users are paying a price for these nominally "free" services. Our fee, of course, is our personal data and browsing histories, and once we agree to a platform's terms, we have little control over them. Frictionless features, then, sabotage the very agency users must trust in to remain faithful to a platform. In the name of enriching user experience through these features, however, Facebook et al. deplete user agency and indirectly endanger their own viability.

This is all to say that since user engagement is thwarted more and more by algorithms, the online experience becomes increasingly "interpassive": agentic activity is circumscribed and undermined by pre-encoded binary operations that offer the illusion of democratic participation but hardly deliver on that promise (Payne 33). Jonathan Sterne notes, "While interactivity can be imagined as the 'like' or 'retweet,' it also encompasses the 'agree to terms' button. The supposedly democratic call to dialogue and participation can turn sour when people have good reasons and desires to retreat." These "good reasons" include feeling manipulated, surveyed, or commodified, disbelieving any news story that shows up in one's feed, or feeling wary of handing over profitable personal data for the umpteenth time. When Sterne presciently asks in the same essay, written in 2012: "What if interactivity is one of the central hinges through which power works?" the 2016 U.S. presidential election asserts itself urgently into the spotlight. In the wake of that election, as we continue to learn the extent to which Facebook user feeds were manipulated by partner corporations who shared data promiscuously, the political dangers and consequences of interpassivity become clear. Animated and circumscribed by interface, platform design, and algorithm, social media users scream into a void that has been rigged to manipulate them. Users debate, like, comment, and share to register their presence, to feel their power, and to stabilize a self that has been deliberately destabilized, exploited, and bamboozled. And while online input might feel like communicative action—i.e., like participation in a democratic public sphere—it is actually unpaid labor exploited by both communicative capitalism's fat cats and nefarious political strategists alike. In the age of social media, then, democracy, in Jodi Dean's phrasing, becomes a neoliberal fantasy (*Democracy*). Self-segregated and self-validating, duped interpassive digital citizens shout into the abyss so as to feel heard, while the corporate platforms encouraging this hullabaloo partner with big data to manipulate election outcomes and sell more products. In short, there is a decreasing amount of oxygen in our pre-packaged, disinformational filter bubbles.

But what if we were to complicate the idea of interpassivity? That is, what if in the m4m media context, "relinquishing control to the promiscuous viral flows of content (37)," as Payne puts it, might be a practice leading to new understandings of agency, interactivity, and even community? Despite the fact that erotic promiscuity has been "rebranded as active sharing and market leadership" in network culture (37), might a vision of queer sociability nonetheless be available in networked experience?[12] Take, for example, again, the humiliating process of creating a profile on an m4m hookup app. Beyond the painful recognition that you are more likely than not handing over your personal data to corporate behemoths that care little about your privacy, security, or happiness, the process is humiliating

---

12. Payne queers the concept of interpassivity by emphasizing the user-subject's capacity to pleasurably disperse itself, or to disintegrate, in the circulative flows of media content. With a nod to Bersani's "Is the Rectum a Grave?," he highlights the "value of powerlessness" and valorizes a queer subject grounded in the abdication of power. In the following chapter, I pick up on this notion of interpassivity, specifically as it relates to Bersanian "self-shattering," and argue that, in terms of ethics, it is merely a beginning. The power of powerlessness is realized only in the centrifugal expansion of the interpassive user-subject seeking to correspond with similar forms.

in some quite interesting ways as well. Creating a profile typically entails choosing a picture that represents you at your most attractive, distilling your personality or interests into a sentence or two, checking some boxes regarding relationship preferences, sexual preferences, and preferred types, and ultimately flattening your 3-D self into a 2-D avatar. Akin to the experience of filling out official documents that do not accurately represent your real-life self—in terms of, say, gender identity, relationship status, title, or pronoun—signing up for the online dating game can be frustrating and humbling: "I'm more than this picture! I'm more than these categories!" In this regard, the process resembles the depersonalizing experience of cruising in real life. Key features of both practices involve self-subtraction and self-marketing: since the spark of attraction often ignites after a flash visual assessment, one's past, politics, feelings, and thoughts—i.e., one's psychic interiority—are somewhat irrelevant, at least initially, in both practices. Of course, the communicative rituals and psychic effects of virtual cruising differ significantly from pre-digital cruising practices. Context (unique vs collapsed), audience (actual vs imagined), social cues (embodied vs discursive/photographic), and risk (online cruising being arguably more risk-averse) are a few significant differences that come to mind.[13] And yet, the virtual cruising context affords opportunities that cannot occur in physical space. For one, the visual experience of mediated self-objectification, of viewing oneself from a third-party perspective as a piece in a virtual collection of optional objects: this aesthetic experience is unavailable in the tearoom or the back room. Willfully becoming the object of an imagined audience's thirsty gaze is an interpassive experience also different from liking and retweeting: users are indeed circumscribed and animated by a hookup app's protocols, but the dehumanizing flattening of the self that this protocol demands encourages a mode of interobjective interaction that lends itself toward an ethics of fungibility. On a purely formal level, the protocol makes all users interchangeable: the profile pic becomes a placeholder for an "I" that can be substituted with any other on the grid. Although subjective passivity has traditionally been understood as the weaker, less desirable half of the activity/passivity binary, that understanding has, of course, been reworked by queer theorists, such as Bersani. For him, "losing one's manhood" in the interpassive act

---

13. For more on the differences between face-to-face and virtual socializing, see boyd, 29–43.

of receptive anal sex, for example, might be the best thing a guy could do: it is an embodied opportunity to disavow the sadistic, masculine ego ideals that men internalize. "It may, finally, be in the gay man's rectum," Bersani declares, "that he demolishes his own otherwise uncontrollable identification with a murderous judgment against him" (*Rectum* 29–30).

Interpassive promiscuity is a useful concept, then, to complicate loaded conceptual binaries and value hierarchies that have plagued women and queers for centuries: not just active (masculine, dominant, strong) versus passive (feminine, submissive, weak), but also productive (hetero-sexual, reproductive, healthy) versus unproductive (homosexual, infertile, diseased). One way to reach an understanding of the self as substitutable is to embrace erotic interpassivity: to learn to relish the relinquishment of self-mastery. "Bottoming" may be one path to this self-understanding as might the recognition that, at least on the Grindr grid, we're nothing special: we may just be, in Hocquenghemian terms, a part that plugs or gets plugged. The very act of willfully handing ourselves over to both an app's protocols and to an unknown audience's judgment is itself a vulnerable, even generous gesture: we trust, however naively, that nei-ther app nor audience will harm or exploit us. Like other services in the sharing economy—taking an Uber or Lyft, for instance, and effectively putting your life in the hands of a driver about whose skills or history you know little to nothing—signing up for an m4m app is an act of entrustment. Although an ego-aggrandizing illusion of agentic control and life-optimization may motivate m4m app profile creation, the reality of digital cruising is precisely the opposite: once you are part of the grid, you have little control over who looks at you, let alone what they think of you. As Mowlabocus notes: "The user is seen but does not know by whom. He is the silent object of someone else's narrative, but he cannot reciprocate unless given permission by the browser" (115). In the digital cruise, we not only consent to becoming a character in another's story, however, we are granted the power *not* to be recognized and not to rec-ognize others. If we happen to end up the protagonist in another's erotic fantasy, we are under no obligation to move the plot along; we reserve the right to ignore, to disacknowledge, to ghost, and to block. Conversely, try as we might to influence user perception and feedback, a fellow user's picture viewing, profile parsing, and solicitation is beyond our control: user activity is a one-way street, a unilateral, isolationist activity, until it isn't. Moreover, since digital cruising is frequently a way to kill time, to relieve boredom, or to distract us from the burdens of an overextended neoliberal subjectivity, users tend to approach one another with a non-committal indifference. Indeed, the draw of mere connectivity seems to outweigh the hope of deep connection; a user might feel like he is little more than the passing interest of a fellow user's distracted gaze, barely, if even, more interesting than a game of Solitaire. But the dehumanizing norms and communicative protocols of m4m media lend themselves toward an anti-intersubjective ethics of nonreciprocation. The self-lessening lessons of online interpassivity can train us for an anti-egotistical, impersonally narcissistic self-expansion. As I will argue in the pages to come, centripetal practices of self-subtraction are the prerequisite for the centrifugal movement of corresponding with other substitutable subjective forms—for making connections that radically complicate traditional understandings of intersubjectivity and that hold promise for collective forms that, however indebted to and reflective of neoliberalism, may be imperceptible and inimical to it.

Chapter Five

Becoming Fungible

It's almost too easy to make the case that dating and hookup media are terrible in every way. The laundry list of horrors essentially writes itself. These media are steeped in a consumerist logic. They substitute algorithms for pheromones. They instrumentalize intimacy and mechanize the wily ways of desire. They conjure illusions of privacy, control, and anonymity while simultaneously violating that perceived privacy with insidious practices like data mining and personalized advertising. They exacerbate the same barbarous impulses—hyper-individualism, cutthroat competition, solipsism, and self-aggrandizement—so integral to and rewarded in the marketplace.[1] Indeed, it is difficult to argue that social media at large do little else but construct and fortify what Foucault designates *homo economicus*: that calculating spawn of neoliberalism who perceives himself and others foremost as human capital. If the lived experience of *homo economicus* turns on consumption, enterprise, brand creation, self-optimization, efficiency, aggressive speculation, and, ironically, amid the never-ending workday, the maximization of individualized pleasure, it finds its virtual Elysium in the profile pages of online dating sites. m4m media are especially toxic. They are the arch breeding ground for neoliberal subjectivity, communication, and relational forms. Like I said, condemning the media and the monsters they reward is almost too easy.

---

1. For a basic discussion of the illusion of anonymity and privacy on the Internet as well as social media's encouragement of impulsive, socially inappropriate behavior, see Bruni.

In contrast to the chorus of techno-pessimistic queer voices,[2] I assert that to whatever extent social media have transformed the means of queer communing, the ends are generally the same: connection, hooking up. Despite significant differences between bathhouse cruising and profile browsing, between dark rooms and chat rooms, the anti-intersubjective, antisocial ethical principles constituted in the former practices can nonetheless be found and fostered in the latter.

I write this chapter as a counterpoint to thinkers such as Samuel Delany and Tim Dean, both of whom value public contact over private networking. In *Times Square Red, Times Square Blue*, Delany laments the loss of a public sex culture in the sanitization and Disneyfication of Times Square. He argues that a vibrant public sex culture encourages an interclass contact that cuts through hierarchical social strata and ultimately contributes to a city's safety and viability. In this discussion, he marks a key distinction between contact and networking, a distinction Tim Dean seizes upon in his praise of public cruising and his critique of online connection. Contact for both authors refers to public, social interaction: bodies mingling among bodies with the potential for chance encounters and happy accidents. Its opposite is networking: an instrumental, means-end form of communication, more bounded, focused, and purposeful. Although Delany notes that these two communicative forms are not simple binaries and do not fit tidily into the moral categories of good versus evil, he clearly prefers contact to networking. For him, networking is the privatization, mechanization, and domestication of public contact. Dean, using the same logic, contends that networking is the discursive form dominating m4m media. Staying at home to "order in" a hookup on computers and phones; becoming ever more tethered to private screens instead of public communities; learning to be more efficient, focused, and opportunistic in interpersonal interactions; closing ourselves off to serendipity, and corralling our desire into rigid sexual or anatomical confines—all of this is perfectly consonant with the logic and practice of networking in neoliberal capitalism. However, in looking a bit more closely at the discursive norms as well as the forms of connection and belonging produced in these forums, I find that there is something in excess of solipsistic, self-serving networking traversing the ether of

---

2. For a succinct formulation of a queer techno-pessimistic line of thought, see Gross. For a more nuanced critique of m4m online cruising, see Dean, *Unlimited Intimacies* 176–212.

m4m media. Indeed, precisely because m4m media are so thoroughly saturated in neoliberal market relational norms, they offer an opportunity to reconceive liberal-humanist notions of the social altogether.

The third key interlocutor in this chapter is Greg Goldberg, whose work has helped immensely in shaping *Screen Love*'s arguments. In "Meet Markets," Goldberg argues that "Grindr's marketization of what might otherwise be properly social relations may be its most politically useful accomplishment" (13). What the market encourages is "loose association and separation instead of bondedness" (12), and Grindr users typically follow suit and relate in this manner. But, for Goldberg, the market-relational practices endemic to Grindr are a model for politics: if citizens were to relate to one another as Grindr users do—interobjectively, impersonally, nonviolatively—the singular difference of each citizen would be respected. Given how rote critiques of neoliberalism are in leftist scholarship, Goldberg's moxie here is refreshing. Ultimately, however, his uncritical embrace of market relationality seems a bit of a dead end. Goldberg's political vision amounts to something we might call Absolute Neoliberalism: a brazenly antisocial form of sociality thoroughly and inescapably saturated in market rationality and relationality. If the market itself—with its inherent exploitative and annihilative tendencies—weren't part of this picture, Goldberg's political vision might hold promise. But, as is, it's hard to distinguish his speculative politics from actually existing libertarian theory and policy. With fungibility, I am attempting to appropriate one aspect of neoliberalism to exploit it for its anti-neoliberal, collectionist potential. With all due respect to Audre Lorde, I am attempting to use the tools of neoliberalism to conceive of a way to dismantle the master's house: a house that should not merely be renovated to shelter historically excluded groups but destroyed and built anew. Instead of resisting neoliberalism in the form of dialectical antagonism, I seek to push neoliberal relational forms to the point at which they are no longer productive for, or reproductive of, the system that birthed them. What a "beyond" neoliberal sociality may look like is difficult to conceptualize, but I turn in this chapter to the work of Proust, Warhol, Magritte, and Foucault to begin that work.

Before that turn, it's important to note that m4m media illuminate some ugly truths about the gay community that mainstream LGBTQ political lobbies aim to suppress. For one, the social institutions of marriage and military, along with the deadened concept of sexual identity that grounds them, cannot harness unruly desires or squelch socially unacceptable beliefs and practices. Moreover, the deep currents of racism, classism, sexism, transphobia, effemephobia, and patriarchal masculinism that pervade m4m media are antisocial in the most basic and regressive of ways. I understand m4m media, however, as more than reactionary proof of the failure of a respectable politics of assimilation. Rather, I find in them a form of perceptual training for a coming politics that abandon traditional, dialectical conceptions of intersubjectivity and community.

A connection forged through a mediating force—a screen—that simultaneously binds and separates can provoke affective ties that pressure traditional understandings of subjectivity and belonging. As I have been arguing, in the virtual setting of shared estrangement, the destructive ego might be humbled, unknown selves and unusual intimacies born, and respect for the alterity of the other learned. In this chapter, I take a closer look at the efficient yet inarticulate discursive norms of m4m media and its requisite register of free indirect discourse to see if there's anything worth, well, talking about. Even at first glance, there is something to be said for the untimely power of inarticulateness in the age of hyper-communication. Location-based hookup apps and other context-based media—such as Yo, a mobile app whose sole function is to shout "Yo!" at a recipient—take inarticulacy or, more generously, post-articulacy to new heights.[3] The discursive exchanges typical of m4m location-based apps—from the introductory interpellations, "hey," "'sup," "woof," to the inevitable request for "pics"—reduce dialogue to a series of churlish grunts and crass propositions: a nightmare (or perhaps a respite?) for those who pride themselves on eloquence, wit, or emotional expressivity. Adopting the discursive conventions of these forums (e.g., bluntness, eschewal of conversational niceties, near prohibition of confessional candor) is to learn a new language, one in which any acknowledgment of subjective interiority (thoughts, feelings, etc.) becomes a potential liability. If in his inaugural lecture at the Collège de France Foucault longed to "slip imperceptibly" into a discourse that preceded him, he might well feel at home in the

---

3. Context-based messaging relies on an unwritten but preestablished understanding between users. That is, the word or words contained in a message—"Yo," for instance—are meaningless outside a given context and contract between users. As Michael Brodeur states: "Depending on the Yo-er, the Yo-ee, and the circumstances surrounding one's 'Yo,' a 'Yo' could mean just about anything, from 'I'm pulling up outside,' to 'I miss you but I'm in a meeting,' to, 'You were right, he's gay,' to well . . . 'Yo!' Any practical use of Yo is predicated on the assumption that you have something worth Yo-ing about in your real life" ("Real Talk").

world of m4m media, where ventriloquial speakers rehearse utterances that seem to emanate not from any individualized psychobiographical interiority but from the cultural milieu itself ("Discourse" 215).[4]

In this regard, the provocative and prescient words of Gilles Deleuze come to mind. In a conversation with Antonio Negri, published in 1990 as "Control and Becoming," he states: "Maybe speech and communication have been corrupted. They're thoroughly permeated by money—and not by accident but by their very nature. We've got to hijack speech. Creating has always been something different from communicating. The key thing may be to create vacuoles of noncommunication, circuit breakers, so we can elude control" (*Negotiations* 175). Observing that speech and communication, like all modes of representation, are commodifiable, Deleuze also seems to be implying here that *relations* grounded in communicative norms are also "by their very nature" both market-ready and politically bankrupt. If, as Negri asserts, communication fuels the productive processes of postmodern capital,[5] Deleuze's command to "hijack speech" seems a logical strategy to "elude social control." But what would that hijacking look (or sound) like? I do not believe Deleuze has in mind here the whistleblowing tactics of Julian Assange or Edward Snowden. Their work might be better understood as "speaking truth to power" by illuminating secret histories and suppressed information. No, these provocateurs are not necessarily

---

4. The first paragraph of the lecture is worth quoting in full, as it foregrounds my discussion of the "subjectless" speakers in m4m media.

> I would really like to have slipped imperceptibly into this lecture, as into all the others I shall be delivering, perhaps over the years ahead. I would have preferred to be enveloped in words, borne way beyond all possible beginnings. At the moment of speaking, I would like to have perceived a nameless voice, long preceding me, leaving me merely to enmesh myself in it, taking up its cadence, and to lodge myself, when no one was looking, in its interstices as if it had paused an instant, in suspense, to beckon to me. There would have been no beginnings: instead speech would proceed from me, while I stood in its path—a slender gap—the point of its possible disappearance. (215)

5. The idea that abstract knowledge and communication are the principal productive forces of post-Fordist capital is conceptually central to Negri's oeuvre, from his early "Twenty Theses on Marx" to his more recent collaborations with Michael Hardt.

creating new modes of communication, nor are they destroying old ones. Rather, their exposure of governmental cloak-and-dagger tactics reveals (merely?) how power actually speaks and works behind closed doors. Likewise, the information relay and organizational tactics shared among activists through social media in the service of political movements such as Occupy and Spain's *indignados* are likewise not necessarily Deleuzian circuit breakers. In these contexts, social media fulfill their promise of connecting and choreographing vast numbers of people almost instantaneously (Gerbaudo). Although new forms of protest have certainly been invented in social media, Deleuze seems to be implying in this passage that new forms of *articulation* are necessary: ones that might be incomprehensible to the communicative circuits of capital, ones perhaps deemed utterly nonsensical by conventional discursive standards. So, are there any tactical openings, any "circuit breakers," to be found in social networking technologies? Can "vacuoles of noncommunication" be cultivated in the very heart of the communication-technological beast? If such technologies facilitate the construction of Foucault's *homo economicus*, might they also give life to a new figure whose aestheticized superficiality is designed for collectionist fungibility?

By taking seriously the various forms of post-articulation encouraged in m4m media, I assert that what initially, and rightfully, may appear as forums of senseless blather and crass self-interest might also be an active creation of an antirelational discourse struggling to retreat from dominant systems of commodified communication, on the one hand, and reified classifications of sexual identity, on the other. This baldly superficial, anticonfessional discourse is integral to the production of what I call, following Paulo Virno, *connection-as-such*: not a Facebook post oversharing a portion of one's personal life, however fabricated that life may be, but a sensual mingling of interchangeable types (twink, daddy, bear, jock) devoid of subjective interiority. While self-identity by most accounts involves personal history, psychological interiority, and subjective uniqueness, a type is superficial and interchangeable with like others: it is more like a cardboard cutout of a figure than a complex intellectual and emotional creature. The trafficking in surfaces and types—as opposed to selves, individual histories, and identities—can be as liberating as it is dehumanizing. The pleasures of m4m media certainly include the relief afforded by escaping momentarily the self that works, pays bills, and provides; the self held personally accountable for whatever befalls it; even the self burdened with managing its brand across other, more demanding social media platforms.[6] At the same time, delinking desire from identity and treating people as objects of pleasure run the risk of devaluing life in dangerous, albeit quite typical, ways.

Homo economicus himself cares little for biographical history and emotional interiority: he is simply, as Andrew Dilts puts it, "an array of activities" (136–37). These activities are based not on the principle of mutual exchange or civic responsibility, but rather on self-optimization: as a repository of human capital, *homo economicus* invests in others only if a profitable return is likely. In treating virtual cruising as an enterprising practice, however, *homo economicus* is motivated not by a desire that seeks a satisfying telos; instead, he enacts the circuit of the drive. "The drive, unlike desire and demand," Shannon Winnubst writes, "[. . .] does not aim at any object of satisfaction. Structurally ateleological, its circuitous form enlivens repetition, rather than arrival, as the form of pleasure" (*WTC* 88). The repetitive, haptic practices of scrolling, swiping and clicking profiles, of blocking undesirables and starring hotties—all of these are goals in themselves, immanent pleasures of the virtual cruise requiring no external referent. Browsing the skin shots of profile pages, *homo economicus* calculates his moves using cost-benefit analysis, reaching out and responding only to those likely to maximize his interest and optimize his brand. The more "taps" or "woofs" he receives and the more other users indicate that his brand is marketable, the stronger and farther-reaching the tentacles of this virtual Cthulhu grow.

This monster, however, is humiliated in the process: his aggressive ego is tempered by the law of equivalence in a (meat) market of fungible goods. Here, as in the halls of commerce, equivalence is not equality. While all profiles in any given m4m media platform are subject to the same visual and discursive constraints, their popularity tends to correlate with conventional gender and beauty standards, body ideals, and racial, quite

---

6. In *Cruel Optimism*, Lauren Berlant uses the term "lateral agency" to designate practices of self-management interruption. Eating, one such practice, "is best seen as an activity releasing the subject into self-suspension," becoming a site of "episodic intermission from personality" (116). In the biopolitical, neoliberal context in which well-being and self-optimization are encouraged, if not enforced, cruising online can be understood similarly as an exercise of lateral agency.

often racist, cultural norms and expectations.[7] To be clear, the grid of the m4m hookup app is hardly the picture of Whitmanesque camaraderie or Eakinsesque brotherly love. Rather, like the neoliberal market from which it springs and for which it works, "success" depends on the attractiveness and marketability of the brand. Because sexual desires are socially inscribed, the self-brands that receive the most attention in m4m media are typically the ones that project the image of a neoliberal "winner." "The benefits of the [m4m media] market," McGlotten concludes, "tend to accrete to the very few—namely, well to do, young, and very often white, men" (5). In this sense, medical crowdfunding and Grindr have much in common. In the former, personal narratives of deservingness that demonstrate a mastery of neoliberal entrepreneurial skills generate the most income. In the latter, bodies that display all the characteristics of neoliberal success—whiteness, fitness, gender normativity, "straight-appearing"—get the most hits.

Formally speaking, however, this economy functions not on principles of exchange, but on fungibility: the more *homo economicus* abandons a liberal-humanist understanding of belonging, the more success he is poised to achieve.[8] Although one personal brand/profile might "pop" or catch eyes more than others, all are ultimately flattened into a sea of similitude. Recognizing the replaceability of one's brand—that is, understanding oneself and others as merely one transposable, clickable option among many—can certainly provoke egoistic competition ("I must stand out in the pack; I must market my brand better") and consumer frenzy ("The more I shop, the better my chances of scoring a good deal; This product is fine, but let's keep searching for the best"). And yet this entrepreneurial and consumerist behavior is secondary. In fact, it is a response, however unconscious, to the recognition of one's substitutability. Emphasizing the ego-lessening indignities and pleasures that occur in these forums,

---

7. For more on racism in m4m media, see Daroya; McGlotten, 61–78; and Raj. Goldberg critiques the assumption that targets of ageism, classism, and racism on Grindr are powerless victims lacking the agency to speak for themselves—even if that speech takes the form of blocking other users or logging off. He writes: "[W]hy can't we imagine these users [the ones who face discrimination in m4m media] as also interested in rejecting, rather than as the rejected? Why should we assume that the attention of classists, ageists, and white supremacists is a 'benefit?'" ("Meet Markets" 13).

8. For more on the role of fungibility in neoliberalism, see Winnubst, "The Queer Thing" 92–94; *WTC* 103–4.

I venture to claim that a certain modulation of neoliberal practices and principles might transpire. Not at all a "reverse discourse" or a conscientious political project, the modulation here concerns bending, perhaps unwittingly, the contours of market relationality into other-than-neoliberal forms and articulations. The exodus from intersubjective communication and self-/sexual identity I observe in m4m media is not perforce socially progressive: it might just forge a dead-end paved with violent egoism, willed ignorance, or more commodifiable forms of communication and social identity. As a vehicle for connection-as-such, however, that road might also lead beyond contemporary communicative and relational conventions that, in the name of openness, honesty, team building, and interpersonal respect, have not only created the conduits for neoliberal global capital but have also made violent, self-destructive, and socially destructive interactions the norm.

Connection-as-Such

Any significant step toward new relational forms must first entail a disinvestment in traditional communal forms. Founded in commonality (we have x in common), property (I belong to this group), exclusivity (you are not a member of this group), and intersubjectivity (our singular interests dialectically sublate into a common goal), such communities are the remnant of an earlier stage of capitalist development. If *homo economicus*'s principle occupations are entrepreneurship and consumerism,[9] if the affects that motivate him are primarily greed, cynicism, and opportunism, those who wish to put an end to neoliberalism might best learn to traverse the neoliberal landscape as nimbly as he does—but for different reasons and toward different ends. Perhaps the only way to push past the social atomization and inequality wrought by neoliberalism is to appropriate and modulate the methods and affects of its prized figure: to play the game not to "win" (i.e., to accumulate capital) but to gen-

---

9. In *Friendship in an Age of Economics*, Todd May, following Foucault, argues that the consumer and entrepreneur are the two key figures of neoliberalism. Although I find his concept of friendship altogether too indebted to traditional philosophical understandings of belonging and intimacy, and hence ill-equipped to challenge neoliberal relational norms, his staging of the neoliberal scene and its key players is quite useful. See May, 17–55.

erate alternative definitions of success and unorthodox communal and communicative forms.

Paolo Virno's notion of belonging-as-such becomes quite useful in conceptualizing this project. In "The Ambivalence of Disenchantment," Virno argues that the flexibility and mobility required of the contemporary laborer, from the migrant farmer to the jet-setting hedge funder, produces, paradoxically, intense feelings of belonging. In his words: "The impossibility of securing ourselves within any durable context disproportionately increases our adherence to the most fragile instances of the 'here and now' " (31). Unlike an exclusive group membership, this belonging is not tied to a substantial entity or community. Rather, it is a belonging to a *feeling* of belonging, to belonging itself. In a world shot through with precarious labor, contingent attachments, morphing self-identities, and unpredictable financial ebbs and flows, traditional practices of belonging are increasingly untenable, certainly less profitable. Put another way, neoliberalism has little use for belonging in a traditional sense: the more the entrepreneur and consumer abandon a liberal-humanist understanding of belonging, the more success they are poised to achieve. According to Virno, the affects that motivate neoliberal subjects and generate belonging-as-such include cynicism, fear, and resignation in the face of an interminable yet hyper-volatile present. He notes, however, that the affective experience of belonging-as-such is itself ambivalent. Suffusing a diverse range of practices in the communication-technological spectacle of information overload and stimulant surplus, it can spur increased opportunism and competition, or, quite the opposite, engender alternative understandings and experiences of connection, solidarity, and collectivity. Virno thus locates an immanent strategy, neither nostalgic nor utopian, in the irreversible present: the affects produced in neoliberalism can be put to work in the creation of nontraditional assemblages that defect from contemporary arrangements and functions.[10] An abandonment of traditional conceptions of friendship, love, the family, the party, an abandonment of dialectical, transcendent conceptions of intersubjectivity, community, and revolution, might be the only way to deviate from a course dead set on destruction.

---

10. Dilts argues that Foucault discovers a similar ethical opportunity in neoliberal subjectivity: when the subject is reconceptualized as an array of practices and thereby "freed" from psychobiographical interiority, it might formulate regimens of self-care that brush against the grain of the very logic that "liberated" it (140–46).

Although we indeed may be "bowling alone" in our civically disengaged neighborhoods, and although we may be "alone together" in our social media, the alienating experiences that generate belonging-as-such harbor the seeds, if properly propagated, of an impersonal ethics and an anti-relational sociality.[11]

Ironically, it is a centenarian, Charles Swann from Marcel Proust's *In Search of Lost Time*, who, when read against the grain, presages such a futural ethics. A well-heeled socialite with a fondness for buxom working-class lassies, Swann comes undone in his troubled courtship with Odette, "a young woman almost of the *demi-monde*" whom he struggles to find sexually appealing (255–56). Counter to contemporary romantic narrative conventions, Swann's indifference is not magically transformed in a dis-covery of Odette's "true self": her thoughts, feelings, and interests pulsing beneath those uninspiring features. The transformation is in fact motivated by a revelation quite to the contrary. Swann realizes that Odette bears a superficial likeness to another surface that bespeaks his class status and aesthetic sensibility. What sets Swann's heart aflame, to be precise, is Odette's resemblance to Botticelli's rendering of Jethro's daughter, Zipporah, in *Scenes from the Life of Moses*. Through the painting, Odette becomes for Swann a talisman of refined taste, a fetishized bit of cultural capital. "The words 'Florentine painting' were invaluable to Swann. They enabled him, like a title, to introduce the image of Odette into a world of dreams and fancies which, until then, she had been debarred from entering, and where she assumed a new and nobler form" (317). Odette is allowed entrance via "high art" to the world of the titled, the master class. Swann, the urbane bachelor moving gracefully through the upper echelons, requires his beloved to embody a representation of an aesthetic/aristocratic cultural sensibility so essential to his own (quite fragile) sense of self. As a result, Swann, to his own surprise, becomes vulnerable and progressively unhinged. Suspicious of Odette's potential infidelities and susceptible to her power over him, Swann rages murderously against those who stand between him and his beloved. In other words, Swann realizes, in the most self-serving manner, that he is quote-unquote "in love." In accordance with his aristocratic aspirations, he seeks to possess Odette as one would a work of fine art.

---

11. I refer here, tongue firmly in cheek, to two best-selling books bemoaning the lack of traditional civic engagement and communal involvement in contemporary America: Robert D. Putnam's *Bowling Alone* and Sherry Turkle's *Alone Together*.

Although Proust is here mocking the shallowness and narcissism of France's *nouveau riche*, what if we were to read Swann against Proust's critique as a way of emphasizing the effect that the self-shattering and subsequent self-expansion the Zipporah/Odette image engenders? Upon being stood up by Odette, Swann, half-mad, scours the streets of Paris late into the night to locate her. Up to this point he has been stoically playing hard to get so as to keep Odette guessing, to generate in her what he hopes will be a neurotic dependence on him. During this humiliating search, however, Swann becomes not only a new man, but a multiplied one: "He was obliged to acknowledge that now [. . .] he was no longer the same man, was no longer alone even—that a new person was there beside him, adhering to him, amalgamated with him, a person whom he might, perhaps, be unable to shake off, whom he might have to treat with circumspection, like a master or an illness. And yet, from the moment he had begun to feel that another, a fresh personality was thus conjoined with his own, life seemed somehow more interesting" (323). Interesting, indeed: Swann's first folly here is not that he loses and consequently multiplies himself in the frustration of longing, but rather that he conceptualizes love as: (a) a cat-and-mouse chase; (b) as ownership, and (c) as a dialectical fusion of selves. Consequently, both Odette/Zipporah and the neurotic, second self Swann generates in his yearning immediately become suspect, things to monitor "like an illness." When love is perceived as either a master/slave dialectic or as an amalgamation, jealousy, rage, and the will to possess follow naturally. However, if we rewind Swann's courtship narrative a bit and tarry in the moment of love's blossoming, things get "somehow more interesting." For it is only through a mediating image, a painting of a face, that Swann becomes capable of love in the first place. Before being corrupted by fantasies of fusion, this love prompts humiliation and openness, bringing to life a subtracted self extending outward, seeking connection.

Because Swann finds an aesthetic projection of Odette more appealing than her embodied self, because he falls in love with an image and not a person, his love is intriguingly superficial. Like Narcissus himself, Swann, at least initially, has little interest in mining the mystery of the Other. The secrets of Odette's desire fail to move him, but her artificial likeness undoes him. Only in objectifying her—emptying her of interiority by transforming her into an image—can he find a less snobbish, less sadistic, and more equitable manner of relating to her. Once Odette becomes a mediated avatar, Swann can connect with her in a nonhierarchical and nonintersubjective way: their connection is instead a lateral mingling, a brushing of surfaces. Before love becomes mutual psychological torture—in other words, romantic—Swann is awakened to a style of loving that is profoundly antisocial. In depsychologizing Odette, he empties himself too, allowing the pure force of magnetism to move through him and toward her. He relates to Odette interobjectively, as a mere form to which he is attracted, one to which his polarity, for lack of a better word, corresponds. From the vantage point of liberal-humanist notions of interpersonal respect, Swann's love is dehumanizing, irresponsible, and narcissistic. But what is narcissism without psychological interiority? What would narcissism look like if the self were conceived merely as a conduit through which cosmic forces move? And what (queer) form of sociality might emerge from an impersonal narcissism?[12]

Understood through Bersani's ontological framework, Swann's interobjective extensivity—what we might call the discovery of a cosmic "home"—affirms the presence of an asubjective, heterogeneous sameness that undercuts the violent dualism of self and other, male and female, subject and object. Although the (objective) world is conceived in depth psychology as antagonistic to the subject, as something that must be dialectically sublated by the ego to make it manageable, Bersani finds a "deeper," nonsubjective interiority ontologically at home in the world. The subject that opposes the world, then, is secondary, merely a subject-effect; the supposedly aggressive object he or she faces and defends against is a projection of the insecure ego. The actual relationship between these two purportedly distinct entities is a correspondence of forms rather than a contest of rivals or an assimilation of difference. "There is neither a subject/object dualism or a fusion of subject and object," Bersani writes, "there is rather a kind of looping movement between the two. The world finds itself in the subject and the subject finds itself in the world" (*Rectum* 147). The subject's ego-armor is thus a defense against its ontological porosity. The ethical task, then, is to learn to redirect our fascination with psychic interiority to our extensions beyond the self, "our innumerable and imperfect appearances outside" that urge us to "treat the outside as we would a home" (ibid. 62). But how to locate this ethical course? How to learn to divest the self of a destructive ego and recognize the world within and our home without?

---

12. My thoughts on impersonal narcissism are informed by Bersani and Philips, 57–87; Goldberg, "Through the Looking Glass"; and Tuhkanen, 147–75.

For Bersani, two forms of perceptual training that might spur the subject to live less invasively are cruising for sex and studying art. Through these practices, the subject can discover itself in the world not merely as a fantasmatic ego-projection but as something that was always already there: a thing that exists in solidarity with world-being. The self becomes exogenous: it extends beyond ego and corresponds with heterogeneous forms, both human and nonhuman. Never discovering a perfectly rendered self-similitude, the subject learns to respect, not stamp out, difference. "The narcissistic pleasure of reaching toward our own 'form' *elsewhere* has little to do with the flood of an oceanic, limitless narcissism intent on eliminating the world's difference. Rather, it pleasurably affirms that we are inaccurately replicated everywhere, a perception that may help us, ultimately, to see difference not as a trauma to be overcome, but as the nonthreatening supplement to sameness" (ibid. 100). Put another way, through centripetal practices of self-subtraction and the centrifugal pleasures of self-extension, the subject finds its peace with others and its home in the world. "[W]e move irresponsibly among other bodies, somewhat indifferent to them, demanding nothing more than that they be as available to contact as we are, and that, no longer owned by others, they also renounce self-ownership and agree to that loss of boundaries which will allow them to be, with us, shifting points of rest in a mobile communication of being (*Homos* 128).

Which leads me back, first, to Swann and then, at last, to m4m media. Although the mediating image of Zipporah prompts Swann's love for Odette, that love turns out to be "an illness" for two reasons: first, as I argued earlier, because Swann conceives love as dialectical fusion, and second, as Bersani helps us see, because Swann comes to perceive the world's objects and others as ego-projections. Panicked by the prospect of losing himself, he fortifies his ego and turns against the world. Botticelli's painting and Odette herself ultimately become vain fantasies of class power for Swann because they are merely projections of a trembling ego with a voracious appetite. Swann initially experiences love, however, as an impersonal, objectifying force that shoots through his very being and divests his ego of its power. Indeed, "something more interesting" materializes when love comes via a mediating image that connects objectified forms. Before Swann's world becomes ego-projection, he experiences the terror of egolessness in the face of a universal interobjectivity. Such an experience does not perforce result in an agonistic competition between self and other, self and world, for as Bersani shows us, a correspondence of forms between "inner" and "outer" might also prompt a recognition of ontological sameness among patently different others. Objectifying others through a mediating image is not, then, always and only licentious. As Bersani notes, this aesthetic experience can also prompt a revelatory self-undoing that brings into view an antisocial ethical horizon: "Art gives us a model of the world *as the world*, one we know as aesthetic subjects thrown outward, 'defined' by relations that at once dissolve, disperse, and repeat us" (ibid. 101).[13]

Self-dissolution, self-dispersal, and self-repetition: the Grindr user that ogles the kaleidoscope of portraits and body parts while cruising online certainly might experience such sensations. Adrift in a sea of resemblance and difference, lost in a spectacle of others "like me" but distinct in their virtual frames, the self recognizes itself as one of hundreds, thousands, seeking connection. Although the tendency toward Swann-like ego-aggrandizement is palpable here, might this platform also encourage a self-subtraction, a process of humiliation through which one discovers, à la Bersani, the ontological porosity of subjecthood? Wishful thinking, perhaps. But, as I've been implying, in the experience of self-aestheticization, an aestheticization voluntarily performed and shared, one might discover ways of relating founded not on ego-projection, assimilative identification, or defensive differentiation. Instead, through self- and other-objectification, we might develop an indifference to difference that is, counterintuitively, deeply respectful of another's otherness insofar as it is less invasive and controlling.[14] Again following Bersani, whereas the study of art teaches us

---

13. Shannon Winnubst and Jodi Dean argue the opposite: in the neoliberal context aesthetic subjectivation does not open up a space for ethics. For Winnubst, "aesthetics displace ethics as the final arbiter of value" in neoliberalism ("Queer Thing" 87). From this perspective, the self-aestheticization of the sort we see in m4m media is merely another instance of neoliberal accessorizing and self-optimization. While both Winnubst's and Dean's work on neoliberalism have been instrumental to this project, I part ways with them in terms of conceiving other-than-neoliberal subjectivities, relations, and practices. On a fundamental, ontological level, we begin thinking our way through neoliberal relationality in different places: myself, in immanentist conceptions of a heterogeneous sameness; Dean and Winnubst, in psychoanalytic, dialectical understandings of difference.

14. Here, I am essentially rephrasing Goldberg's argument about m4m media in "Meet Markets." "[A]n openness to otherness," he writes, "can be established and maintained through objectification, an approach to relations that is categorically indifferent to and therefore 'respectful' of others' desires and pleasures" (2).

about the correspondence of heterogeneous forms in a universal solidarity, cruising for sex reduces the self to an impersonal rhythm of sociability. For cruising, if anything, is not about personal investment, attachment, or possessiveness. Rather, it is a scattering of the self among superficial acquaintances or strangers. Cruising, in Bersani's conceptualization, puts one in step with the most impersonal of ecological, and even cosmic, rhythms and forces (magnetism, for one) and prompts feelings of "placed-ness" in the world. By this logic, the mingling that occurs in m4m media, the flittering among aestheticized avatar-objects, moves to a music that exceeds the ebb and flow of individualized desire. Aesthetic subjectivation and impersonal sociability, which Bersani values, respectively, as a practice of self-subtraction and an education in respecting difference, merge in the experience of digital cruising. It is the form and movement of this experience that I am designating connection-as-such.

In brief, connection-as-such is the experience of the objectified, divested self becoming pure extension in the online cruising context. From the self-abbreviation involved in profile setup to the distracted glances and ephemeral chats in the play, it is both form and rhythm: aestheticized selves circulating among like others in impersonal cadences. What interests me here is not a virtual "broadening of horizons" (conceived as becoming cosmopolitan or experimenting with new personas), but instead a double movement that might occur in these forums: a centripetal whittling of the self and a consequent centrifugal extension. On Grindr, for example, users are encouraged to identify with a "tribe" (bears, jocks, twinks), to empty themselves, essentially, into a generic type.[15] Dialogue occurs between figuratively, and frequently literally, headless subjects: fragmented and vacated types who mouth seemingly authorless scripts—jumbles of porn dialogue, hip-hop slang, and texting shorthand.[16] The appropriated language here belongs to the contemporary cultural milieu more than any particular individual or social group: one "slips imperceptibly" into a post-articulate discourse to connect with ventriloquial others. For the remainder of this chapter, I pursue the ethical and political potential of connection-as-such by focusing on two features of m4m digital cruising:

---

15. To date, there are twelve Grindr tribe classifications: Bear, Clean-Cut, Daddy, Discreet, Geek, Jock, Leather, Otter, Poz, Rugged, Trans, and Twink.

16. For more on m4m media discursive norms, see Ward, *Not Gay* 119–52.

first, the trafficking in types as opposed to identities, and second, free indirect discourse as a possible "circuit breaker," in the Deleuzian sense, in the neoliberalization of communication. In short, I attempt to answer the following question: If the dream of capital is to co-opt human affect and communication to the extent that we speak no other language, relate on no other terms, and feel nothing beyond that which the market commands, can connection-as-such orient objectified, consumerist, entrepreneurial subjects toward other-than-neoliberal ethical and political articulations?

Whatever Belonging

"To indulge some uncomfortably organic metaphors," Shannon Winnubst writes in "The Queer Thing about Neoliberal Pleasure: A Foucauldian Warning," "if sexuality is the heart and lifeblood of biopolitics, neoliberalism is its birth-mother" (79). While in my previous work I emphasize the integral role of sexuality in the formulation of biopower (*Friendship* 97–122), Winnubst, through a careful reading of Foucault's *Birth of Biopolitics* alongside his *History of Sexuality, Volume 1*, makes an intriguing case for the complementary ("maternal") role neoliberalism plays in this development. As a psychobiographical hermeneutic, so Foucault's story goes, sexuality works to discipline subjects through normalizing discourses concerning health, population, and security. Caught up in the historical sweep of post-normative neoliberalism, however, sexual identity becomes increasingly irrelevant. The sexual self is supplanted by the neoliberal "subject of interest" for whom questions of anthropological interiority matter less than those concerning success, optimization, and maximal profitability (86). The result of this shift, for Winnubst, is the subsumption of ethics into aesthetics. When the market becomes the site of ethical veridiction, right/wrong transcodes to success/failure and the "good life" is achieved through superficial self-fashioning via the accumulation of both financial and characterological interest(s). Winnubst insists: "Neoliberal practices embed us in a mode of rationality that cannot hail us with any normative force: as neoliberals we cannot think ethics" (88).

If Winnubst finds these neoliberal times ethically bankrupt, Dilts locates an ethical opportunity amid the bleakness. If the subject is no longer held captive to a disciplining interiority, if the subject is simply an assemblage of practices and choices, it might, Dilts argues, modulate the rules of the neoliberal game to develop critical practices of self-care.[17] In "'Entrepreneur of the Self' to 'Care of the Self': Neoliberal Govern- mentality and Foucault's Ethics," Dilts is careful not to promote a specific liberatory program that transcends the ethical wasteland of neoliberalism. For him, ethics begins with a critical response to neoliberalism from within neoliberalism. The ethical neoliberal subject, like the entrepreneur, fashions a "lifestyle," but does so with a self-conscious understanding of "the rules of the truth game as a game" (144). For Dilts, critical thinking offers an ethical opening—and quite a convenient one for a critical the- orist. Although sympathetic to his attempt to locate an ethical horizon within neoliberalism, I am left wondering about other ways one might learn that neoliberal concepts of freedom, choice, and the "good life" are empty promises. Reading Foucault is one method, perhaps, but are there other forms less intentional and rational, less "consciousness-raising"? Might the simulated pleasures and humiliations of online cruising move the neoliberal subject—unconsciously, affectively—toward ethical practices of self-fashioning, communicating, and relating? In short, might the aes- thetic experience of becoming fungible afford a view of an ethical horizon beyond neoliberalism?

Although the types that populate the m4m online cruising arena— the twink, the jock, the bear, the leather man—emerge from a history shot through with racism and misogyny,[18] it is their very fungibility as

---

17. Winnubst is not persuaded by Dilts's claim here because, as noted, she believes ethics has been absolutely subsumed by aesthetics in the neoliberal context. Anti-neoliberal strategies that rely on aestheticization or a stylization of self-care hold little promise. Winnubst argues instead that a properly historicized under- standing of *jouissance* might be a point of resistance to neoliberal rationality, specifically, the rationality of fungibility. Because *jouissance* is a limit-experience that "radically disarms the self, not the identity-confirming, self-enhancing domes- ticated pleasure that saturates neoliberal culture" ("The Queer Thing" 96–97), the experience is nonfungible, unsubstitutable. By contrast, I find fungibility itself ambivalent: just as, for Virno, belonging-as-such might be put to work in the service of revolutionary goals, fungibility could serve as an immanent strategy for modulating neoliberal relationality toward other-than-neoliberal ends.

18. For a discussion of the misogyny of the "not gay" type as well as the masculinist hetero-eroticism of m4m forums, see Ward, *Not Gay* 1–50. For a discussion of racist stereotyping in online m4m cruising forums, see Rodriguez, "This Is What It's Like to Log onto Grindr as a Person of Color."

superficial types, not unique interiorities, that I find intriguing. Fungibility, according to Winnubst, plays a more crucial role than exchange in neoliberal economies, becoming "the singular barometer" of social value. She writes: "To be fungible is to have all character and content hollowed out. It is a relationship of equity that requires purely formal semblance. In economic terms, fungibility refers to those goods and products on the market that are substitutable for each other. [. . .] This is different from exchangeable goods, which must be related to a common standard (such as money) in order to judge their differing or similar values" (92).

Seeking a nonfungible site of queer pleasure/resistance that might confound the calculating logic of neoliberalism, Winnubst puts stock in a thoroughly historicized concept of *jouissance*, "to engage it as a way to intervene in the rationality of fungibility" (96). While this strategy is quite logical and tactical—exemplifying in some ways what Foucault calls "reverse discourse," in this case, seeking a nonfungible point of resistance in a world that values fungibility—I contend that relations and interobjective exchanges based *in* fungibility harbor ethical potential. Specifically, the practice of trafficking in substitutable types on m4m media holds the capacity to set off on other-than-neoliberal trajectories. The transposition of interiority to surface in these forums, the delinking of erotic desire from sexual identity—the latter, for Foucault, a tactic marking an exodus from biopolitical management (Roach, *Friendship* 123–44)—can be understood as the striving toward what I designate "whatever belonging": the affirmation of an impersonal heterogeneous sameness in the gathering of nonidentitarian types. The "whatever" to which I refer here, and which I adapt from Giorgio Agamben's notion of "whatever being,"[19] denotes a common asubjective substance that finds expression in variegated modes. "Whatever" is that which seethes beneath social identity, seeking to locate its place in the world and assemble singularities in anti-identitarian collections.[20]

---

19. See Agamben, 1–4; for an elaboration on the political viability of this concept, see Roach, *Friendship* 149–51.

20. Bersani also helps envision what I am calling whatever belonging. His clearest, and quite beautifully rendered, articulation of an antisocial collective assemblage grounded in sameness appears in *Homos*: "[W]e move irresponsibly among other bodies, somewhat indifferent to them, demanding nothing more than that they be as available to contact as we are, and that, no longer owned by others, they also renounce self-ownership and agree to that loss of boundaries which will allow them to be, with us, shifting points of rest in a mobile communication of being" (128).

To clarify the connection between m4m media and whatever belonging, I propose a visual analogy. As discussed in previous chapters, the profile grid of many geosocial hookup apps is composed of distinct blocks: an expanded grid of tic-tac-toe, but with photographs of faces and body parts instead of Xs and Os. Although the variety and distinctness of the individual profiles are noteworthy, the grid creates the optical effect of flattening profile pictures into a homogeneous, somewhat Borg-like cube, each unit being merely a facet of a larger whole wherein difference evaporates in similitude. The profiles, moreover, come to resemble one another in their conformity with dominant cultural figures and archetypes: the beefcake flexing as if a cover model for *Men's Fitness*; the bear doing his best Paul Bunyan impersonation; the twink posing like a supermodel; the jock/bro displaying his allegiance to whatever sports team; the boy-next-door, often admittedly an "average guy," devoid of any specifically gay cultural signifiers, fueling hetero-erotic conversion fantasies. All of it obviously borrowed, banal, willful reversions to types. Although Grindr emphasizes the internationalism and multicultural diversity of its users (*Kindr*), its original profile grid, the standard for m4m apps, seems to have more in common with Andy Warhol's soup cans than with any imagined "global village." This is precisely what makes it interesting. (See figures 5.1, 5.2, and 5.3.)

As literally objectifying as this analogy may seem, the Warhol print envisages the form of whatever belonging: difference becomes similar yet remains discreet; units "touch" but do not violate; similitude dissolves individuality, yet singularity remains intact; relating is not a Venn diagram but bounded. The constituent parts of this assemblage have everything and nothing in common. They cohere for an instant purely in the form and movement of their connectivity. During that time, they are mere pieces of an aesthetic collection.

Screen-based media are widely criticized for desensitizing users to real-world horrors: video games desensitize players to violence; porn desensitizes viewers to misogyny and sexual abuse; social media desensitize users to others' feelings, resulting in cyberbullying and moblike public shaming. I assert, by contrast, that becoming a piece of a Warhol-esque collection of aestheticized avatar-objects on m4m media activates the mimetic force and thereby *sensitizes* users to perceive sameness. Because Grindr users are forced to squeeze their complex selves into little boxes that "all look just the same," as Malvina Reynolds might put it,[21] they are

---

21. Here I am referencing her hit song, "Little Boxes," which critiques the social conformity rampant in post-WWII American life.

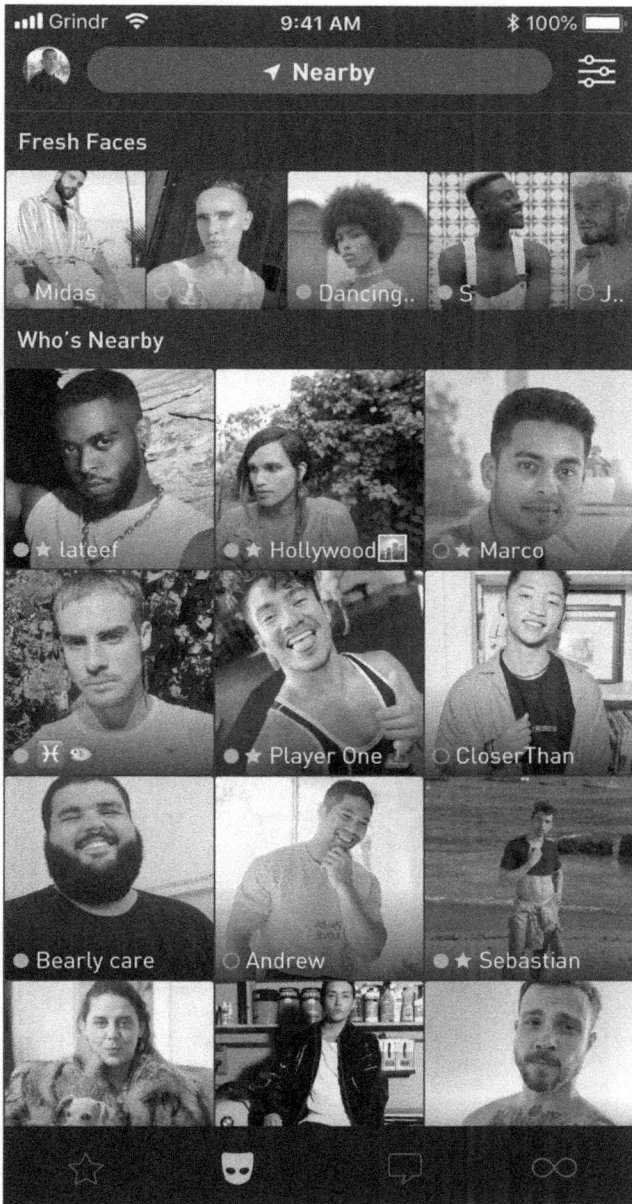

Figure 5.1. Grindr promotional image (2020) emphasizing the cultural, racial, and gender diversity of its users. The interface featured in this advertisement deviates from Grindr's original grid layout of user profile pictures because it features "Fresh Faces," a selection of new user profiles that can be left-right swiped.

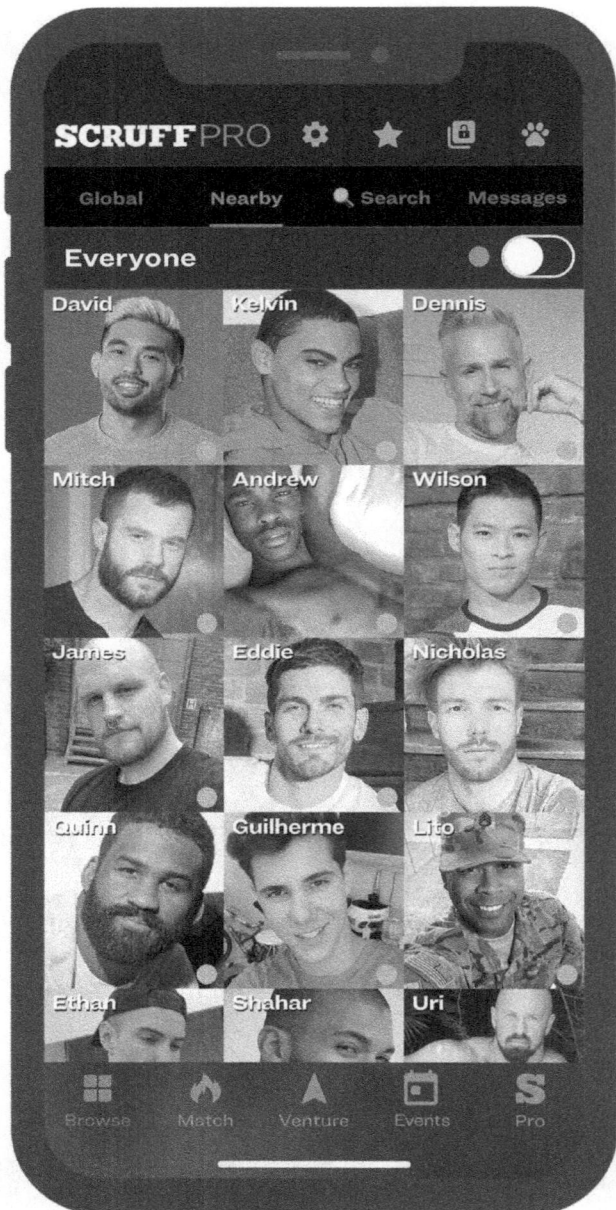

Figure 5.2. Scruff promotional image (2020) also emphasizes the cultural and racial diversity of its users. Unlike Grindr, however, Scruff highlights the cisgender-maleness of its clientele. The interface featured in this advertisement better represents the classic grid layout of profile pictures that Grindr introduced.

Figure 5.3. The original Grindr grid interface, best represented by Scruff's promotional image here, bears resemblance to Andy Warhol's *100 Cans* (1962).

visually compelled to recognize likenesses among socially differentiated others. Although these users are so often critiqued for their conformist adherence to dominant gender norms and for their allegiance to the sartorial, gestural, and embodied norms of the gay male "tribe" with which they identify, such conformity empties users of their individuality and flattens them into generic types. Whether or not these types correspond with one another, they nonetheless comprise an aesthetic collection that visually emphasizes commonness and resemblance. "Resemblance, or 'acting alike,'" Jonathan Flatley argues, "implies a relation of mutuality and enacts a shared being-in-common, a 'we-centricity,' that has been seen as the basic element of emotional connection, even affectivity itself, more generally" ("Like" 74). Citing neuroscientific studies on mirror neurons, Flatley contends that our compulsion to be like others, to mimic and impersonate, trumps any desire to stand out as individuals. Being alike and finding likenesses, moreover, prepare us for liking and being liked: for opening ourselves to another's affections. In their very form, then, m4m media feed an ontological mimetic force and help it flourish. By signing up, users agree to become like others—aestheticized, digitized, divested—and this sets the stage for liking others. Akin to the way that Swann makes Odette likable by transforming her into Zipporah, users prep themselves for liking and "likenessing" via an aesthetic mediation that awakens both the mimetic faculty and the pleasures of connective self-extension. The pieces in this visual collection are not the same, but they are similar; they are not treated equally, but they are functionally equivalent. As bounded objects, they relate in a manner that respects personal boundaries—the photographic frame surrounding each profile pic in the grid becomes a visual metaphor for a nonviolative, interobjective touch. Moreover, because revealing "too much information" about one's interior life or probing another's "personal space" are normative no-nos here, one's own and another's otherness is respected. In short, becoming fungible seekers of corresponding forms in a ceaselessly changing space of commonality attunes us to the political potentialities of serial likenesses and excessive liking.

Flatley analyzes the life and work of Warhol to flesh out a politics of mimesis. For example, at the heart of Warhol's promiscuous collecting habits—his practice of creating likenesses between things and people and gathering them in assemblages (everything from the famous soup cans to the less-celebrated cock books and Sex Parts series)—Flatley discovers "commonism": not merely the leveling of cultural taste hierarchies for which pop art is renowned, but a political vision that "replaces the opposition between capitalism and communism" (ibid.) because it is so reliant on elements of both systems. Commonism entails "creating spheres of likeness, realms of practice, perception, and affect that can be held in common" (ibid.), and Warhol's collecting practice rests on an indiscriminate desire to make everything at once familiar and foreign: everything becomes, to use a word Warhol certainly liked, "interesting." Gathering disparate things under a categorical rubric orients us to appreciate objects anew, to discover new connections among them, and to search for new additions to our collections. It encourages an openness to the world, its objects, and its others that undercuts normative identitarian barriers. Although it would seem that the uniqueness of each collectible diminishes when situated among like objects, that is, when the unique object becomes genericized, to the contrary, singularity is highlighted in a collection. In Warhol's screen prints of serialized objects and people, for example, each component is unique in its imperfections: a blurred line, a smeared patch of color, a blank space. Serialized people and objects are distinct insofar as they stray from the collection's representational norms or the extent to which they fail to accurately replicate the archetype to which they refer. Importantly, every replication in a Warholian series succeeds at failing to be both the real and the ideal; they all "misfit together," and this is the constitutive ground of their being-in-common (92–93). As a political theory, then, commonism conceptualizes a citizenry as an assemblage of serial singularities: inasmuch as they deviate from their categorical sameness and in their particular style of failing to fit, they are distinct. They are united in their inability to be identical and ideal, and yet, because of this, they cannot be unified. The space of nonrelation between them is the constituent ground of their assemblage (94–95).[22]

Foucault also explores the radical possibilities of "misfitting together" in his analysis of Magritte's most famous work, *The Treachery of Images* (see figure 5.4). What intrigues Foucault about this painting is that the words "*Ceci n'est pas une pipe*," enter into an uncertain relationship with the figure of a pipe, and that the two ultimately share no common ground save their "misfittingness." In the painting, neither word nor thing refers

---

22. For more on the space of nonrelation between singularities, see Ricco.

Figure 5.4. René Magritte, *La Trahison des images (Ceci n'est pas une pipe)*. [*The Treachery of Images (This is Not a Pipe)*], 1929.

to the conceptual model they supposedly designate. Rather, both exist as their own models: they resemble only themselves, refer only to themselves, and represent nothing. Foucault designates the empty region between Magritte's text and image a "crevasse," an "effacement of the 'common place' between signs of writing and the lines of image" (*This Is Not* 28–29). This crevasse is a site of nonrelation: words do not speak for or stand in for things and vice versa. Like the forcefield balancing Lawrence's lovers in a star-equilibrium, like the frames that bind and separate the serial singularities of Warhol's grids, this is a space of disconnected connection.

Foucault argues that two principles dominate Western painting from the fifteenth to the twentieth centuries: (a) the separation between plastic representation and linguistic reference; and (b) the equivalence between the fact of resemblance and the affirmation of the representative bond. He asserts that in classical works "verbal signs and visual representations are never given at once" (33), that a hierarchy between text and image always exists: either the image (which implies resemblance) subordinates the text (which excludes resemblance) or vice versa. Modern artists such as Paul

Klee abolish this principle by juxtaposing representational shapes (boats, buildings, landscapes) with linguistic signs (letters, words) in a single work. Like Magritte, Klee destabilizes the connection between words and things and ultimately declares painting's autonomy from textual discourse and representational reality. Similarly, the implicit command within classical paintings that "what you see is that"—i.e., that the painted image unproblematically represents the essence of an object or figure—is refuted by abstract artist Wassily Kandinsky. In painting lines, objects, and color fields that only refer to the gestures that form them—the act of painting itself—Kandinsky dissociates resemblance and affirmation, and thus ruptures the transparent relation between language/signs and reality (36–42).

Magritte complements yet one-ups the modernist provocations of Klee and Kandinsky. Though Magritte's paintings deploy largely familiar images "wedded to exact resemblances" (35), Foucault contends that Magritte uses literalism to undermine the laws of representation. Incorporating both resemblances and linguistic signs within his paintings—signs which often call into question the transparency of representation—Magritte opens a network of similitudes that play with the classical equivalence between resemblance and affirmation, producing "an art of the Same, liberated from the 'as if' " (43). Foucault distinguishes resemblance from similitude to gauge what we might anachronistically call the queer antisocial possibilities manifest in Magritte's work. While resemblance "presupposes a primary reference that prescribes and classes" (44), similitude erases the notion of an original, unmoors representation, and forges lateral, as opposed to vertical, relations. "The similar develops in series that have neither beginning nor end, that can be followed in one direction as easily in another, that obey no hierarchy, but propagate themselves from small differences among small differences. Resemblance serves representation which rules over it; similitude serves repetition, which ranges across it" (ibid.). What is most disconcerting about Magritte's paintings, then, is neither that they meld incongruous images (e.g., *L'explication* in which a wine bottle metamorphoses into a carrot; *La philosophie dans le boudoir* in which articles of clothing merge with female body parts) nor that they produce contradictory statements. What is most radical is that they resist the order and categorizations that are imposed upon them by dominant, "sensible" discursive frameworks of intelligibility. Commenting on the instability of discursive categorizations themselves in *The Order of Things*, Foucault writes: "[T]here is a worse kind of disorder than the incongruous [. . .] I mean the disorder in which fragments of a large number of possible orders glitter separately in the dimension, without law or geometry, of the heteroclite [. . .] [I]n such a state things are 'laid,' 'placed,' 'arranged' in sites so very different from one another that it is impossible to find a place of residence for them, to define a common locus beneath them all" (xvii–iii).

The social and political implications of this "dimension of the heteroclite" are profound. Only in a site "without law or geometry" in which it is impossible "to define a common locus beneath" singular constituents, does it become *possible* to dream up new orders, categorizations, and, indeed, forms of collecting and relating. Such dreams "glitter" with the promise of a queer sociality not founded on liberal-humanist conceptions of belonging and community. If there is no common ground between constituents, if the crevasse between one and another is a site of non-relation, the (Habermasian) public sphere, the deliberative democratic process, and representational democracy itself are lost causes: all of these depend on fictitious models of representation and intersubjective relations grounded in dialectics. Magritte, by contrast, opens a window onto a world in which perfect, monadic singularities exist on a level plane and relate to one another laterally. Because there is no model or original to which they aspire, there is no hierarchy regarding good, better, or best copy. Because there is no evaluative hierarchy, these singularities relate first and foremost as "similars": they are disinterested in probing the differences between them, be they in shape, form, or identity. These parts relate in a noninvasive manner. They extend themselves outward to touch one another, but refuse to claim knowledge of or to speak for one another: difference is thus preserved. "A day will come," Foucault predicts, "when, by means of similitude relayed indefinitely along the length of a series, the image itself, along with the name it bears, will lose its identity" (54). Mining the crevasse for its heterotopic potential, Foucault welcomes the multiplication of nonidentical similitudes and seems to long for their transformation into nonidentitarian assemblages. Fittingly, the last four words of his essay on Magritte are a clear reference to Warhol: "Campbell, Campbell, Campbell, Campbell" (54).

This is all to say that I believe both Warhol and Foucault would be quite intrigued with Grindr. Nurturing the mimetic force and operating according to a logic of serial similitude, Grindr assembles users into an aesthetic collection that renders them functionally equivalent and encourages a form of connection that "can be followed in one direction as easily in another." So as not to belabor my point about the connections between Warhol's commonism, Foucault's concept of the crevasse, and the Grindr grid, I turn now to an analysis of the post-articulate discursive norms of m4m media. With an understanding of the antisocial, nonrelational terms of the Grindr assemblage, the language of seeking in this context can be understood as an attempt to articulate a discourse of whatever belonging.

The monosyllabic, often grunt-like propositions and rejoinders traversing online cruising forums, hardly expressions revealing interior states or personal histories, signal weariness with two currently dominant discursive forms: a discourse of transparency so valued in neoliberal communication, and a confessional discourse foundational to the invention and deployment of sexuality.[23] Although comparable to, perhaps deriving from, the businessman's pitch that works to "seal the deal" as efficiently as possible, the often brutally honest exchanges in cruising forums might also be read as a rejection of both the "good communication skills" extolled in the workplace and the tell-all imperatives of gay identity politics. If twenty-first-century capitalism values team building based in clear written and verbal expression, digital cruising forums, in all of their inarticulateness, reveal disenchantment with this skill set. The forced social niceties of the business world are typically absent here: affects are not instrumentalized into "service with a smile" but permitted to take alternative forms; competitive resentments are not sublimated in "cooperative innovation" but are put, sometimes disarmingly, on display. Indeed, it takes a thick skin, an armor with little or nothing in the way of subjective interiority beneath it, to negotiate this terrain. But rather than bemoaning the death of eloquence, moralizing about the barbaric rudeness of "kids these days," or finding in the discourse of online cruising only more evidence of capitalism's triumph over all aspects of human sociality, we might also discover in this discourse an attempt to invent a language not yet captured by capital, a pared-down and context-based discourse that undercuts or brushes up against the obligatory transparency and expressivity of communicative capitalism. For creating a personal, marketable brand is an arduous and never-ending task: optimizing the self by choosing "interesting" hobbies,

23. For more on a neoliberal discourse of transparency, see Read. For more on confession and the invention of sexuality, see Foucault, *HoS Vol. 1* as well as my elaboration of Foucault's insights in the next chapter.

maintaining an employer-friendly online presence, being in touch with and expressing appropriately one's feelings—all of it requires an enormous expenditure of time and energy. Put frankly, it seems that even the most networked of people, those supposedly screen-crazy Millennials and Gen Zers, are growing tired of the laborious image management and expressive transparency required of platforms like Facebook.[24] For a life in which leisure means only more labor is hardly an ideal life. Thus, both the inarticulacy witnessed in online cruising forums and the increasingly pared-down forms of dialogue in context-based apps might signal an unwillingness to play by communicative capitalism's rules of discursive transparency and clear expression. With any luck, they might also be the rudiments of that "circuit breaker" Deleuze urged us to create.

In "Rejecting Friendship: Toward a Radical Reading of Derrida's *Politics of Friendship* for Today," Irving Goh likewise seeks a relational language beyond the contemporary communicative norms of the knowledge-based economy. For him, however, social media are the last place one might find it: networked friendship not only holds no promise for a new ethics but poses a primary obstacle to it. The networked friend, according to Goh, accumulates contacts as a hoarder does merchandise. He or she only friends others if they share cultural interests or acquaintances; he or she avoids "truly knowing" another by keeping conversational topics and inquiries as superficial as possible (97). The nonsensical blather and, in Goh's words, "hyper-gregariousness" of social media produce a form of friendship that is always and only complicit in the capitalist cooptation of communication. In Goh's words: "The 'concept' of friendship proclaimed by digital social networks, then, is no less corrupt than the mode of communicative sociability that Deleuze analyzed in the late '80s and early '90s. And users of contemporary social networks, caught up in, or bought into the friendship archive fever and the ecstasy of hyper-gregariousness that

---

24. A September 2018 Pew research survey found that 44 percent of Facebook users between the ages of eighteen and twenty-nine "say they have deleted the Facebook app from their phone in the past year, nearly four times the share of users ages 65 and older (12%) who have done so" (Perrin). Massive privacy breeches and unethical use of personal data certainly have something to do with Millennials and Gen Zers ditching Facebook, but one can't help but wonder if a weariness with the labor of image management and expressive transparency also play a role in this Facebook exodus.

digital social networks offer, are equally complicit in sustaining capitalist ideology and its network apparatuses" (96). Goh's rejection of friendship, then, begins with a specific rejection of networked friendship and the utterly commodified, communicative forms through which it materializes. His quite compelling alternative to these debased forms originates in an "anti-gregarious solitariness," the likes of which Nietzsche theorized as the foundation of friendship, that might blossom into relations that, among other things, evade capitalist capture (98). However, because Goh conflates all forms of social media into one monstrous entity (forgivable, given the dizzyingly fast pace at which such media develop), he overlooks what I have been designating the impersonal ethical possibilities emergent in m4m media. In this context, online presence is not a direct expression of an individual's "inner self" that one can "truly know," but rather a highly mediated aestheticization of that self seeking connection in similitude. Understanding, then, the desubjectified subject of m4m social media and the confounding subject-position from which it speaks is the final step in articulating these ethical possibilities.

The chatting something (bot? marketer? horny human?) in the online cruising forum speaks in the register of free indirect discourse. This rhetorical form makes the subject of an utterance mysterious: the speaker's words occupy a middle ground between author and character. Martin Jay describes the event of free indirect discourse as "an experience without a subject: one is never quite certain of who exactly is saying what, if that 'who' is sincere, interested, or simply having a laugh" (qtd. in Hillis, 154). Compounded by the fact that profile photos are often direct references to cultural types and that online cruising repartee seems more the property of whatever cultural milieu than any one person in particular, the words expressing intention and motivation in m4m forums must be parsed both for sincerity and source: not only "Is that someone speaking to me sincere?" but, even more perplexing, "Who exactly is the subject of these incomplete sentences?"

Free indirect discourse became a cause célèbre in the 1857 obscenity trial of Gustave Flaubert's *Madame Bovary*. The conundrum posed by free indirect discourse, specifically the impossibility of knowing for certain the source and tone of statements, outraged France's moral and religious authorities. Dumbstruck by the novel's narrative style and scandalized by its content, these authoritarians forced Flaubert onto the stand precisely because they could not distinguish author from character. Was Flaubert condoning, even encouraging, Emma's adulterous behavior and sexual fantasies, or merely recording them?[25] Ken Hillis asserts that the actual "threat" of free indirect discourse in nineteenth-century France lay not in its capacity to promote an immoral sexual libertinism but in its pre-saging of a form of subjectivity unanswerable to industrial capitalism's then disciplinary norms. "Through its production of a middle voice," he writes, "free indirect discourse infers the truth of emerging forms of plural, hybrid or possibly even fragmented subjectivities ready to challenge, or at least unsettle, the idea of the unitary subject so central to Enlighten-ment principles, capital formation and the nation state" (151–52). That fragmented subjectivity, that flexible, mutating, multitasking self becomes, as we have seen, the Janus-faced entrepreneur/consumer of neoliberalism, the selfsame calculating agent that cruises online profiles. Hillis notes, however, that free indirect discourse in the virtual arena allows users "to give voice to something exceeding representation, to an emergent future and what is at the threshold of imagination and cannot yet be thought. [. . .] In this sense, the middle voice does not function as a disguise. [. . .] Instead, to reiterate, it may point to, 'speak' more of, the ineffable and constitute a nascent effort on the part of an author to symbolize or potentialize that which still remains virtual, incipient, not fully thought" (158). Free indirect discourse, the requisite discursive register of online cruising, thus affords the user the opportunity to articulate an unknown, embryonic "something exceeding representation." That something—emer-gent in the evanescent affects produced in connection-as-such, striven for in the ephemeral and post-articulate chattering of subjectless speak-ers—can be understood as the blueprint for a collective form beyond the

---

25. The following excerpt from *Madame Bovary*, which moves from a report of Emma's adulterous thoughts to an authorially ambivalent statement concerning adultery, was particularly scrutinized during the trial: "She repeated: 'I have a lover! A lover!' delighting at the idea as if a second puberty had come to her. So at last she was to know those joys of love, that fever of happiness of which she had despaired! She was entering upon a marvelous world where all would be passion, ecstasy, delirium" (quoted in Hillis, 154). Lacking the contextual phrase "she repeated," the latter sentences position readers in a space in which it is unclear whether the thrill prompted by adultery belongs to Emma, the narrator, or the author. For more on the trial in relation to free indirect discourse, see Hillis, 152–56, and Huffer, 33–34.

scope of neoliberal relationality: a collection founded on the principle of whatever belonging.

The desire for whatever belonging is nothing new: one can sense it in various encounters with queer cultural and intellectual history. Lynne Huffer locates this desire in Foucault's use of free indirect discourse in *The History of Sexuality, Volume 1*, in which "the radical disorientation of Foucault's headless sentences exposes the illusory stabilities of the present, the subject, and repressive sexuality" (38). In the work of a thinker so critical of the insidious effects of a psychobiographically conceived sexuality, Huffer finds a "self-releasing" style that holds the promise of outliving sexuality and potentially its kin, biopolitics and neoliberalism: "Outliving is our continually renewed encounter with the concrete traces of queer modes of belonging that exceed the oppositional logic of repression-liberation and the continuous ontology of biopolitical gradation" (40). The queer mode of belonging I have sketched in this chapter, a whatever belonging rooted in connection-as-such, resonates with the anti-intersubjective impersonal ethics emergent both in the anonymous public cruising rituals of the gay liberationist era and in the friendships of shared estrangement cultivated in the AIDS crisis. And while it remains perfectly sensible to condemn m4m media for anchoring us ever more firmly to the neoliberal present, for its service in commodifying once and for all human intimacy and affect, and for transforming us all, willingly or not, into "businessmen," sometimes it is necessary to probe the *nonsense* to locate the rudiments of whatever belonging, to discover an ambivalence that signals a desire for something more: alternative presents, other futures. In this regard, we might understand digital cruising as a contemporary site in which a queer ethics, long in the making, seeks to outgrow the present, outlive sexuality, and outsmart, or, perhaps, "outdumb," the maneuverings of neoliberal rationality.

Chapter Six

Shut Up! in the Digital Closet

The Age of Nonsense

It is difficult these days to believe in the power of rational argument, coherent speech, and logical consequence. In the "Age of Trump," as mainstream U.S. media have taken to calling it—thereby validating the troll-in-chief's megalomania—nonsense, inarticulacy, and bald-faced dishonesty prevail. The weight of history and the factuality of events or statements appear to matter little. To misquote, or at best misrepresent, Marx and Engels, "All that is solid melts into air" (476). Of course, Marx and Engels are not referring here to inauguration attendance numbers, the alleged millions of illegal American voters, fictional massacres, presidential wiretapping, or any of the other 2,140 falsehoods concocted, packaged, and tweeted by the Trump administration in its first year in office (Kessler and Kelly).[1] No, in this famous quip from the *Manifesto*, Marx and Engels praise, however backhandedly, the bourgeoisie's revolutionary capacity to obliterate both the instruments of production and social relations of an earlier industrial era. And though Marx and Marxism have seemingly been reduced to a footnote in the neoliberal rewriting of history, "all that is solid melts into air" resonates in Trump's pseudo-revolutionary and denialist nihilism, a force that lays waste

---

1. I began this chapter about a year and a half into the Trump presidency. As I make final edits, Trump's impeachment trial is underway. However changed the political landscape may be by the time this book is published, Trump's disdain for historical fact, reasoned debate, and material reality are indicative of what I'm referring to as the Age of Nonsense.

to claims grounded in the scientific method and humanities-based, critical analysis alike. Amplified in the social media vortex and shat out of alt-right news outlets, Trump's "alternative facts" gain traction and contribute to the destruction of the moderately progressive gains achieved during the Obama presidency—not to mention the destruction of the planet.

Nonetheless, U.S. news media would better serve the public by rebranding the "Age of Trump" with the catchier and farther-reaching "Age of Nonsense." This slogan more accurately designates a moment when facts and history dematerialize or mutate into magical reality, when reasoned argument fails, and when astute analysis competes for airtime with willfully ignorant claptrap. This age, of course, predates the political rise of the short-fingered man with the immoderately long and pathetically overcompensatingly phallic necktie. Number Forty-Five is at least in part the logical consequence of neoliberal *ressentiment* and despair, itself a result of massive income inequality, a news and social media culture that traffics in conspiracy theory and disinformation, systemic racism, and institutionalized misogyny, among other factors. Try as progressives might to counter Trump's bilious nonsense with nonalternative facts and investigative reports that reveal the emperor's nakedness, it is folly to wait for Hegel's heroic rational spirit to swoop in to right the wrongs of the world anytime soon. Indeed, the Trump problem cannot be countered with reason because an overvaluation of reason is part of the problem.

Gilles Deleuze's thoughts on the corruption of rational communication in contemporary control societies are here illuminative. As mentioned in the last chapter, communication is a principal commodity and a primary force of economic production in control societies. Education, the erstwhile training in rational thought, functions chiefly today as the accumulation of marketable skill sets. Although at first glance control societies seem more open—especially in contrast to disciplinary societies, which operate on the principle of confinement in spaces like factories, schools, barracks, and hospitals—the foremost technology in a control society is incessant monitoring. One's productivity, effectiveness, and health (i.e., human capital) must be known and evaluated so as to be optimized. Deleuze asserts that representational politics are compromised once communication is subsumed by capital. In "Control and Becoming," he counters Antonio Negri's techno-optimistic speculation that communism may be "less utopian" (i.e., more realistic) in a context in which new communication technologies permit individuals to "speak out and thereby recover a greater degree of freedom" (175). Deleuze responds: "You ask whether control or communication societies will lead to forms of resistance that might reopen the way for a communism understood as the 'transversal organization of free individuals.' Maybe, I don't know. But it would be nothing to do with minorities speaking out" (ibid.). He finishes his thought with the prescient words I quoted in the last chapter: "Maybe speech and communication have been corrupted. They're thoroughly permeated by money—and not by accident but by their very nature. We've got to hijack speech. Creating has always been something different from communicating. The key thing may be to create vacuoles of noncommunication, circuit breakers, so we can elude control" (ibid.).

To put it frankly, all the communicative freedom in the world cannot topple the billion-dollar industries—and lapdog governments—specifically invested in the commodification of communication. Gently squashing Negri's dream of a Marxian communicative communism, Deleuze makes clear here that resistance in the form of "speaking out"—specifically, the creation of a reverse discourse by minority groups, or, in the current political context, speaking truth to power via reasoned debate—is not the guarantor of greater freedoms in a control society. A liberatory politics grounded in resistant discourses will only go so far: like all systems of representation, language is inevitably commodified and corrupted; as in all dialectical struggles, reverse discourse is merely a stepping stone to future becomings (Roach, *Friendship* 63–77). Instead of investing in a discursive politics of representation, then, "eluding control" might involve the creation of sites of noncommunication, perhaps the creation of non-sensical communication, that work as "circuit breakers" in the capitalist consumption/subsumption of ideas. In other words, perhaps it is time again, or, at last, to heed David Byrne's directive from the Reagan 1980s: *Stop Making Sense*. Byrne is the lead singer and lyricist of the post-punk/rock group Talking Heads; *Stop Making Sense* (Demme) is the group's 1984 concert film. Given the political-economic context of the early '80s, the film's title, a command, is astute and prescient. Reagan's trickle-down economics and his gutting of the welfare state coupled with his celebrity spectacle, which carried more weight than his political experience or education, set the stage for the neoliberal tragedy. The film's title, then, can be interpreted as a clarion call to resist the neoliberal tendency to rationalize, quantify, and actuarialize—so as to commodify—all aspects of human life. Thirty-plus years later, diving into the wreck of neoliberalism, I find Byrne's command more relevant than ever. Trump's nonsense, and, by extension, the neoliberal commodification of communication, might best be negotiated, thwarted, and ultimately vanquished by "better" nonsense:

not a smarter nonsense per se, but a *sensual* nonsense that, however unwittingly and however ironically, might pave the way for an exodus from these nonsensical times.

By "sensual nonsense," I am referring to the haptic practice of cruising m4m media as well as the typically inarticulate, post-grammatical discourse circulating therein. Hunter Hargraves emphasizes the tactile sensuality of the iPhone in his dissertation chapter "iTouch Therefore iAm: The iPhone as Masturbation." He writes: "What I am envisioning here is a total explosion of tactile vision into a synthesis of hand/iPhone sexual contact: when hand and phone become inextricably tethered to each other, the iPhone becomes a masturbatory aid, a blurring of flesh and cellular technology that demands immediate gratification of both tactile and visual pleasure" (3). According to Hargraves, the sensual and masturbatory fusion of human/machine, enhanced by geosocial cruising apps, restructures queer social relations and communities (22). It is the *form* of this restructured, posthuman community and the discursive nonsense binding it that interest me most in this chapter.

One need only read the words of a Grindr spambot to ascertain the absurdity of a typical m4m media exchange. (See figure 6.1.) A spambot is malicious software designed to lure users to websites that infect phones with malware or steal personal information. Grindr has been plagued in recent years by spambots, what users call "Grindrbots," causing much frustration and at times defection from the app (McCormick). To clarify, a Grindrbot is only as effective as it is convincingly human; the moment a user realizes that a "conversation" is in fact a phishing scam is the moment the bot fails. Hence, "ive have a really nice dick broand i love showing it off" is a perfectly credible statement in m4m media, a statement that many would follow down the rabbit hole.

And yet precisely because of such laughable enticements and inarticulate gobbledygook geosocial m4m apps might be understood as Deleuzian "circuit-breakers." In the last chapter, I argued that the production of discursive nonsense in m4m media brushes against both the neoliberal commodification of communication and the reified, sexological classifications of sexual identity. Though dominated by transactional exchanges that would make any salesperson (or phisher) proud, the post-articulate call-and-response of m4m media counterintuitively eschews two hegemonic discursive forms: (1) the language of transparency so valued in corporate and governmental settings; and (2) a confessional discourse so necessary for the invention and perpetuation of modern sexuality. Indeed,

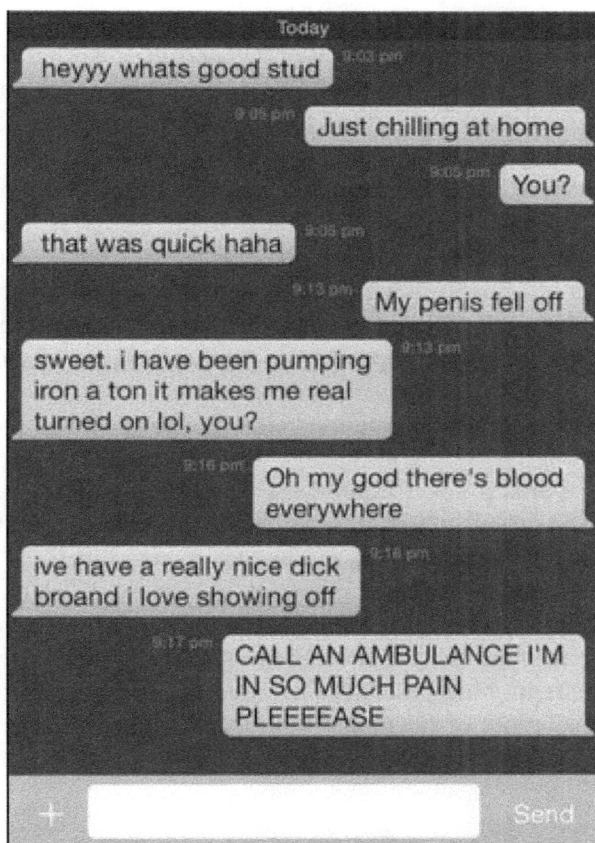

Figure 6.1. This Grindr user clearly recognizes a Grindrbot when he encounters one.

in the world of m4m hookup apps, the revelation of an interior life—emotions, intellect, eloquence—is more often than not a liability. Moreover, Grindr users are encouraged to identify not as unique individuals but as members of a "tribe" or type: bear, twink, daddy, jock. This subjective deferral de-emphasizes the psychic life of sexuality and arguably works to delink erotic desire from social identity: a link forged fundamentally through the confession "I'm gay." The type, then, serves as a mask, even a puppet, that deflects the significance and deep-seatedness of sexual desire. Users become ventriloquists of a sort, speaking not primarily of their personal histories or "deep thoughts" but rather the clichéd lexicons of the porn star, the bro, the businessman, or whatever tribe.

The logical conclusion of this anti-confessional and ventriloquial subjective deferral comes in the form of (my personal favorite) Grindr user "Emily Dickinson."[2] While the poet died over a century ago, her poetry is indeed immortal, thanks in part to a Grindr user who responds to potential suitors exclusively in Dickinsonian verse. (See figures 6.2, 6.3, and 6.4.)

The silliness of this performance not only brings levity to the typically transactional, often woefully banal m4m media scripts but also underscores the fact that there are no "people" on Grindr: everyone, in one way or another, is speaking through an avatar and negotiating discursive norms that mask selfhood. Be they the bluntest of porn-esque pickup lines or hetero-erotic slang ripped from hip-hop and sports cultures, the language of m4m media emanates from the broader cultural milieu more so than from any authentic, singular voice. In Grindr nation, then, we are all, to some degree, "Emily Dickinson."

In these final pages, I explore the ethical and political potential of m4m media's sensual nonsense, focusing on three main points: (1) the confession as the discursive crux of identitarian sexuality, itself the nexus of disciplinary and biopolitical power in modernity; (2) human capital trumping depth-psychological models of sexuality in neoliberalism and its influence in m4m media; and (3) the sublime digital closet of m4m media as a site in which users are afforded the opportunity to practice an impersonal ethics of fungibility that opens onto nondialectical, post-representational political imaginaries.

The Fantastical Confession

A final note of clarification: I do not believe m4m media are any sort of "training grounds" for a resistant politics. I understand resistance as a force intrinsic to dialectical struggle, ultimately subject to the discursive terms of that struggle. Without diminishing the importance of a politics of resistance—acting up, fighting back, and working to expand the scope of civil rights and political representation are perhaps more imperative than ever in the "Age of Trump"—I glimpse in m4m media a nascent, immanentist political project "growing sideways."

---

2. "Emily Dickinson" is not, in fact, the handle of the Grindr user who responds only in Emily Dickinson's verse. I chose this pseudonym in order to, as they say, "protect the innocent." An archive of Grindr texts from "Emily Dickinson" can be found at http://Grindrtextsfromemily.tumblr.com.

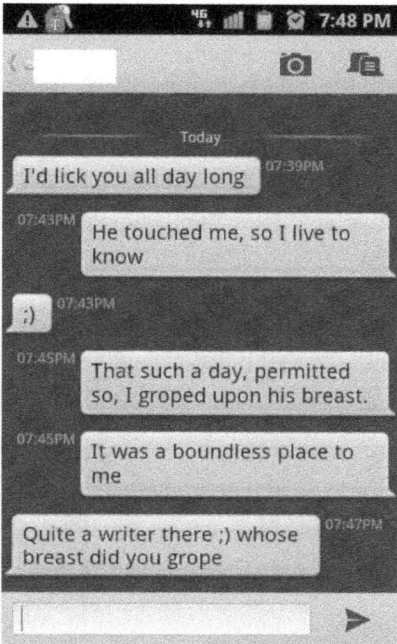

Figures 6.2, 6.3, and 6.4. "Emily Dickinson" chats with fellow Grindr users.

Resistant and immanentist political strategy are often counteractive yet coterminous. On the one hand, the struggle to legalize same-sex marriage in the U.S. can be understood as a resistant sexual-political project seeking to expand civil rights and political representation. On the other hand, friendships immanent to queer cultural formations, ones that breach boundaries of normative institutional and relational classification systems, erupt in cultural creations and innovative activisms that contribute to a perhaps farther-reaching political project beyond rights and representation. I see in these queer friendships, as I see in m4m media, the germ of a powerful politics: one that will not perforce blossom into resistance per se but one whose form and development are notable for "growing sideways" and potentially circumventing neoliberal logics. The concept, "growing sideways," appears in Kathryn Bond Stockton's book, *The Queer Child, or Growing Sideways in the Twentieth Century*, and concerns "a mode of irregular growth involving odd lingerings, wayward paths, and fertile delays" (back cover). In contrast to a resistant politics that works progressively and linearly towards a telos, m4m media grows sideways insofar as the virtual cruise is typically meandering, repetitive, circular, and unproductive—more of a thumb-twiddling time sink than a motivated, goal-oriented form of engagement. The sideways communicative and relational practices encouraged in these media—imperceptible or perhaps superfluous from the vantage point of a resistant politics—anticipate a queer erotics beyond the discursive frameworks of sexuality as we have come to know it. That said, a "post-sexual" erotics is by no means endemic to m4m media: any media born of and steeped in neoliberal logics might in the end affirm contemporary sexual and neoliberal paradigms. However, it is worth running the risk to think otherwise: to explore m4m media cruising as a form of sensual training for an antirepresentational, noncommunicative politics that seeks relational and ethical freedoms beyond those afforded in neoliberal control societies.

This exploration begins with the confession, a discursive rite historically inextricable from the conceptual implantation of a sexual essence in individuals and the population at large.[3] Foucault, of course, credited

---

3. To avoid rehashing an oft-told tale, I offer this quotation from my previous work, *Friendship*, summarizing the intrinsic link between confession and modern sexuality: "When in the nineteenth century sexuality was constituted as a problem of truth, the confession became the lynchpin between sexuality and truth, the discursive rite that provided the subject a knowable, manageable self. Historically

this "perverse implantation" to a *scientia sexualis* that secured a link between sexual desire and subjective truth. Forged primarily by forcing sex to speak through confession, this link becomes paramount in the functioning of modern biopolitics (Roach, *Friendship* 78–80). Throughout his late interviews, Foucault repeatedly, almost polemically, instructs readers to distrust this link. He counsels against investing in a concept of sexuality created to substantiate, and thereby manage, bodies and pleasures. In terms of sexual politics, the declaration of one's truth via the sexual confession—for example, coming out—not only validates but arguably celebrates the imprisonment of erotic desire in a marked subject and a manageable demographic. A political project erected on the basis of the sexual confession is at best a reactive and quite limited strategy because it remains ensnared within a rigged discursive/dialectical struggle set in motion by biopolitical administrates. As an alternative, Foucault suggests that a creative exodus from biopolitical administration begins with the severance of the link between sexual desire and self-truth. In his lived friendships, work, and politics, he strove to prompt such an exodus by, among other things, minimizing the psychological and identitarian significance of sexual desire and avoiding the confessional register altogether (ibid. 17–42).

Unfortunately, despite the valiant efforts of gender studies and queer theory professors worldwide, the belief that humans are born with a core, intractable sexual orientation—one invested with enormous identitarian and social significance—has gained in popularity since the publication of Foucault's seminal work.[4] Aided by mainstream LGBTQ political efforts, the work of the *scientia sexualis* is indeed implanted, perhaps more firmly than ever, into the psyches, laws, and censuses of the U.S. citizenry. No matter

---

rooted in the Christian pastoral, the ritual has become so familiar in modern Western life that 'we no longer perceive it as the effect of a power that constrains us' (Foucault *HoS Vol. 1* 60). We view confessions instead as liberatory, redeeming, and purifying rather than as systems of regulation and surveillance" (21). I understand the anticonfessional register typical of m4m media as antagonistic to a modern (homo)sexual identity grounded in a confession.

4. Jane Ward notes, "The number of Americans who believe that sexual orientation is biologically determined has been steadily increasing from 13 percent in 1977, to 31 percent in 1998, to 52 percent in 2010" (*Not Gay* 83). For more current information on American beliefs in biologically determined sexual orientation, see Jones.

how often we stray from our sexual "home" via drunken, experimental, or ritualized homosocial behavior, all too many of us remain confident that a solid foundation—a biological substructure of genes, hormones, and chromosomes—grounds the frisky sexual self. Especially for dominant social groups, being "born this way" is a comforting, even liberating fact.

In *Not Gay: Sex between Straight White Men*, Jane Ward notes that medical/scientific conceptions of sexuality, both past and present, grant straight-identified white men more than a few queer freedoms. Confident in the biological certainty that they are "not gay," men create elaborate rituals (fraternity hazing, military "bonding," *Jackass*-style tomfoolery) to touch one another. Outrageous rationalizations, frequently backed by the medical/psychiatric community, follow: the *unheimlich* behavior is justified as circumstantial (in prison, for example), homosocial (in the frat house and barracks), or pure accident (intoxication). Through it all, not-gay men remain devoted to both a stigma-free heterosexual identity and a hetero-normative politics frequently peppered with homophobia, misogyny, and racism. In this mindset, the social identity of heterosexuality is achieved not necessarily through heterosexual practice but by declaring loyalty to a white, heteronormative politics. Because the desire for "normalcy" is so strong, Ward argues that heteronormativity is itself a socially constructed *erotic* desire. She writes: "The investment in heteronormativity is itself a *bodily desire*; in fact, I believe it is *the* embodied heterosexual desire [. . .] It is the desire to be sexually unmarked and normatively gendered. It is a desire that people may well feel in their genitals" (*Not Gay* 35). The bod-ily desire for heteronormativity need not find fulfillment in heterosexual sex. So long as not-gay men remain faithful to white heteronormative politics, and so long as out gays continue to validate the deep-seatedness and identitarian significance of all sexualities, straight white men can do what they please with their bodies and remain politically and socially in the driver's seat.

Compounding the irony, in the age of "born this way" sexuality, "gay love" comes to emblematize ideal, romantic love. In what might cynically be deemed just deserts, the conjugal gay couple is held captive in a house of its own making. This unexpected plot twist is one consequence of same-sex marriage legalization: "love wins" only when it is domesticated, dyadic, and nuptial. Marriage becomes the compulsory telos of all romantic love, and the new poster children for this toxic myth are those fresh-from-their-honeymoon (white) husbands. The upshot of the bait-and-switch is that queer sex is appropriated by straights, rebranded as heteroflexibility

for white women and "str8 dude sex" for white men,[5] and queer public
cultural spaces become playgrounds for bachelorette parties and (often
barely) gay-friendly bros. The script, at its best, goes something like this:
"I'm straight, but I totally support gay rights and marriage. You guys are
a cute couple; you should definitely get married. Now move aside and
allow me to invade your bars, co-opt your sex practices, and colonize your
culture. You can stick around to provide style advice and entertainment."

In sum, the popular notion that there exist authentic gays—those
born with a homosexual essence—works to the benefit of straight white
male hegemony and hetero-/homonormative politics. Coming out as gay,
consequently, is not necessarily an antinormative or countercultural act
insofar as it is consistent with the sexual logic serving the status quo.[6]
For this reason, Ward places a great deal of emphasis on the current
importance of cultivating a queer *political* identity. She writes:

> Certainly to imagine that queerness is an option for all people—
> to consider that anyone could, technically, choose to get off
> the tired, beaten path of heterosexuality or homonormativity
> and relocate him- or herself among the freaks and perverts,
> among the leather daddies and fat dykes in San Francisco rav-
> enously filling each other's orifices with organic squash—is to
> highlight that most straight-identified people are "straight" not
> because they don't ever want to have a same-sex encounter, but
> because, in their view, queer modes of homosexual relating do
> not constitute an appealing way of life. Because their allegiance,
> ultimately, is to normativity. (208)

---

5. Ward elaborates on str8 dude sex and female heteroflexibility on 119–52 and
12–21, respectively. On a side note, the popularity of the *50 Shades of Grey*
franchise likewise speaks to the appropriation of queer sex cultures by the heterosexual mainstream. Only in a cultural context in which heterosexuality is
authenticated by science can kinky sex be so utterly disengaged from the queer
sex cultures in which it blossomed. As long as it is not *gay* sex, the expression of
a biologically incongruent essence, queer sex is permissible, even popular, among
the straight-identified.

6. I complicate this statement in this chapter's third section by discussing the
continued importance of coming out, despite the fact that it is not a solution to
the problem of dialectical sexual politics.

The idea of queerness being "an option for all people," of queerness defined solely as a cultural and political affiliation, returns us to an issue that plagued early queer theorists: Is queerness merely antinormative politics? If so, are we back in the conceptual realm of the "lesbian continuum" or the "straight but not narrow?"[7] What happens to bodies and pleasures—to queer sex practices—that might ground a queer politics? Ward, fully aware of this conundrum, closes her book with a call to "re-center sex acts themselves" (211), to invest queer sex with a sincerity and a significance shrugged off by (straight white male) practitioners of not-gay sex. Nonetheless, questions remain: Is *more* significance in sex acts a canny strategy? Will not a reinvestment in the meaningfulness of queer sex place us squarely within the jaws of the trap set by the *scientia sexualis*? What happens to Foucault's call to de-emphasize the social and subjective significance of sex? To delink sex from identity? What becomes of the sincere (homo)sexual confession if it ultimately works to enhance the power of a seemingly intractable power bloc?

Because the *scientia sexualis* has persuaded the majority of Americans with its concepts and categories, the sexual confession is currently, paradoxically, more banal and more loaded. If sexual behavior and social identity are essentially biological destiny, speaking our sexual truth seems at once like reading aloud the results of a DNA test and handing out a life sentence. Although many folks sleep more soundly knowing that homosexuals are "born this way," the political investment in this essentialist claim affects not only individual life trajectories but also the future of sexual politics. Regardless of whether one embraces a homonormative ideology bolstering the status quo or a resistant, antinormative stance, the terms of the debate have been established as a dialectical back-and-forth. Lest we forget, it was biopolitical administrates, not queers, that set this struggle in motion; the best we can do within this debate is react. In this regard, the sexual confession, while crucial to gay rights campaigns, might be

---

7. I refer here to the pioneering work of Adrienne Rich and a common "gay-straight alliance" slogan from 1990s activism. Rich's concept of the lesbian continuum includes the "range [. . .] of woman-identified experience, not simply the fact that a woman has had or consciously desired genital sexual experience with another woman" ("Compulsory" 239). Both Rich's concept and the ally slogan run the risk of desexualizing queer life and politics so as to increase the ranks of a feminist and LGBTQ political bloc. This conceptual move was met with much resistance, most notably by Leo Bersani in *Homos*.

considered a trap for a queer politics seeking freedoms beyond the scope of a dialectical, sexual-political struggle. So what power, if any, does the confession hold for a contemporary queer politics?

This question becomes more interesting when considered in relation to neoliberal policies and practices. As Thomas Waugh and Brandon Arroyo note: "Confession has become the last space for individual self-actualization, the enduring fantasy where we can imagine that we exist outside of the neoliberal ethos" (7). According to this neoliberal ethos, the self is merely a bundle of activities, a collection of skill sets, and a fungible vessel of human capital whose personal history and interior life matter little. By assertively bringing to the foreground issues concerning subjective interiority, the sexual confession potentially disrupts a neoliberal "business as usual" that wilfully overlooks personal histories and thus purposefully exacerbates social inequalities based in race, gender, class, and sexuality. In highlighting the importance of the interior life and identitarian histories, then, the confession humanizes and diversifies an increasingly automated workplace and public sphere . . . or so the story goes. The key word in Waugh and Arroyo's previously quoted statement is "fantasy": the confession offers the *fantasy* that we can actualize ourselves beyond the constraints of neoliberal subjectivity. Shannon Winnubst, however, reminds us:

> Once the principles of neoliberalism are absorbed into a culture, as they increasingly are in the U.S., we are all succumbing to the social rationality of neoliberalism: despite ideological or political differences, we are all speaking the same language, drinking the same Kool-Aid, breathing the same air. Consequently, the question of identity, which involves laying claim to a substance, is turned inside out, becoming a matter of process that is absorbed into this neoliberal grammar of success. One does not ask, "who are you?" in neoliberalism. Rather, one asks, "how good are you at what you do? How successful are you?" And the true bottom line: "*how much and how well do you maximize your interests?*" ("The Queer Thing" 86)

The diversity so celebrated in neoliberal publics—specifically, a diversity of sexual orientations that rests on confessions—is hence purely formal, "a matter of process." Success, be it financial, health-related, or popular, is constituted as the fundamental evaluative principle for all social identities. Although the subjectifying confession might superficially diversify a social milieu, it is in the end merely a stage in the process of neoliberal self-actualization, most certainly not a break from it. And while the sexual confession "I'm gay" might augment one's social "interest" and more readily translate into an anyone-can-do-it, rags-to-riches success story, it does little to unsettle the underlying conceptual premise of neoliberalism: radical individualism and cutthroat competition will produce a society of few winners and innumerable losers.

One need only look to the success of Donald Trump to understand the social hierarchy that neoliberal theorists had in mind. Born with a silver spoon, obsessed with self-brand marketing and maximization of self-interest, committed to intensifying political, economic, and social divisions, Trump, the quintessential neoliberal "winner," will ensure that the so-called free world he leads remains riven by the obscene social inequalities wrought by forty years of neoliberal policy. "Losers" like the poor, the elderly, and the undocumented will be sadistically punished because they weigh down a trickle-up economic system. People of color will continue to be murdered by Trump-backed storm troopers, whose witness-stand tears will be rewarded with exoneration, police protection, and a pension.[8] Emergent within this social wreckage, indeed in the very romantic heart of it, are media that arguably distill the zero-sum, winner-take-all imperatives of neoliberalism: Grindr, Scruff, Jack'd. Counterintuitively, these media might also prepare us for finding a way out of this mess.

Shut Me Up in the Digital Closet

To summarize, the sexual confession is historically instrumental to the formation of identitarian sexuality and, by extension, the functioning of a biopolitical governmentality. At present, the scientific notion that sexual orientation is biologically hardwired into our psyches is more popular than ever. We have apparently become the docile subjects that biopolitical administrates wished to create. However, in a neoliberal context, human capital trumps any depth-psychological model of subjectivity. The confession and identitarian sexuality become increasingly insignificant in neoliberalism;

---

8. I refer here to the numerous U.S. police officers who murdered unarmed Black men and were acquitted of any crime. For an incomplete (because it is ever-expanding) list of acquitted officers, see Barbara Goldberg's "Factbox: Trials of U.S. Police Officers Charged with Killing Black Men."

both are "absorbed into the neoliberal grammar of success," as Winnubst so aptly puts it. Instead of subjective truth and personal history, then, a neoliberal conception of sexuality emphasizes surfaces, visuals, skill sets, and branding. A neoliberal sexual subject works to optimize and maximize his or her sexual interest: sex is less a question of who one is than how successful one is in practicing it, less an expression of a deep-seated essence than a marketing strategy to achieve profitable returns.

Two distinct concepts of sexuality, therefore, currently compete for our attention: a neoliberal sexuality evaluating how well we "employ" our sexual desires, and an identitarian sexuality concerned with how authentic we are in our sexual beingness. Depending on the context, whom or what we desire paradoxically reveals nothing and everything about who we are and what we are capable of. We daily navigate a course between the rock of scientific sexuality and the hard (work)place of neoliberal sexuality. We adapt, somewhat schizophrenically, to the illogical and incommensurate demands of relational norms and romantic myths, on the one hand, and, on the other, we slug it out in an unforgiving marketplace in which such norms and myths are liabilities. Our lives as striving individuals and biopolitical subjects become more manageable knowing "who we are," and yet we are encouraged to check our self-truth at the office door lest we risk playing the "gay card," the "race card," the "gender card." Neoliberal subjectivity is at once, impossibly, too much and nothing at all: we are paradoxically required to authenticate our psychosocial essences and disown them in the same breath. In this age of nonsense, then, what might we glean from m4m media to help chart a course through a sexual-political Scylla and Charybdis?

For starters, in m4m media we can witness neoliberalism stripped bare, so to speak. The discursive, relational, and self-presentation norms of these media exemplify some social ideals of neoliberalism: hyperindividualism, self-branding, anticonfessional, transactional exchange, and the instrumentalization and commodification of intimacy. Yet in this hotbed of neoliberal sexuality, new subjective and relational freedoms, however negatively conceived, also emerge. These include: (a) freedom from a deep-seated, psychic sexual core, substantiated historically by linking erotic desire to self-truth; (b) freedom from a confessional imperative inextricable from identitarian sexuality; (c) freedom from romantic myths shackling sex to love and marriage; and, (d) freedom from corporate/workplace communicative norms that demand expressivity, transparency, articulacy, and team building. As a result, I discern in m4m media a restlessness with essentialist, scientific models of sexuality and a yearning for connection beyond romantic and neoliberal relational norms. Specifically, the former two freedoms afford an escape from the trap laid out by the *scientia sexualis*, whereas the latter signal a longing for intimacies beyond romantic and neoliberal limits. Thinking optimistically, we may have here the basic rudiments of both a Foucauldian "exodus" from biopolitical sexuality and a Deleuzian "circuit breaker" in the commodified communicative flows of control societies. If not, then m4m media at least express disenchantment with the present. But do they offer more than a desire to escape these bleak times?

The sage verse of Emily Dickinson, wittily appropriated by Grindr user "Emily Dickinson," is illuminative here. Specifically, the following Dickinson poem, surely quoted by "Emily Dickinson" in one Grindr exchange or another, speaks to the limited discursive confines of m4m media and the ecstatic excess produced precisely because of such confinement:

> They shut me up in Prose—
> As when a little Girl
> They put me in the Closet—
> Because they like me "still"—
>
> Still! Could themself have peeped—
> And seen my Brain—go round—
> They might as wise have lodged a Bird
> For Treason—in the Pound—
>
> Himself has but to will
> And easy as a Star
> Abolish his—Captivity—
> And laugh—No more have I—

Countering common understandings of closets as dark, even shameful sites of punishment and personal misery, Dickinson's poem emphasizes the enraptured imagination and unbridled willpower a closet might produce. Forced into "Prose," a genre deemed more appropriate for "a little Girl" by the masculinist literary gatekeepers of the nineteenth century (Galvin), the narrator refuses to let this gendered "Closet" contain her poetic creativity. In defiance of her jailers' wishes, her imagination ("Brain") flies like a bird through the bars of its prison; her "will" shines like a "Star" to reveal the boundaries of "Captivity" abolished. This "little Girl" surely has the last laugh (Casarino 186–88).[9] Dickinson's poem sheds light on the artistic invention and affective production taking place in the "Closet": artistry and affect perhaps birthed *only in* the closet.

If we were to commit the dreaded biographical fallacy and interpret this work as Dickinson's own plight, the poem itself becomes her closeted production, one might say her secret weapon: the rebellious poetry written in the "Closet" of "Prose" is made visible and public in this verse. In this regard, the poem is also, in the Austinian sense, a performative (Austin). The poem *qua* poem perforce abolishes the "Prose" closet to which Dickinson was relegated; through poetic form, Dickinson herself not only exits the closet but destroys it altogether by becoming-poet in the poem's utterance. Although the literary gatekeepers of her day attempted to shut her up—that is, to silence Dickinson's poetic voice—that voice "comes out," declares itself, and speaks loudly and proudly of its existence. Or does it?

It is tempting to appropriate this poem for a sexual or feminist liberationist project: to read the poem as evidence of unruly women making history, as the public confession of a closeted secret, as a coming-out narrative, and even as an ode to the moral necessity of coming out. Indeed, it is tempting to compare the performative utterance "I am gay" to Dickinson's performative enactment of "I am poet." But might Dickinson's verse instead be a paean to the sublime pleasures, affects, and intellects produced *in* the closet? Might the poem be a song of praise *for* the closet, a space productive of an imaginative and sensual potential that knows no bounds? Is the closet a jail ultimately inaccessible to the jailers themselves, in that it explodes dualistically conceived notions of in/out and incarcerated/liberated altogether?

In *Modernity at Sea*, Cesare Casarino interprets the poem precisely in this manner: "For (Dickinson's poem seems to be saying) you can 'shut me up in' the 'Closet,' but then you no longer have control over the blazing and star-like *potentia* that can be produced within it, thus effectively

---

9. Cesare Casarino's chapter section "Preliminary Remarks on Emily Dickinson's Last Laugh" deeply informed my interpretation of both Dickinson's poem and the digital closet of m4m media. See Casarino, 186–95. I discuss his work in detail in the following paragraphs.

exceeding it and abolishing it from the inside" (186). For Casarino, the sexual closet is the "privileged locus of an as yet untapped excess of same-sex desire" (ibid.) that "marks the threshold of an other-becoming" (187). This becoming is more than a transformation into an identifiable (gay) subject because the closet itself, like Walt Whitman, contains multitudes: molecular desires, sublime pleasures and affects, a potential to become anything.[10] Dickinson herself exemplifies this multitudinous becoming: in her Closet of Prose, she becomes a bird, a star, and, indeed, a poet. Using Dickinson as a starting point, Casarino thus complicates sexual-political understandings of being "in" or "out" of the closet by arguing that the immanent excesses of being "in" serve no purpose for, in fact, overcome the limitations of, a dialectically conceived "out" politics. Like Foucault, however, Casarino is adamant about the "dire necessity" (188) of coming out. Although a resistant gay politics might ultimately affirm a biopolitical dialectical social order in which antiheteronormative resistance was conceived and foretold, it is nonetheless imperative to participate in such dialectical struggle and to embrace a public LGBTQ social identity despite the risk of affirming precisely what that identity theoretically opposes. That said, coming out will not ultimately afford an escape from the quagmire of dialectical sexual politics: "Just because the act of coming out is necessary and inevitable at a given conjuncture in both the life history of particular sexual subjects and in the larger-than-life history of modernity, it does not necessarily follow that such an act is the solution to the problem that produced the closet in the first place" (189).

So, what might the closet offer that a public "outness" cannot? Unnamed and unclassified libidinal energies, affective sensualities, and

---

10. In *Foucault*, Gilles Deleuze distinguishes molecular sexuality from molar sexuality. The molecular involves multiple desires of radical difference that are irreducible to the molar, binary code of sexual opposition. The molecular is reined in and territorialized by the molar into representational forms, primarily hetero- and homosexuality. He writes: "But always [. . .] a molecular sexuality bubbles away beneath the surface of the integrated sexes" (76). Although most m4m hookup apps attempt to "molarize" sexuality by offering specific identity categories (orientation, tribe, type, etc.), preferences (top/bottom), and a host of other markers that users are encouraged to assign themselves, I nonetheless find in these media the circulation of molecular desires exceeding the codes created to represent them. I discuss this point further in relation to Casarino's concept of the sublime of the closet.

molecular sexualities; invisibility, imperceptibility, fraught with and intensified by anxiety, loneliness, and other ecstatically unbearable somatic sensations; the pleasures of enclosure, a finite space yielding to an imaginative infinity, a claustrophilia; the welcoming security of finitude itself, of finality, a tomb, extinction. All such excess cannot be assimilated into a manageable social identity or recognized as a coherent political stance. Casarino goes so far as to argue that the closet ultimately houses the waste of modernity's dominant mode of production, the dialectic itself, including its primary product, the homo-/heterosexuality binary: "In the sublime of the closet one confronts nothing less than the excess of the onto-epistemological production of modernity. Such an excess constitutes an escape from modernity as we know it—a cunicular network of a subterranean history of the body threatening suddenly to erupt through the ground of modernity and to materialize that which never would or will be modern" (192). That which "never would or will be modern" is precisely that which is unrecognizable and unrepresentable from the standpoint of "out" politics: the sensual *potentia* that exceeds social identity and escapes demographical, economic, or quantitative evaluation; a *potentia*, in other words, that forges a course between and beyond identitarian and neoliberal sexualities.

It requires now only a small conceptual leap to understand m4m media as a contemporary digital manifestation of Casarino's, or Dickinson's, sublime closet. First, in m4m media one need not "come out" of, or as, anything: although providing virtual space for men to connect with other men (an activity, like poetry writing), these media are not necessarily or solely for "gay men" (a social demographic). Nonidentitarian desires circulate freely in this closet, some surely inassimilable to the sexual codes and categories created "in real life" to represent them. Second, the discursive conventions of m4m media encourage anticonfessional, crassly sexual exchanges—typically *not* proud declarations of gay identity or cultural affinity. One discovers in the stammering and inarticulate chatter instead a sensual, depersonalized, even impersonal, discourse. If we neoliberals are shut up in a closet of discursive transparency and personal accountability, that closet also produces its opposite in m4m media: opacity and unreliability.[11] Just as Dickinson's Closet of Prose unintentionally

---

11. For more on opacity and unreliability as queer strategies, see de Villiers, especially 89–116.

produces poetry, the m4m media closet, ostensibly created to connect users at least preliminarily through conversation, inadvertently generates an impersonal discourse of ventriloquists. The form of intimacy emergent in this discourse, long familiar to queers, is what I understand as shared estrangement. Manifest historically in practices such as anonymous cruising and friendships emergent in the AIDS crisis, shared estrangement finds its contemporary home in the digital closet. Here, the ache of longing, the loneliness of isolation, even the shame of socially disreputable acts and intimacies, are (un)shared in a nondialectical, disconnected mingling. If "vacuoles of noncommunication" are needed to circumvent the com-modified communicative forms in control societies, then an antirelational, queer ethic of shared estrangement might be one such "circuit-breaker." Its past implementation in queer culture has proven prescient, resilient, and politically strategic; as cultivated in m4m media, it may hold the capacity, like Dickinson's rebellious imagination, to abolish our captivity in dialectical struggle.

Third, m4m media require users to create a profile: a digital self-representation that characteristically features an invented name, photos of faces or body parts, lists of sexual preferences or skills, and references to a type or tribe. As with the dialogic norms, profiles typically steer clear of personal history and emotional interiority. They are often perfunctory when it comes to (nonsexual) self-description and cautious in terms of socially identifying markers. Since "out" politics has rendered same-sex desire so blindingly visible and thoroughly individualized, becoming "invisible" in profile creation can be understood as a (re-)enactment of the anxious anonymity of the closet as well as a form of voluntary self-dissolution. More than simply nostalgia, however, such imperceptibility lends itself to the establishment of unconventional collective forms.[12] The Grindr grid, for instance, can be understood as the visual representation of a nonidentitarian collection affirming a common, asubjective substance

---

12. In figure 6.4, "Emily Dickinson" proclaims that she is "nobody" and welcomes another "nobody" into her closet. The mental image of a closet full of anony-mous, perhaps indistinguishable "nobodies" mingling sensually not only calls to mind the queer sex space of the dark room but also envisages the form of whatever-belonging: a nonidentitarian collectivity affirming a common, asubjective substance. In this sense, the work of "Emily Dickinson" is useful for more than a laugh.

that seethes beneath identifiable individuals—libidinal energies, affective intensities, molecular desires. Such sensual *potentia*, as Casarino reminds us, threatens to explode the very conceptual framework in which the closet was conceived in modernity.

Finally, claustrophilia: it is gratifying, even liberating, to feel in control of one's confines, no matter how oppressive that entrapment may be, no matter how illusory such control is. Within that finite space, one can likewise dream up fantasies, scenarios, and worlds unimaginable—or more often than not, unrealizable—outside of it. The unbridled imagination produced in and by Dickinson's closet finds its complement in m4m media in flights of fancy and fugitive desires.

Of course, the above descriptions of m4m media protocols and conventions might also likely appear in a self-help book entitled "How to Brand Yourself and Find a Mate in Neoliberalism," or even "How to Repudiate the History of Struggle and Sacrifice That Paved the Way for M4M Media." In other words, we cannot simply ignore the ways that m4m media affirm neoliberal logics and potentially belittle the agonizing, life-threatening work of queer activists. However, I also discern in these media an ambivalence that signals a desire for something more: alternative presents, other-than-neoliberal futures. Unlike Jane Ward's not-gay men who want homosexual sex without the stigmatizing label "homosexual," we can, of course, experience the sublime pleasures of the digital closet *and* embrace a public queer identity. In cultures for which "gay" increasingly signifies domestic, dyadic love, however, one lure of m4m media surely lies in the "shame" of returning to the closet. The shamelessly crass, dehumanizing, and transactional discourse typical of m4m media is not only often shamefully erotic but also surges with affective, nonsensical, and sensual *potentia*. The abject, self-negating pleasures produced in this digital closet are anathema to both rights-seeking politics and neoliberal injunctions to self-optimize. In this space, we might be training for a politics that exceeds rights-seeking and neoliberal "winning" altogether, a politics beyond the dialectical trap set by the *scientia sexualis* and incomprehensible to quantitative, neoliberal metrics. The sensual nonsense coursing through m4m media might be, like Dickinson's poem, a secret weapon that explodes sensible, representational politics altogether. Using an imagination produced only in the closet, we too might become astral, avian, indeed, poetic. If all systems of representation—linguistic, scientific, political—are, at best, artistic renderings of a finally unrepresentable outside, then the conversion of the closet's sublimity into a representational form may, at best, be a poetic politics.[13] For this translation and transition, let the verse of "Emily Dickinson" be our guide.

---

13. Here I have in mind Friedrich Nietzsche's critique of Cartesian dualism in "On Truth and Lying in the Extra-Moral Sense," perhaps best encapsulated in this quotation: "On the whole it seems to me that the 'right perception'—which would mean the adequate expression of an object in the subject—is a nonentity full of contradictions: between two utterly different spheres, as between subject and object, there is no causality, no accuracy, no expression, but at the utmost an *aesthetical* relation, I mean a suggestive metamorphosis, a stammering translation into quite a distinct foreign language, for which purpose however there is needed at any rate an intermediate sphere, an intermediate force, freely composing and freely inventing" (263).

Bibliography

Agamben, Giorgio. *The Coming Community*. University of Minnesota Press, 1993.

Ahmad, Asam. "A Note on Call-Out Culture." *Briarpatch Magazine*, 2 March 2015, https://handbook.law.utoronto.ca/sites/handbook.law.utoronto.ca/files/users/alzner/A%20Note%20on%20Calling%20Out.briarpatch.pdf. Accessed 20 May 2019.

Aristotle. *Nicomachean Ethics*. Cambridge University Press, 2000.

Arpacia, Ibrahim, Süleyman Barbaros Yalçınb, Mustafa Baloğluc, and Şahin Kesicib. "The Moderating Effect of Gender in the Relationship between Narcissism and Selfie-posting Behavior." *Personality and Individual Differences* 134, 1 November 2018, pp. 71–74, https://doi.org/10.1016/j.paid.2018.06.006. Accessed 20 May 2019.

Arthur, Charles. "Text messaging turns 20—but are their best years behind them?" *The Guardian*. 3 December 2012, https://www.theguardian.com/technology/2012/dec/02/text-messaging-turns-20. Accessed 20 May 2019.

Austin, J. L. *How to Do Things with Words*. Harvard University Press, 1962.

B & H Photo and Video. "What is a Modular Synthesizer?" 23 May 2018, https://www.youtube.com/watch?v=RIeTgmxju6Y. Accessed 20 May 2019.

Ballard, Jamie. "17% of People Using Dating Apps/Websites Are There to Cheat on Their Partner." *YouGov*. 6 February 2019, https://today.yougov.com/topics/relationships/articles-reports/2019/02/06/dating-apps-websites-cheating-romance-sex. Accessed 20 May 2019.

Bechdel Test Movie List. 2019, https://bechdeltest.com. Accessed 20 May 2019.

Beckett, Samuel. "Worstward Ho." *Nohow On: Three Novels*. Grove, 1996, pp. 87–114.

Bennett, Jessica. "When Saying 'Yes' Is Easier Than Saying 'No.'" *The New York Times*. 16 December 2017, https://www.nytimes.com/2017/12/16/sunday-review/when-saying-yes-is-easier-than-saying-no.html. Accessed 20 May 2019.

Berlant, Laura. *Cruel Optimism*. Duke University Press, 2011.

Berliner, Lauren S., and Nora J. Kenworthy. "Producing a Worthy Illness: Personal Crowdfunding amidst Financial Crisis." *Social Science & Medicine* 187, 2017, pp. 233–242, https://doi.org/10.1016/j.socscimed.2017.02.008. Accessed 20 May 2019.

Bersani, Leo. *Homos.* Harvard University Press, 1995.

———. *Is the Rectum a Grave? and Other Essays.* University of Chicago Press, 2010.

———. *Receptive Bodies.* University of Chicago Press, 2018.

———. *Thoughts and Things.* University of Chicago Press, 2015.

Bersani, Leo, and Ulysse Dutoit. *Arts of Impoverishment: Beckett, Rothko, Resnais.* Harvard University Press, 1993.

———. *Caravaggio's Secrets.* MIT Press, 1998.

Bersani, Leo, and Adam Phillips. *Intimacies.* University of Chicago Press, 2008.

Binyam, Maya. "Letter of Recommendation: Ghosting." *The New York Times,* 3 August 2017, https://www.nytimes.com/2017/08/03/magazine/letter-of-recommendation-ghosting.html. Accessed 20 May 2019.

Board of Governors of the Federal Reserve System. "Changes in U.S. Family Finances from 2013 to 2016: Evidence from the Survey of Consumer Finances." *Federal Reserve Bulletin* 103, no. 3, September 2017, https://www.federalreserve.gov/publications/files/scf17.pdf. Accessed 20 May 2019.

Bond Stockton, Kathryn. *The Queer Child, or Growing Sideways in the Twentieth Century.* Duke University Press, 2009.

Bordenstein, Seth R., and Kevin R. Theis. "Host Biology in Light of the Microbiome: Ten Principles of Holobionts and Hologenomes." *PLoS Biology* 13, no. 8, 2015, https://doi.org/10.1371/journal.pbio.1002226. Accessed 19 January 2020.

Borg. *Wikipedia.* 13 May 2019, https://en.wikipedia.org/wiki/Borg. Accessed 20 May 2019.

boyd, danah. *It's Complicated: The Social Lives of Networked Teens.* Yale University Press, 2014.

Brammer, John Paul. "#Pride30: Physician Jack Turban Is Dedicated to Trans Kids' Health." *NBC News.* 14 June 2017, https://www.nbcnews.com/feature/nbc-out-pride30/pride30-physician-jack-turban-dedicated-trans-kids-health-n763171. Accessed 20 May 2019.

Brennan, Timothy. *Wars of Position: The Cultural Politics of Left and Right.* Columbia University Press, 2006.

Brodeur, Michael Andor. "Real Talk: The Rise of Context." *Boston Globe,* 28 June 2014, http://www.bostonglobe.com/arts/2014/06/28/real-talk-the-rise-context/3gL3gcg3eW1eLNs8KPOW0M/story.html. Accessed 20 May 2019.

Bromwich, Jonah Engel. "Tinder and Bumble Are Hungry for Your Love." *The New York Times,* 18 December 2018, https://www.nytimes.com/2018/12/18/style/dating-apps-tinder-bumble-content.html. Accessed 20 May 2019.

Brown, Wendy. "Neoliberalism and the End of Liberal Democracy." *Theory and Event* 7, no. 1, 2003, https://muse.jhu.edu/article/48659. Accessed 20 May 2019.

Bruni, Frank. "Our Hard Drives, Ourselves." *New York Times*, 18 November 2012, http://www.nytimes.com/2012/11/18/opinion/sunday/Bruni-Our-Hard-Drives-Ourselves.html. Accessed 20 May 2019.

Cai, Belinda. "I Moved to LA for a Tinder Relationship that Lasted Two Weeks, but I Don't Regret It—Here's Why." *Swipe Life*, 24 September 2018, https://swipelife.tinder.com/post/i-moved-to-la-for-a-tinder-relationship-that-lasted-two-weeks-but-i-dont-regret-it-heres-why/. Accessed 20 May 2019.

Campbell, John Edward. *Getting It on Online: Cyberspace, Gay Male Sexuality, and Embodied Identity*. Harrington Park, 2004.

Casarino, Cesare. *Modernity at Sea: Melville, Marx, Conrad in Crisis*. University of Minnesota Press, 2002.

Chu, Andrea Long. "On Liking Women." *n+1* 30, Winter 2018, https://nplusonemag.com/issue-30/essays/on-liking-women/. Accessed 20 May 2019.

Cohen-Sheffer, Natalie. "Text Message Response Times and What They Really Mean." 6 November 2017, https://www.viber.com/blog/2017-11-06/text-message-response-times/. Accessed 20 May 2019.

Combahee River Collective. "A Black Feminist Statement." *The Second Wave: A Reader in Feminist Theory*. Routledge, 1997, pp. 63–70.

Congress.gov. "H.R.5—Equality Act." 13 March 2019, https://www.congress.gov/bill/116th-congress/house-bill/5/text. Accessed 20 May 2019.

Crimp, Douglas. "How to Have Promiscuity in an Epidemic." *AIDS: Cultural Analysis, Cultural Activism*, edited by Douglas Crimp. MIT Press, 1987, pp. 237–271.

Daroya, Emerich. "Erotic Capital and the Psychic Life of Racism on Grindr." *The Psychic Life of Racism in Gay Men's Communities*, edited by Damien W. Riggs. Lexington Books, pp. 67–80.

Dash, Julie, director. *Daughters of the Dust*. Kino International, 1991.

Dating Sites Reviews. "Grindr Information, Statistics, Facts and History." 22 April 2019, https://www.datingsitesreviews.com/staticpages/index.php?page=-Grindr-statistics-facts-history. Accessed 20 May 2019.

Davidson, Arnold. "Ethics as Ascetics: Foucault, the History of Ethics, and Ancient Thought." *The Cambridge Companion to Foucault*, edited by Gary Gutting. Cambridge University Press, 2006.

Davis, Nicola. "The Human Microbiome: Why Our Microbes Could Be Key to Our Health." *The Guardian*. 26 March 2018, https://www.theguardian.com/news/2018/mar/26/the-human-microbiome-why-our-microbes-could-be-key-to-our-health. Accessed 19 January 2020.

Dean, Jodi. *Democracy and Other Neoliberal Fantasies: Communicative Capitalism and Left Politics*. Duke University Press, 2009.

Dean, Tim. *Beyond Sexuality*. University of Chicago Press, 2000.

———. *Unlimited Intimacy: Reflections on the Subculture of Barebacking*. University of Chicago Press, 2009.

Delany, Samuel R. *The Motion of Light in Water*. New American Library, 1988.

———. *Times Square Red, Times Square Blue*. New York University Press, 1999.

Deleuze, Gilles. "Control and Becoming." *Negotiations, 1972–1990*. Translated by Martin Joughin. Columbia University Press, 1995.

———. *Foucault*, translated and edited by Seán Hand. Minneapolis: University of Minnesota Press, 1988.

Deleuze, Gilles, and Félix Guattari. *Anti-Oedipus: Capitalism and Schizophrenia*. Translated by Robert Hurley, Mark Seem, and Helen R. Lane. University of Minnesota Press, 1983.

———. *What Is Philosophy?* Translated by Hugh Tomlinson and Graham Burchell. Columbia University Press, 1994.

Demme, Jonathan, director. *Stop Making Sense*. Palm Pictures, 1999.

Deresiewicz, William. "Faux Friendship." *The Chronicle of Higher Education*. 6 December 2009, https://www.chronicle.com/article/Faux-Friendship/49308. Accessed 20 May 2019.

De Villiers, Nicholas. *Opacity and the Closet: Queer Tactics in Foucault, Barthes, and Warhol*. University of Minnesota Press, 2012.

Dickinson, Emily. "They Shut Me Up in Prose (445)." 1862, https://www.poetry-foundation.org/poems-and-poets/poems/detail/52196. Accessed 20 May 2019.

Dilts, Andrew. "From Entrepreneur of the Self to Care of the Self: Neoliberal Governmentality and Foucault's Ethics." *Foucault Studies* 12, 2011, pp. 130–146, https://rauli.cbs.dk/index.php/foucault-studies/article/view/3338/3643. Accessed 20 May 2019.

Dolgoy, Erin, Kimberly Hurd Hale and Bruce Peabody. *Political Philosophies of Aging, Dying, and Death*. Routledge, 2021 (forthcoming).

Ebo, Bosah. *Cyberghetto or Cybertopia: Race, Class, and Gender on the Internet*. Westport, CT: Praeger, 1998.

Farrow, Ronan. "From Aggressive Overtures to Sexual Assault: Harvey Weinstein's Accusers Tell Their Stories." *The New Yorker*. 10 October 2017, https://www.newyorker.com/news/news-desk/from-aggressive-overtures-to-sexual-assault-harvey-weinsteins-accusers-tell-their-stories. Accessed 20 May 2019.

Fischel, Joseph J. *Screw Consent: A Better Politics of Sexual Justice*. University of California Press, 2019.

———. "What do we consent to when we consent to sex?" *Aeon*. 23 October 2018, https://aeon.co/ideas/what-do-we-consent-to-when-we-consent-to-sex. Accessed 20 May 2019.

Fischer, Nancy L. "Purity and Pollution: Sex as a Moral Discourse." *Introducing the New Sexuality Studies: 2nd Edition*, edited by Steven Seidman, Nancy L. Fischer, and Chet Meeks. Routledge, 2011, pp. 38–44.

Fishbein, Rebecca. "The 'Men React to Cat Person' Twitter Account Is Screen-shotting Men's Posts about the Short Story 'Cat Person' in *The New Yorker*." *Bustle*. 11 December 2017, https://www.bustle.com/p/the-men-react-to-cat-person-twitter-account-is-screenshotting-mens-posts-about-the-short-story-cat-person-in-the-new-yorker-7531850. Accessed 20 May 2019.

Flatley, J. "Like: Collecting and Collectivity." *October* 132, Spring 2010, pp. 71–98.

———. *Like Andy Warhol*. University of Chicago Press, 2017.

Foucault, Michel. *The Birth of Biopolitics*. Translated by Graham Burchell. Palgrave Macmillan, 2008.

———. "The Discourse on Language." *The Archaeology of Knowledge*. Translated by A. M. Sheridan Smith. Pantheon Books, 1972, pp. 215–238.

———. *The Essential Works of Michel Foucault, Volume One: Ethics: Subjectivity and Truth*, edited by Paul Rabinow. New Press, 1997.

———. *The History of Sexuality, Volume 1: An Introduction*. Translated by Robert Hurley. Vintage, 1990.

———. *The Order of Things: An Archaeology of the Human Sciences*. Vintage, 1994.

———. *Society Must Be Defended": Lectures at the Collège de France, 1975–1976*. Translated by David Macey. Picador, 2003.

———. *This Is Not a Pipe*. Translated and edited by James Harkness. University of California Press, 1983.

Franzen, Jonathan. "Liking Is for Cowards: Go for What Hurts." *The New York Times*, 28 May 2011, http://www. nytimes.com/2011/05/29/opinion/29franzen.html. Accessed 20 May 2019.

Freud, Sigmund. "Leonardo DaVinci and a Memory of His Childhood." *The Freud Reader*, edited by Peter Gay. W. W. Norton, 1989, pp. 443–480.

———. "Mourning and Melancholia." *General Psychological Theory: Papers on Metapsychology*. New York: Collier Books, 1963, pp. 164–170.

Galloway, Alexander R. *Protocol: How Control Exists after Decentralization*. MIT Press, 2004.

Galvin, Mary C. "Poltergeist of Form: Emily Dickinson and the Reappropration of Language and Identity." *Queer Poetics: Five Modernist Women Writers*. Greenwood Press, 1999, pp. 1–20.

Gandhi, Leela. *Affective Communities: Anticolonial Thought, Fin-De-Siècle Radicalism, and the Politics of Friendship*. Duke UP, 2006.

Geiger, A. W. and Gretchen Livingston. "8 Facts about Love and Marriage in America." *Pew Research Center*. 13 February 2019, https://www.pewresearch.org/fact-tank/2019/02/13/8-facts-about-love-and-marriage/. Accessed 20 May 2019.

Gerbaudo, Paul. *Tweets and the Streets: Social Media and Contemporary Activism*. Pluto, 2012.

Goh, Irving. "Rejecting Friendship: Toward a Radical Reading of Derrida's *Politics of Friendship* for Today." *Cultural Critique* 79, Fall 2011, pp. 94–124.

Goldberg, Barbara. "Factbox: Trials of U.S. Police Officers Charged with Killing Black Men." *Reuters*. 5 October 2018, https://www.reuters.com/article/us-chicago-police-killings-factbox/factbox-trials-of-u-s-police-officers-charged-with-killing-black-men-idUSKCN1MF2K8. Accessed 20 May 2019.

Goldberg, Greg. *Antisocial Media: Anxious Labor in the Digital Economy*. New York University Press, 2018.

———. "Meet Markets: Grindr and the Politics of Objectifying Others." *Convergence: The International Journal of Research into New Media Technologies*, July 2018, pp. 1–16, doi:10.1177/1354856518787305. Accessed 20 May 2019.

———. "Through the Looking Glass: The Queer Narcissism of Selfies." *Social Media + Society*. January–March 2017, pp. 1–11, https://doi.org/10.1177/20563051 17698494. Accessed 20 May 2019.

Grindr. http://www.Grindr.com/about/. Accessed 20 May 2019.

———. "Grindr Takes A Stand Against Sexual Racism and Discrimination with 'Kindr' Initiative." 18 September 2018, https://www.prnewswire.com/news-releases/Grindr-takes-a-stand-against-sexual-racism-and-discrimination-with-kindr-initiative-300714327.html. Accessed 20 May 2019.

———. "What Is Grindr Xtra?" 2019, https://help.Grindr.com/hc/en-us/articles/115008879108-What-is-Grindr-XTRA-. Accessed 20 May 2019.

Gross, Michael Joseph. "Has Manhunt Destroyed Gay Culture?" *Out Magazine*. 4 August 2008, http://www.out.com/entertainment/2008/08/04/has-manhunt-destroyed-gay-culture? Accessed 20 May 2019.

Halberstam, J. "The Anti-Social Turn in Queer Studies." *Graduate Journal of Social Science* 5, no. 2, 2008, pp. 140–56.

———. *Gaga Feminism: Sex, Gender, and the End of Normal*. Beacon, 2013.

———. *The Queer Art of Failure*. Duke University Press, 2011.

Halperin, David. "Is There a History of Sexuality?" *The Lesbian and Gay Studies Reader*, edited by Henry Abelove, Michèle Aina Barale, and David M. Halperin. Routledge, 1993, pp. 416–431.

Halperin, David, and Trevor Hoppe, editors. *The War on Sex*. Duke University Press, 2017.

Hardt, Michael, and Antonio Negri. *Commonwealth*. Harvard University Press, 2009.

———. *Empire*. Harvard University Press, 2000.

———. *Multitude: War and Democracy in the Age of Empire*. Penguin, 2004.

Hargraves, Hunter. "iTouch, Therefore iAm: The iPhone as Masturbation." "Viscerally Uncomfortable TV: Affective Spectatorship and Televisual Neoliberalism." PhD Dissertation, Brown University, 2015.

Hart-Landsberg, Martin. "The 2016 Survey of Consumer Finances Paints a Grim Picture of Working Class Finances." *Monthly Review Online*, 11 December 2017, https://mronline.org/2017/12/11/the-2016-survey-of-consumer-finances-paints-a-grim-picture-of-working-class-finances/. Accessed 20 May 2019.

Hartman, Saidiya V. *Scenes of Subjection: Terror, Slavery, and Self-Making in Nineteenth-Century America*. Oxford University Press, 1997.

Haver, William. "A Sense of the Common." *South Atlantic Quarterly* 111, no. 3, 2012, pp. 439–452.

Hillis, Ken. *Online a Lot of the Time: Ritual, Fetish, Sign.* Duke University Press, 2009.

Hocquenghem, Guy. *Homosexual Desire.* Translated by Daniella Dangoor. Duke University Press, 1993.

Huffer, Lynne. "Foucault and Sedgwick: The Repressive Hypothesis Revisited." *Foucault Studies* 14, 2012, pp. 20–40, https://rauli.cbs.dk/index.php/foucault-studies/article/view/3888/4231. Accessed 20 May 2019.

Illouz, Eva. *Cold Intimacies: The Making of Emotional Capitalism.* Polity, 2007.

Iqbal, Mansoor. "Tinder Revenue and Usage Statistics (2018)." *Business of Apps.* 27 February 2019, http://www.businessofapps.com/data/tinder-statistics/. Accessed 20 May 2019.

Irwin, Neil, Claire Cain Miller, and Margot Sanger-Katz. "The Upshot: America's Racial Divide, Charted." *New York Times.* 20 August 2014, http://www.nytimes.com/2014/08/20/upshot/americas-racial-divide-charted.html. Accessed 20 May 2019.

Jack'd. https://jackdapp.com. Accessed 20 May 2019.

Jones, Jeffrey M. "Majority in U.S. Now Say Gays and Lesbians Born, Not Made." *Gallup Social & Policy Issues*, 20 May 2015, https://news.gallup.com/poll/183332/majority-say-gays-lesbians-born-not-made.aspx. Accessed 20 May 2019.

Karlan, Sarah, J. Lester Feder, and Michelle Rial. "Here Are the World's Most Popular Dating Apps for Gay Dudes." *BuzzfeedNews*, 17 December 2015, https://www.buzzfeed.com/skarlan/here-are-the-worlds-most-popular-hook-up-apps-for-gay-dudes. Accessed 20 May 2019.

Kessler, Glenn, and Meg Kelly. "President Trump Made 2,140 False or Misleading Claims in His First Year." *The Washington Post*, 20 January 2018, https://www.washingtonpost.com/news/fact-checker/wp/2018/01/20/president-trump-made-2140-false-or-misleading-claims-in-his-first-year/. Accessed 20 May 2019.

Kindr. 2018, https://www.kindr.Grindr.com. Accessed 20 May 2019.

King, Tiffany Lethabo. "The Labor of (Re)Reading Plantation Landscapes Fungible(ly)." *Antipode* 48, no. 4, Sept. 2016, pp. 1022–1039. *EBSCOhost*, doi:10.1111/anti.12227. Accessed 19 January 2020.

Kipnis, Laura. *Against Love: A Polemic.* Vintage Books, 2003.

Koedt, Anne. "The Myth of the Vaginal Orgasm." *The Chicago Women's Labor Union Herstory Project.* 1970, https://www.cwluherstory.org/classic-feminist-writings-articles/myth-of-the-vaginal-orgasm. Accessed 20 May 2019.

Konstan, David. "Aristotle on Love and Friendship." *ΣΧΟΛΗ* 2, no. 2, 2008, pp. 207–212.

Kotsko, Adam. *Neoliberalism's Demons: On the Political Theology of Late Capital.* Stanford University Press, 2018.

Kuhnreich, Chaim. "Grindr Profile Pics Are All about the Hookup." *The Conversation.* 18 June 2018,http://theconversation.com/Grindr-profile-pics-are-all-about-the-hookup-96839. Accessed 20 May 2019.

Lacan, Jacques. *Book XI: The Four Fundamental Concepts of Psychoanalysis, 1964.* Edited by Jacques-Alain Miller. Translated by Alan Sheridan. W. W. Norton, 1977.

Lawrence, D. H. *Women in Love.* Penguin, 1987.

Levy, Ariel. "Lesbian Nation: American Chronicles." *The New Yorker* 85, no. 3. 2 March 2009, https://www.newyorker.com/magazine/2009/03/02/lesbian-nation. Accessed 20 May 2019.

Lewis, Mary Grace. "Study Says Only Two Thirds of Gen Z Is Straight." *The Advocate.* 6 July 2018, https://www.advocate.com/youth/2018/7/06/study-says-only-two-thirds-gen-z-straight. Accessed 20 May 2019.

Li, Yun. "Nearly Half the U.S. Population Is without a Job, Showing How Far the Labor Recovery Has to Go." *CNBC.com*, June 29, 2020, https://www.cnbc.com/2020/06/29/nearly-half-the-us-population-is-without-a-job-showing-how-far-the-labor-recovery-has-to-go.html. Accessed 22 July 2020.

Liptak, Adam. "Civil Rights Law Protects Gay and Transgender Workers, Supreme Court Rules." *The New York Times*, June 15, 2020. https://www.nytimes.com/2020/06/15/us/gay-transgender-workers-supreme-court.html. Accessed 2 August 2020.

Lorde, Audre. "The Master's Tools Will Never Dismantle the Master's House." *Sister Outsider: Essays and Speeches.* Crossing, 2007, pp. 110–114.

Luo, Michael. "The Twenty-Five Most-Read *New Yorker* Stories of 2017." *The New Yorker*, 19 December 2017, https://www.newyorker.com/culture/2017-in-review/the-twenty-five-most-read-new-yorker-stories-of-2017. Accessed 20 May 2019.

Madrigal, Alexis C. "What Facebook Did to American Democracy." *The Atlantic*, 12 October 2017, https://www.theatlantic.com/technology/archive/2017/10/what-facebook-did/542502/. Accessed 20 May 2019.

Marx, Karl, and Friedrich Engels. "Manifesto of the Communist Party." *The Marx-Engels Reader*, edited by Robert C. Tucker. W. W. Norton, 1978, pp. 473–500.

Match Group. "Singles in America: Match Releases Largest Study on U.S. Single Population for Eighth Year." 1 February 2018, https://www.multivu.com/players/English/8264851-match-singles-in-america-study/. Accessed 20 May 2019.

Mastroyiannis, Alexis. "Gay dating apps: A comprehensive guide to Jack'd, Grindr, Hornet, Scruff and the rest." *Pink News*, 5 March 2018, https://www.pinknews.co.uk/2018/03/05/best-gay-dating-apps-jackd-Grindr-hornet-scruff/. Accessed 20 May 2019.

May, Todd. *Friendship in an Age of Economics: Resisting the Forces of Neoliberalism.* Lexington Books, 2012.

McCormick, Joseph Patrick. "WARNING: These Grindr Profiles Are Actually Robots Trying to Steal Your Info." *Pink News*, 8 November 2015, http://

www.pinknews.co.uk/2015/08/11/warning-these-Grindr-profiles-are-actually-robots-trying-to-steal-your-info/. Accessed 20 May 2019.

McGlotten, Shaka. *Virtual Intimacies: Media, Affect, and Queer* Sociality. State University of New York Press, 2013.

Meeker, Martin. *Contacts Desired: Gay and Lesbian Communications and Community, 1940s–1970s*. University of Chicago Press, 2005.

Mendus, Elaine and Trudy Ring. "Is Anyone Immune to HIV?" *Plus*, 23 March 2016, https://www.hivplusmag.com/research-breakthroughs/2016/3/23/anyone-immune-hiv. Accessed 20 May 2019.

Mitchell, Joni. "Woodstock." *Ladies of the Canyon*. Reprise Records, 1970.

Moby. "We Are All Made of Stars" *18*. Mute Records, 2002.

Monbiot, George. "Neoliberalism—the Ideology at the Root of All Our Problems." *The Guardian*, 15 April 2016, https://www.theguardian.com/books/2016/apr/15/neoliberalism-ideology-problem-george-monbiot. Accessed 20 May 2019.

Mowlabocus, Sharif. *Gaydar Culture: Gay Men, Technology and Embodiment in the Digital Age*. Ashgate, 2010.

NAMES Project Foundation. "The AIDS Memorial Quilt." 2019, https://www.aidsquilt.org/about/the-aids-memorial-quilt. Accessed 20 May 2019.

Nancy, Jean Luc. *Being Singular Plural*. Translated by Robert Richardson and Anne O'Byrne. Stanford University Press, 2000.

National Association for the Advancement of Colored People. "Criminal Justice Fact Sheet." 2019, http://www.naacp.org/pages/criminal-justice-fact-sheet#. Accessed 20 May 2019.

Negri, Antonio. "Twenty Theses on Marx: Interpretation of the Class Situation Today." *Marxism beyond Marxism*, edited by Saree Makdisi, Cesare Casarino, and Rebecca E. Karl. Routledge, 1996, pp. 149–180.

Nietzsche, Friedrich. "On Truth and Lying in the Extra-Moral Sense." *Literary Theory: An Anthology*, edited by Julie Rivkin and Michael Ryan. Blackwell, 2005, pp. 262–266.

Oppel, Richard A., Jr., and Robert Gebeloff, K. K. Rebecca Lai, Will Wright, Mitch Smith. "The Fullest Look Yet at the Racial Inequity of Coronavirus." *The New York* Times, July 5, 2020, https://www.nytimes.com/interactive/2020/07/05/us/coronavirus-latinos-african-americans-cdc-data.html. Accessed 22 July 2020.

Payne, Robert. *The Promiscuity of Network Culture: Queer Theory and Digital Media*. Routledge, 2014.

Pepper, Thomas. *Singularities: Extremes of Theory in the Twentieth Century*. Cambridge University Press, 1997.

Perrin, Andrew. "Americans Are Changing Their Relationship with Facebook." *Pew Research Center*. 5 September 2018, https://www.pewresearch.org/fact-tank/2018/09/05/americans-are-changing-their-relationship-with-facebook/. Accessed 20 May 2019.

Proust, Marcel. *In Search of Lost Time, Volume I: Swann's Way.* Translated by C. K. Scott Moncrieff and Terence Kilmartin (Revised by D. J. Enright). Modern Library, 2003.

Putnam, Robert D. *Bowling Alone: The Collapse and Revival of American Community.* Simon and Schuster, 2000.

Ra, Chaelin, Junhan Cho, Matthew D. Stone, et al. "Association of Digital Media Use with Subsequent Symptoms of Attention-Deficit/Hyperactivity Disorder Among Adolescents." *Journal of the American Medical Association* 320, no. 3, 2018, pp. 255–263, doi:10.1001/jama.2018.8931. Accessed 20 May 2019.

Race, Kane. "Speculative Pragmatism and Intimate Arrangements: Online Hook-up Devices in Gay Life." *Culture, Health & Sexuality* 17, no. 4, pp. 496–511.

Raj, Senthorum. "Grindring Bodies: Racial and Affective Economies of Online Queer Desire." *Critical Race and Whiteness Studies* 7, no. 2, 2011, pp. 1–12.

Raskin, Jamin. "A Last Interview with French Philosopher Michel Foucault." *City Paper*, July 27, 1984, p. 18, https://monoskop.org/images/5/54/Raskin_Jamin_1984_A_Last_Interview_with_French_Philosopher_Michel_Foucault.pdf. Accessed 19 January 2020.

Rattner, Steven. "The Mystery of High Stock Prices." *The New York Times*, July 3, 2020, https://www.nytimes.com/2020/07/03/opinion/stock-market.html. Accessed 22 July 2020.

Read, Jason. "A Genealogy of Homo-Economicus: Neoliberalism and the Production of Subjectivity." *Foucault Studies* 6, 2009, pp. 25–36, https://rauli.cbs.dk/index.php/foucault-studies/article/view/2465/2463. Accessed 20 May 2019.

Redd, Noah Taylor. "Main Sequence Stars: Definition & Life Cycle." *Space.com*, 24 February 2018, https://www.space.com/22437-main-sequence-stars.html. Accessed 20 May 2019.

Reynolds, Malvina. "Little Boxes." *Sings the Truth.* Columbia Records, 1967.

Rheingold, Howard. *The Virtual Community: Homesteading on the Electronic Frontier.* MIT Press, 2000.

Ricco, John Paul. *The Decision between Us: Art and Ethics in the Time of Scenes.* University of Chicago Press, 2014.

Rich, Adrienne. "Compulsory Heterosexuality and Lesbian Existence." *The Lesbian and Gay Studies Reader*, edited by Henry Abelove, Michèle Aina Barale, and David M. Halperin. Routledge, 1993, pp. 227–254.

Roach, Tom. "Becoming Fungible: Queer Intimacies in Social Media." *Qui Parle: Critical Humanities and Social Sciences* 23, no. 2, 2015, pp. 55–87.

———. *Friendship as a Way of Life: Foucault, AIDS, and the Politics of Shared Estrangement.* State University of New York Press, 2012.

———. "Shut Me Up in Grindr: Anticonfessional Discourse and Sensual Nonsense in MSM Media." *I Confess: An Anthology of Original Essays on Constructing the Self within the Third Sexual Revolution*, edited by Thomas Waugh and Brandon Arroyo. McGill-Queens University Press, 2019, pp. 549–571.

Rodriguez, Matthew. "Grindr President Says Marriage Is 'Holy Matrimony between a Man and a Woman' in Deleted Social Media Post." *Into.* 29 November 2018, https://www.intomore.com/impact/Grindr-president-says-marriage-is-holy-matrimony-between-a-man-and-a-woman-in-deleted-social-media-post. Accessed 20 May 2019.

———. "This Is What It's Like to Log into Grindr as a Person of Color. *Mic.* 18 September 2018, https://mic.com/articles/125417/this-is-what-it-s-like-to-log-into-Grindr-as-a-person-of-color. Accessed 20 May 2019.

Rosoff, Matt. "Facebook Exodus: Nearly half of young users have deleted the app from their phone in the last year, says study." *CNBC.* 5 September 2018. https://www.cnbc.com/2018/09/05/facebook-exodus-44-percent-of-americans-age-18-29-have-deleted-app.html. Accessed 20 May 2019.

Roupenian, Kristen. "Cat Person." *The New Yorker.* 4 December 2017, https://www.newyorker.com/magazine/2017/12/11/cat-person. Accessed 20 May 2019.

Rubin, Gayle. "Thinking Sex: Notes for a Radical Theory of Sexuality." *The Lesbian and Gay Studies Reader*, edited by Henry Abelove, Michèle Aina Barale, and David M. Halperin. Routledge, 1993, pp. 3–44.

Schorr, Collier. "Racing the Dead," interview by Howard Halle. *TimeOut New York.* September 2007, pp. 13–17.

Scott, Eugene. "The Marginalized Voices of the #MeToo Movement." *The Washington Post.* 7 December 2017, https://www.washingtonpost.com/news/the-fix/wp/2017/12/07/the-marginalized-voices-of-the-metoo-movement/. Accessed 20 May 2019.

Scruff. "ScruffPro Features." 2019, https://support.scruff.com/hc/en-us/articles/202623364-SCRUFF-Pro-Features. Accessed 20 May 2019.

Seidman, Steven. "Theoretical Perspectives." *Introducing the New Sexuality Studies: 2nd Edition*, edited by Steven Seidman, Nancy L. Fischer, and Chet Meeks. Routledge, 2011, pp. 3–13.

Sen, Mayukh. "Torso Junkie." *Real Life.* 16 August 2016, http://reallifemag.com/torso-junkie/. Accessed 20 May 2019.

Seneca, *Epistulae Moralis, Books I–LXV.* Translated by Richard M. Gummere. Harvard University Press, 1917.

Serano, Julia. "Trans Woman Manifesto." *Whipping Girl: A Transsexual Woman on Sexism and the Scapegoating of Femininity.* Seal, 2016, pp. 11–22.

Shadel, Jon. "Grindr Was the First Big Dating App for Gay Men. Now It's Falling out of Favor." *The Washington Post.* 6 December 2018, https://www.washingtonpost.com/lifestyle/2018/12/06/Grindr-was-first-big-dating-app-gay-men-now-its-falling-out-favor/. Accessed 20 May 2019.

Slouka, Mark. "Dehumanized: When Math and Science Rule the School." *Harpers Bazaar.* September 2009, pp. 32–40.

Snorton, C. Riley. *Black on Both Sides: A Racial History of Trans Identity*. University of Minnesota Press, 2017.

Spade, Dean, and Craig Willse. "Marriage Will Never Set Us Free." *Organizing Upgrade*. 6 September 2013, http://archive.organizingupgrade.com/index. php/modules-menu/beyond-capitalism/item/1002-marriage-will-never-set-us-free. Accessed 20 May 2019.

Spillers, Hortense J. "Mama's Baby, Papa's Maybe: An American Grammar Book." *Diacritics* 17, no. 2, 1987, pp. 65–81. *JSTOR*, www.jstor.org/stable/464747. Accessed 19 January 2020.

Spinoza. *Ethics*. Translated by G. H. R. Parkinson. Oxford University Press, 2000.

Sterne, Jonathan. "What If Interactivity Is the New Passivity?" *Flow Journal*. 9 April 2012, https://www.flowjournal.org/2012/04/the-new-passivity/. Accessed 20 May 2014.

Stone, Brad Elliot. "The Down Low and the Sexuality of Race." *Foucault Studies*, no. 12, 2011, 36–50, https://rauli.cbs.dk/index.php/foucault-studies/article/view/3208/3402. Accessed 19 January 2020.

Treisman, Deborah. "Kristen Roupenian on the Self Deceptions of Dating." *The New Yorker*. 4 December 2017, https://www.newyorker.com/books/this-week-in-fiction/fiction-this-week-kristen-roupenian-2017-12-11. Accessed 20 May 2019.

Tuhkanen, Mikko. *The Essentialist Villain: On Leo Bersani*. State University of New York Press, 2018.

Turban, Jack. "We Need to Talk about How Grindr Is Affecting Gay Men's Health." *Vox*, 4 April 2018, https://www.vox.com/science-and-health/2018/4/4/1717 7058/Grindr-gay-men-mental-health-psychiatrist. Accessed 20 May 2019.

Turkle, Sherri. *Alone Together: Why We Expect More from Technology and Less from Each Other*. Basic Books, 2011.

———. *Reclaiming Conversation: The Power of Talk in a Digital Age*. Penguin, 2015.

Twitter. "Men React to Cat Person." @MenCatPerson. December 2017, https:// twitter.com/MenCatPerson. Accessed 20 May 2019.

Tye, Larry. *Rising from the Rails: Pullman Porters and the Making of the Black Middle Class*. Henry Holt, 2004.

Virno, Paolo. "The Ambivalence of Disenchantment." *Radical Thought in Italy*, edited by Paolo Virno and Michael Hardt. University of Minnesota Press, 1995, pp. 13–34.

Wacquant, Loïc. "Actually Existing Neoliberalism: Three Steps to a Historical Anthropology of Actually Existing Neoliberalism." *Social Anthropology* 20, no. 1, 2012, pp. 66–79.

Ward, Jane. "Dude Sex: White Masculinities and 'Authentic' Heterosexuality among Dudes Who Have Sex with Dudes." *Sexualities* 11, 2008, pp. 414–433.

———. *Not Gay: Sex between Straight White Men*. New York University Press, 2015.

Warner, Michael. *The Trouble with Normal: Sex, Politics, and the Ethics of Queer Life*. Harvard University Press, 1999.

Waugh, Thomas, and Brandon Arroyo, editors. *I Confess!: Constructing the Sexual Self in the Internet Age*. McGill-Queens University Press, 2019.

Weigel, Moira. *Labor of Love: The Invention of Dating*. Farrar, Strauss, and Giroux, 2016.

Wiegman, Robyn, and Elizabeth A. Wilson. "Introduction: Antinormativity's Queer Conventions." *Queer Theory without Antinormativity*, special issue of *differences: A Journal of Feminist Cultural Studies* 26, no. 1, May 2015, pp. 1–25.

Winnubst, Shannon. "The Queer Thing about Neoliberal Pleasure: A Foucauldian Warning." *Foucault Studies* 14, 2012, pp. 79–97. https://rauli.cbs.dk/index.php/foucault-studies/article/view/3889/4235. Accessed 20 May 2019.

———. *Way Too Cool: Selling Out Race and Ethics*. Columbia University Press, 2015.

Woo, Jaime. *Meet Grindr*. CreateSpace, 2013.

Wood, Molly. "How Facebook Is Ruining Sharing." *CNet*. 18 November 2011, https://www.cnet.com/news/how-facebook-is-ruining-sharing/. Accessed 20 May 2019.

Zacharek, Stephanie, Eliana Dockterman, and Haley Sweetland Edwards. "Person of the Year: The Silence Breakers." *Time Magazine*, 18 December 2018, http://time.com/time-person-of-the-year-2017-silence-breakers/. Accessed 20 May 2019.

Index